Aazheyaadizi

Aazheyaadizi

Worldview, Language, and the Logics of Decolonization

Mark D. Freeland

MICHIGAN STATE UNIVERSITY PRESS | *East Lansing*

⊖ The paper used in this publication meets the minimum requirements
of ANSI/NISO Z39.48 1992 (R 1997) (Permanence of Paper).

Michigan State University Press
East Lansing, Michigan 48823-5245

LIBRARY OF CONGRESS CATALOGING-IN-PUBLICATION DATA
Names: Freeland, Mark D., author.
Title: Aazheyaadizi : worldview, language and the logics of decolonization / Mark D. Freeland.
Description: East Lansing : Michigan State University Press, [2020?]
| Series: American Indian Studies Series | Includes bibliographical references and index.
Identifiers: LCCN 2020007019 | ISBN 9781611863802 (paperback)
| ISBN 9781609176556 | ISBN 9781628954159 | ISBN 9781628964165
Subjects: LCSH: Ojibwa language. | Ojibwa Indians—Government relations.
| Ojibwa Indians—Politics and government. | Indians, Treatment of—Social aspects—North America.
Classification: LCC E99.C6 F675 2020 | DDC 497/.333—dc23
LC record available at https://lccn.loc.gov/2020007019

Book design by Charlie Sharp, Sharp Designs, East Lansing, Michigan
Cover design by Erin Kirk
Cover art: "We R Of The Land (crane)," by Keitha Keeshig-Tobias.

Michigan State University Press is a member of the Green Press Initiative and is
committed to developing and encouraging ecologically responsible publishing
practices. For more information about the Green Press Initiative and the use of
recycled paper in book publishing, please visit www.greenpressinitiative.org.

Visit Michigan State University Press at *www.msupress.org*

CONTENTS

PREFACE

For most Indigenous peoples, the year marked as 2007 in the eurowestern calendar will not be remembered as a watershed year for decolonization.[1] However, for Anishinaabeg in what is now Northern Michigan, there was a significant shift in relationships. For the first time in my life, the practice of hunting in my homeland was not mediated by the State of Michigan, treating me as a citizen of the United States. That year, I paid a nominal fee to the Bahweting Anishinaabe Nation (federally recognized as the Sault Ste. Marie Tribe of Chippewa Indians), which licensed my hunting, fishing, and gathering practices as a citizen of my own Indigenous Nation. The State of Michigan no longer held final authority over my Indigenous practices. I shot a large whitetail doe that year in September and was able to feed my family in ways that are meaningful to us. While my actual practices shifted only a little, allowing me to take a few more deer and fish and extending a few of the seasons, practicing those rights as an Indigenous person was a significant shift. We now participate in activities passed down from our ancestors, in our ancestral land, as coequal inhabitants of those places. We have the vision of our ancestors who insisted on the inclusion of Article 13 of the Treaty of Washington in 1836 to thank for this ability.

In 2007 the Inland Consent Decree, a contemporary implementation of the 1836 Treaty of Washington, was put into effect. At issue were the hunting and fishing rights stated in Article 13 of the treaty: "The Indians stipulate for the right of hunting on the lands ceded, with the other usual privileges of occupancy, until the land is required for settlement."[2] The fishing rights on the Great Lakes had already been settled with *U.S. v. Michigan* in 1979, returning to the Treaty of Washington as the guiding legal principle outlining Anishinaabe rights for fishing.[3] Since the treaty language focuses on the question of what land as "required for settlement" means, the hunting and inland fishing parameters would wait until that legal language could be worked out. Of particular interest here are the methods of decolonization that are present. When it comes to negotiating our Indigenous lives and cultures in our own homelands, there are different logics associated with how we assert ourselves as Indigenous peoples. When implementing a treaty right, we engage in what I would term the logics of indigeneity. We signed treaties as free Indigenous peoples with the U.S. Government, and the continued sociopolitical-economic praxes associated with those treaties represent an ongoing practice of freedom. The reestablishment of the Treaty of Washington for Anishinaabe peoples functions to provide that praxis of indigeneity as passed down from our ancestors.

Indigeneity is not the only possible action when it comes to our engagements with our homelands. Other legal strategies are often employed that represent the logics of inclusion into the nation-state apparatus. For example, in response to a lack of protection for American Indian relationships to our homelands, in 1978 the United States Congress passed the American Indian Religious Freedom Act (AIRFA) to much fanfare among Indigenous peoples and their allies.[4] This act was supposed to be the linchpin allowing us to legally protect our ceremonial relationships to the land. However, as the efficacy of this act was adjudicated throughout the 1980s, the hope for greater protection from legal structures soon dwindled. Then in 1988, Sandra Day O'Connor penned the *Lyng v. Northwest Indian Cemetery Protection Association* decision, stating that "Even assuming that the Government's actions here will virtually destroy the Indians' ability to practice their religion, the Constitution simply does not supply a principle that could justify upholding respondent's legal claims."[5] While there continue to be legal challenges to lumber, mining, energy, and recreational interests that effectively destroy the land and our relationships to it, consistently, the courts favor those economic interests over Indigenous cultural uses. This was true in Anishinaabe Akiing, when in January 2010 the Department of Environmental Quality in Michigan granted a permit to open a copper mine over an objection that the Environmental Impact Assessment (EIA) did not properly address the impacts to the Eagle Rock area of northern Michigan as a "place of worship."[6] According to this report, the Eagle Rock area "is not a building used for human occupancy, [hence] there is no basis to require the EIA [to] identify and describe the feature as a 'place of worship.'"[7] On the face of it, one may argue that the courts and governmental agencies are misapplying or misunderstanding the concepts of religion, or they are simply disregarding our cultural traditions because the lumber, mining, energy, and recreational interests are simply too economically and politically powerful. While these arguments have merit, instead, I am asking a deeper set of questions of this quandary. If there is a desire to be included under the protections of the First Amendment, can our relationships to land be accurately translated as religious? What if religion and its associated concepts are not universally applicable, and Indigenous relationships to the land are so different from the eurowest that the First Amendment cannot effectively comprehend and protect these differences? More importantly, how might we as Indigenous peoples perpetuate the colonization of our own minds by continually working to force-fit our cultural ceremonies and relationships into categories of religion that are indicative of fundamentally different sets of cultural logics?

We are dealing with a number of complex issues in these cases; however, I am most concerned with the problems in translation that are present here. It is interesting to note that after more than five hundred years of contact between eurowestern and Indigenous peoples, there still exists a significant gap in effective communication between the two cultures. Even though, as Clifford Geertz has suggested, the "aim" of anthropology "is the enlargement of the universe of human discourse," this academic discipline has failed to enlarge the discourse of human communication, and as I will demonstrate, has actually done the opposite.[8] By imposing a eurowestern cultural framework of understanding on Indigenous (and other) peoples, anthropology has significantly narrowed the universe of human discourse by representing all cultures through a culturally particular lens.

As the language of the court proceedings suggests, Indigenous peoples and their allies have attempted to include themselves under the umbrella of the First Amendment to the Constitution and its free exercise clause. However, even with the addition of a special congressional act, we have yet to find any consistent protection under these legal proceedings.[9] While there are numerous forces at work and means of analysis with which to view this phenomenon, ultimately this strategy of inclusion relies upon the conviction that "religion" and "worship" are universally applicable concepts. At the same time, there has been much decolonization work done among Indigenous scholars and activists that demonstrates that concepts around religion may not have cultural equivalents in Indigenous cultures. For example, in the twentieth anniversary edition to his classic text *God Is Red*, Vine Deloria Jr. points to a further problem in the intersection of U.S. law and American Indian culture. In this updated version he states, "Much more thought needs to be given to the question of whether the Indians had 'gods' in the same sense as Near Eastern peoples."[10] Similarly, Tink Tinker notes that the terms faith and religion are entirely western constructs "since neither category applies to any American Indian cultural equivalent."[11] What these scholars point to is the necessity for Indigenous conceptual decolonization. For too long we have been forced into the categories of cognition of the eurowest, and most of us, both Indigenous and non-Indigenous alike, have internalized these categories as universal. As Kwasi Wiredu, an Akan scholar from Ghana, has pointed out in *Cultural Universals and Particulars*, when we unreflectively translate our cultural traditions into western categories, "the outcome is likely to do violence (though not premeditatedly) to [our] indigenous categories of thought."[12]

We have relied too heavily upon the English language and its associated cultural concepts as the lingua franca to communicate our ceremonies and relationships; however, with the ongoing regeneration of our languages and our cultural traditions, we also have the tools available to further this work of decolonization. It is this combination of our Indigenous languages with their respective conceptual fields of knowledge that holds a significant next step in this process. Within this combination of language, concepts, and praxis, Indigenous peoples can construct a cultural framework of understanding, which I am naming worldview, that can communicate to other people an accurate depiction of our culture and traditions. I define worldview as an interrelated set of cultural logics that fundamentally orient us to space (land), time, the rest of life, and provides a prescriptive methodology for how to relate to that life. This definition is designed to provide a corrective to the lack of consistent use of the term. Worldview as a concept is often used but rarely defined. This lack of precision undermines the ability of the term to communicate cultural difference at a deep level. Since there is so much misinformation and misunderstanding about Indigenous relationships to land, I privilege a definition of worldview that can communicate those fundamental relationships to time and space.

I employ this definition of worldview as a way of effectively communicating deep cultural differences between Indigenous and eurowestern cultures. I have three primary goals. First, my thesis is that an Anishinaabeg worldview is an intimate relationship to a localized space, cyclical time, living in a web of relatedness with the rest of life, with a prescribed methodology of balance for that life.[13] I devote a chapter to each of these four components of worldview, demonstrating how this theory provides a cogent understanding of Anishinaabeg relationships to land, time, life, and a methodological lens. Together, the four interrelated logics of worldview provide a framework of knowledge to better understand our complex sets of relationships and will reinforce the necessity for a consistent definition of worldview to be used. Second, by defining worldview as a set of logics, I will show how the addition of this theory as a test for translating Indigenous languages provides a firm cultural grounding to engage a process of retranslating our culture with integrity.[14] Too often we are still using translations for our languages that have been passed down to us from missionaries and other colonial agents who used eurowestern culture as a universal framework of thought. The logics of worldview help us to root out the colonization of our own languages and concepts by demonstrating the logical inconsistency of some of our translations. Finally, by demonstrating an Indigenous worldview as manifest in a particular culture, I will show the futility of engaging in the logics of inclusion. As the above examples of the attempted use of the First Amendment show, our concepts of relationship to land are not comprehensible within legal statutes and religious language. For a more effective defense of our homelands, we will have to find more creative means of engagement, like the "radical resurgence" projects outlined by Anishinaabekwe Leanne Simpson.[15]

Cognitive Freedom

The work of decolonizing and reinterpreting our relationships to land demands a sophisticated linguistic and conceptual methodology, and Kwasi Wiredu provides this foundation. He has been on the forefront of African conceptual decolonization for several decades, and his work provides the type of linguistic and conceptual decolonization that I am attempting. Wiredu gives the example of translating the concept of god in his native Akan language, demonstrating that the concept itself is shot through with particular cultural meaning and concepts. God, in its eurowestern form, functions as a creator of the universe, as a creator out of nothing. However, the Akans do not have a concept of creation out of nothingness, and their concept *oboade*, which is the closest translation to god as creator, is thought of as an "Excavator, Hewer, Carver, Creator, Originator, Inventor, Architect."[16] These categories of cognition presuppose a material already in existence, so "'constructing, hewing, fashioning out something without using anything' . . . carries its contradictoriness on its face."[17] God, in its eurowestern form, cannot be translated into Akan without doing damage to the concept or cultures involved.

However, Wiredu also points out that language is an "infinitely flexible framework capable of being bent to any purpose of communication or symbolism in general."[18] While this flexibility demonstrates some positive power for languages and their ability to adapt to new situations, when combined with the problems of colonial power and domination, there is also a proclivity for the colonization of our languages and thought. As Wiredu demonstrates, the concept of god can be thought of and translated into Akan when one is unthinkingly participating in the colonial culture. In this instance, rather than a dissonance being recognized between the two different conceptualizations of god and *oboade*, the concept of the creation out of nothingness is simply attached to the Akan language, thereby subverting an Indigenous meaning. In Wiredu's words, "For an African to think in a Western language in this way is a mark of what might be called the colonial mentality."[19] Unfortunately, the colonial situation both in Africa and in the Americas is thick with this type of linguistic and conceptual colonization.

This colonial mentality is at work when we attempt to protect our relationships to lands under the guise of religion and the free exercise thereof, without fully thinking through the consequences.[20] By attempting to include our conceptual understandings and our relationships to land under the legal definition of religion, we can inadvertently come to understand ourselves, our concepts, and our relationships to the land with these eurowestern religious fields of knowledge. At some level, we are attempting to include ourselves, our cultures, and our relationships to the land within these eurowestern concepts, and without a consistent cultural, linguistic, and experiential mechanism to keep our relationships to our lands imbued with a sense of Indigenous integrity, we are in constant threat of negotiating our lives and our ceremonies from within a eurowestern conceptual framework. Stated in another way, if we naively attach our Indigenous categories of thought to colonial, religious, and legal language that does not have the ability to understand those concepts, then we are at risk of participating in our own cultural genocide.

While one could argue that protecting our lands may be worth this stretch and that the U.S. legal system is the only such vehicle for this protection, there are two glaring problems. First, if we actually had some success in protecting our lands from eurowestern development, then one could argue that participating in these legal cases could be worth the stretch. However, there has been little to no protection thus far. Second, if we negotiated these legal cases from a place of cultural and communal functionality where the colonial mentality did not exist, then again, one could say the risk of colonizing our thought would not exist. However, none of our communities negotiates the world from a place of functional balance where we are consistently in charge of our own children's education, or even our own cultural categories of thought. The historical trauma in our communities makes the colonial mentality even more dangerous when we begin to translate our languages and concepts of land into eurowestern religious language. Therefore, I believe that it is essential to identify methods of engagement that do not compromise our Indigenous categories of thought, and to develop new and better methods of land protection.

Recent developments in Indigenous scholarship have demonstrated the need to recalibrate our efforts away from the politics of the colonial state apparatus and focus more closely on our own methods of engagement. As Anishinaabekwe Leanne Simpson has stated,

> Indigenous scholarship has recently experienced crucial interventions into how we account, frame, and tell the truths of the political and cultural lives of Indigenous peoples that move away from a constriction of our intelligence within the confines of Western thought and the dumbing down of the issues for the non-Indigenous outside to a meticulous, critical, robust and layered approach that accurately contextualizes and reflects the lives and the thinking of Indigenous peoples on our own terms, with the clear purpose of dismantling colonial domination.[21]

In chapter 10 of *As We Have Always Done*, titled "I See Your Light," Simpson engages Dene scholar Glen Coulthard's work on refusing the politics of recognition in *Red Skin, White Masks* and Mohawk scholar Audra Simpson's discussion of the politics of identity in *Mohawk Interruptus*, elaborating on the need for "the potentialities of organizing and mobilizing within a radical resurgent politic by beginning to reconceptualize these concepts within Indigenous intelligence or within the diverse nation-based practices of grounded normativity."[22] While this project of critically defining worldview to demonstrate cultural difference could be used in the ongoing politics of recognition with the state, I am more interested in the need for translational methodologies grounded in our Indigenous languages and experiences with the land. As I demonstrate throughout the book, the translations for our languages that have been passed down from missionaries and anthropologists continue to force-fit our experiential Indigenous intelligence into eurowestern frameworks of knowledge that do not have the capacity to communicate Indigenous relationships to land and life. Without a grounded methodology to continually root out these problems, even our best efforts for radical resurgence could be derailed by the reproduction of foreign frameworks and relationships to our own lands. For our decolonizing efforts to gain traction, it is imperative that we pull the colonial strains of thought out at the root to get to our own Indigenous logics of relationship. This theory of worldview helps us towards this goal of Indigenous resurgence and is how I position this project.

In this study, I will use a particular sociocultural-political moment as a conceptual starting place to demonstrate an Anishinaabeg worldview. The Treaty of Washington in 1836 provides a cogent point of analysis as it represents both a moment of Anishinaabeg cultural integrity as living as free, intact communities, and the contemporary basis for the 2007 Inland Consent Decree, providing the ongoing manifestation of those logics of indigeneity. For this treaty, a contingent of Anishinaabeg *ogimaag* (leaders) traveled to Washington, DC, to negotiate a treaty, essentially signing away about one-third of the land mass that would become the state of Michigan. Like many other treaties in this era, the power balance had tipped heavily in favor of the U.S. Government, and their negotiators were eager to use that power to impose land cessions from Indigenous peoples for the growing onslaught of eurowestern colonists to those lands. The primary *ogimaa* for that contingent was an Odawa named Eshkwagenabi (little feather). According to law professor Matthew Fletcher, during these negotiations this *ogimaa* insisted on the inclusion of Article 13, which states, "The Indians stipulate for the right of hunting on the lands ceded, with the other usual privileges of occupancy, until the land is required for settlement."[23] Originally, this treaty was only supposed to be between the United States and the Odawa Nations of what is now the northern lower peninsula of Michigan. However, Henry Schoolcraft was embedded in the Sault Ste. Marie community as the Indian agent and brought along several Ojibwe from northern Michigan who were considered friendly to Schoolcraft's desires to promote statehood for Michigan. Early in the treaty negotiations, Eshkwagenabi was successful in holding a strong position, but Schoolcraft then inserted a different narrative into the negotiations. According to Matthew Fletcher, Schoolcraft told Eshkwagenabi that it does not matter if he actually signs the treaty, because he will have his Ojibwe friends sign the treaty, and when he takes the treaty to the U.S. Senate, they will not care who signed the treaty. The Senate will ratify it anyway and Eshkwagenabi's people will receive nothing from the treaty. Article 13 then became a compromise in the negotiations, which would be incredibly important to succeeding generations of Anishinaabeg in this area of Michigan. This treaty stipulation would become an essential decolonizing tool from the fishing wars of the early 1970s to the signing of the 2007 Inland Consent Decree. Citing Article 13 of the Treaty of Washington, this decree reestablished Indigenous control over hunting and fishing for the signatories of that treaty in the ceded areas. Since much of the ceded land, almost 14 million acres, still remains public in ownership, we are able to exercise our treaty rights on those public lands.

This treaty and Article 13 provide a useful conceptual grounding as we think through the difficult questions embedded in the process of decolonization. Article 13 asks these questions: What were Eshkwagenabi and other *ogimaag* trying to preserve when they insisted on its entry into the treaty language? What relational concepts were they relying upon to discuss hunting? What does it take to continue those relationships to hunting? Were they talking about subsistence, or were they referring to something much more holistic? Just what are we talking about with the "other usual privileges of occupancy?" Does this refer to ceremony, travel, medicine? Throughout this book, I will use this returning as an Anishinaabeg linguistic-conceptual starting place for retranslating our relationships to land, time, the rest of life, and the prescribed lens for negotiating those relationships to life. This methodology in concert with this theory of worldview will provide the cultural integrity necessary for the testing of Anishinaabemowin translations important to this study.

In chapter 1, I will begin this study with an in-depth discussion of the concept of worldview and set up the comparative analysis between Anishinaabeg culture and the eurowest. While the use of worldview as a concept has a long and sordid history in the academy, there are two main problems. First, there is an inconsistency with the usage of the word as a demonstration of a communal or cultural notion and its use as a descriptor of an individual's personal view of the world. When the analysis of worldview is dependent on the view of a single person, the power of the concept to describe any amount of theoretical and analytical components of culture significantly decreases. The second problem is that it vacillates between describing deep cultural frameworks of understanding and describing ideological influences at the conscious level of human ideas and institutions. When worldview is confused with ideology, there is a lack of consistent communication present. To understand the depth of cultural difference, the concept of worldview must have a clearer definition and be differentiated from other concepts. In this chapter I will make a case for the definition of worldview that I will be using throughout this book, which is that worldview is an interrelated set of logics that fundamentally orient a culture to space, time, the rest of life, and provides a prescriptive logic for relating to that life.

In chapter 2, I will begin my application of this definition of worldview within Anishinaabeg culture to discuss our fundamental orientation to space, Anishinaabe Akiing. I will begin with our origin narratives to demonstrate how they relate us to our space and continue to provide a means of keeping us grounded in a particular place. I will also begin the process of retranslating our traditional Anishinaabe words that relate us to our lands. Here I will analyze some traditional definitions and their respective conceptual fields for *aki*, or land, and *Mazikaamikwe*, Earth Mother. By going into further depth on these two concepts, our orientation to particular places will come into greater focus. This analysis will demonstrate that the connections to our particular spaces are integrated into the structure of our society and act as moorings for our everyday conceptualizations and interactions with the land on which we live. This analysis will allow us to understand how the eurowestern concepts of land, sacredness, and the holy fail to conceptualize our relationships to the land of our ancestors.

In chapter 3, I will discuss Anishinaabeg understandings of time as cyclical and give a deeper understanding of those conceptualizations in Anishinaabemowin. All cultures understand both cyclical and chronological relationships to time. What makes Indigenous culture different from its eurowestern counterparts is that cyclical logics shape culture and thought. I will again demonstrate this Anishinaabeg reality by discussing the relationships to celestial and atmospheric phenomena such as *giizis* (sun), *dibiki giizis* (moon), seasons, and star knowledge. The chapter will finish with a brief discussion of time involving the land. As we will see, the eurowestern notion of linear time and its compatriots, development and progress, drive the land-use policies of the U.S. Government and corporations, whereas in Anishinaabeg culture we have no such fundamental drive for development around land with a cyclical understanding of time.

In chapter 4, I will move the discussion of worldview into the Anishinaabeg concepts of relatedness, beginning with the concept of *chidibenjiged*, or "that which makes all things belong." This concept provides a foundation for understanding the complex set of Indigenous relationships. In combination with a discussion of our origin narratives, I will demonstrate how our relationships to human, nonhuman, and other-than-human linguistically conceptualize a large kinship system.[24] With a deeper understanding of kinship, I then move to decolonize Anishinaabemowin by providing spatially cogent definitions of the often-used concepts of *doodemag* (clans) and *manidoog* (other-than-human beings.) This discussion further develops the relatedness of worldview logics and provides a foundation for understanding Indigenous kinship as an essential component of the culture.

Finally, in chapter 5, I can move the discussion of worldview into a deeper understanding of Anishinaabe balance. I will discuss our cultural ceremonies as a method of keeping balance in our societies and in our lands. This function of ceremony will highlight the logics of balance at the level of worldview. I will also include in this chapter an analysis of the concept of *mino bimaadiziwin*, or the good life. Much has already been written about *mino bimaadiziwin*, and I will be able to add to that literature the recognition of the concept as an ideological manifestation of the logic of balance. Finally, I will do the comparative work and discuss the Manichean dualism of the eurowest and its function as a logic to structure eurowestern relationships to life.

I will then conclude this project with a discussion of the importance of this study, summing up how this process of retranslating our culture with our own language and concepts can help us to better understand ourselves, as well as create the possibility of developing better methods of protecting our relationships to our lands. I will describe how the logics of worldview and our relationships to land with its associated ideological, institutional, and experiential functions can help to bring about a different way of relating to the land for all of the people who are here now, both Anishinaabe and non-Anishinaabe alike. By demonstrating the significant differences that exist between the two cultures, it is possible some of the wisdom inherent in the Indigenous traditions can come into clearer focus and be put to better use.

ACKNOWLEDGMENTS

As I attempt to demonstrate in this book, we are all part of a large web of relationships. This work is no different. It is the culmination of years of experiences in multiple places, for which I am very grateful. Chi g'miig-wech'inin (a big thanks) goes out to all of those who have enriched this project with their involvement in many ways. I would not be able to produce this work without their genius and steadfast desire for the return of Indigenous freedom. However, the responsibilities for the mistakes and the conclusions that I offer are all mine.

I would like to start to say chi g'miigwech'inin to the staff and faculty at the Iliff School of Theology in Denver, Colorado, where I made my home for thirteen years. Thank you in particular to Katherine Turpin for insisting that we learn how to teach as PhD students. Thanks also goes out to Loring Abeyta for sharing her research on worldview. One of my intellectually formative experiences happened in a seminar on comparative religious philosophy with Edward Antonio and Tink Tinker. This course, a critique of religious philosophy through a comparison of American Indian and South African Indigenous ceremony and culture, provided foundational knowledge and methodologies to pursue the problems associated with religious language and Indigenous peoples. Edward, who is Zebra clan from the Shona

Nation in what is now Zimbabwe, demonstrated the role of foundational logics of indigeneity through very common ceremonial frameworks cultural knowledge of his own people. Throughout my time at Iliff, his wisdom and knowledge of cultural theory helped me to sort out these very complex relationships to land and life. For his wisdom I will be forever grateful. At the same time, Tink provided the localized versions of ceremonies and helped to bring indigeneity of these lands into clearer focus. He also provided consistent engagement and feedback on this manuscript.

Like many Indigenous scholars, Tink not only works as a professor but also in the local community. In Denver this took place at the Four Winds American Indian Council, and this place provided further encouragement and learning in the form of political action and community organizing. I am in debt to Glen Morris, Robert Chanate, Troy Lynn Yellow Wood, Alistair Bane, Calvin Eagle, and many others. The reality of Indigenous brilliance and beauty comes out in the face of colonization in places like these, in many shared meals and ceremonies. Tink's influence goes far beyond the walls of Iliff, and he has helped to carve out a special place of decolonization at Four Winds for many people.

In addition to areas around Denver, like Tall Bull Ceremonial Grounds, I was able to be in relationship to other places as well during the writing of this. I spent considerable time in Cayuga and Onondaga territory, around Oswego, New York. A special thanks to Kevin White at SUNY Oswego for providing space to teach. Also, chi g'miigwech'inin to Mama Bear Louise Herne for providing space, knowledge, and hospitality in Akwesasne when my spouse and I needed it. Chi g'miigwech'inin for the land around Martville, New York, for taking care of my oldest two kids by playing with them and embracing these young ones in meaningful experiences walking along the creek, learning to hunt, and helping to raise them.

Chi g'miigwech'inin to Michigan State University Press for their support in seeing this project to publication. A special thanks to Julie Loehr for her dedication and patience, and to Anastasia Wraight and Bonnie Cobb for their detailed reading of this text.

Chi g'miigwech'inin to South Dakota State University for providing the space to teach this material in a substantive way. A special thanks to Dean Lynn Sargeant, Christi Garst-Santos, and Will Prigge for supporting this work in numerous ways and to President Barry Dunn for his leadership in connecting the land of Oceti Sakowin peoples (Lakota, Dakota, Nakota) to the support of Indigenous students in the land grant mission of the university with the Wokini Initiative. It is an honor to be a part of this effort.

Chi g'miigwech'inin to the grounding from my parents, Jim and Donna Freeland, whose unwavering support has been a constant source of wisdom. It is with them in Anishinaabe Akiing where relationships with our extended family annually include wawageshkag (white tail deer) in hunting camp and aninatigoog (maple trees) for sugarbushing. I continue to learn from the relationships with the deer and the maples for their generosity in offering themselves to feed us. These relationships in Anishinaabe Akiing continue to ground this work in ways in which I will continue to find language for throughout my life.

M'chi g'miigwech'inin to *n'wiidjiiwagan* (my spouse) Sharity Bassett for more than I could possibly name here. I work hard to keep up with her intellectual abilities and her acute analysis has made significant contributions to this work. Furthermore, her unwavering love for our family has provided a foundation that I work hard every day to reciprocate. And for our children, Payton, Lian, Gavin, Violet and Giizhik, may you find your place in Anishinaabe Akiing.

Chi g'miigwech'in to Margaret Noodin and Mike Zimmerman for their unwavering love for Anishinaabemowin. Their critical insight and knowledge of our language and decolonial translations have enriched this project immensely. *Chi g'miigwech'inin* for engaging in this discourse with me, agreeing to help me learn our language, the random calls during road trips, and your leadership in language revitalization efforts.

This book is dedicated to Lillian (Pond) Lockwood and Violet Lillian (Lockwood) Freeland, my great-grandmother and grandmother respectively. Anishinaabemowin was violently taken from Lillian at the Mount Pleasant Indian Boarding School and was denied to Violet. Yet desire and actions to be Anishinaabe, to be goodhearted people, lived on in many other ways. This work, *Aazheyaadizi*, or "living in a way that extends back in time," is for those people in our communities who have been denied the abilities to speak our languages and live in ways that are conducive to our cultural understandings. This is not a book of hope, because hope is not a method. This is for developing effective methodologies to both return to our languages and decolonize them in the process.

CHAPTER 1

Worldview

T reaties are widely accepted to be one of the more effective means to defend our relationships to land. They provide a legal basis to demonstrate Indigenous occupation and actions within our homelands. One of the challenges before us as Indigenous peoples is to continually live into our ancestral relationships with these lands. The 1836 Treaty of Washington offers this challenge as we work to defend what it means to "stipulate for the right of hunting on the lands ceded, with the other usual privileges of occupancy, until the land is required for settlement."[1] Embedded in Article 13 is a worldview, a set of logics that provide a framework of thought for us to understand what it means to be in relationship with Anishinaabe Akiing. The *ogimaag* who signed that treaty were not colonized peoples. They still lived in intimate relationship to the land, enveloped by cyclical time, in a web of relatedness with the rest of life, and always working towards balance. A successful defense of that treaty will provide protections for us to continue that same lifestyle as best we can. A clear articulation of the relationships associated with this worldview is crucial to the reproduction of that worldview in our contemporary negotiations of Anishinaabeg life. Just what were Eskswagenabi and others who fought for Article 13 experiencing with the land? How might we more effectively translate those actions and meanings? How can we describe this deep sense of cultural difference at the level of worldview in a way that allows for a better understanding of this set of issues?

An Indigenous Genealogy

Considering worldview's more than two-hundred-year history in both Europe and the United States, its multiple definitions are not surprising. With a significant breadth of usage to cover, doing a formal genealogy could easily get out of hand. Luckily, others have already done some of the philological and genealogical work on the term worldview, so I am spared from doing that type of exhaustive work. While I will describe some of the trajectories of the term in academic play in this genealogy, I will focus my attention on Indigenous uses. In this genealogy then, I will demonstrate some of the trajectories of thought on worldview within several disciplines, critique the uses of worldview as a theoretical lens, and begin to build a useful definition of worldview with some critical precision. A critical definition of worldview is necessary to effectively communicate an Anishinaabe relationship to land, and this genealogy is a means to that end.

Weltanschauung

Immanuel Kant was the first person to use *weltanschauung* in his 1790 *Critique of Judgment*, using this new term to mean "the sense perception of the world."[2] From this beginning in Kant, it was first the field of philosophy that embraced this new concept. A brief list of those who deployed weltanschauung in their work would include Fichte, Schelling, Hegel, Dilthey, and Nietzsche. Each one of these philosophers used weltanschauung in their own way, nuancing its meaning throughout the nineteenth century. Fichte followed Kant's meaning of the term as the perception of the sensible world, but Schelling makes a shift from the sensory world of Kant to the "intellectual perception of the cosmos."[3] In Hegel, who used the concept of weltanschauung more consistently throughout his writings, we can see a greater development of the word to mean a "shared view which one acquires automatically by participation in the times and society which one forms with one's fellows."[4] Dilthey's work followed the skepticism that there is no ultimate reality that can be found in metaphysics, but there are worldviews that "seek to elucidate the riddle of life."[5] This line of thought ends up in a relativist bind where one's perspective dictates how one is able to know. Nietzsche takes up this relativist trajectory and uses the concept of weltanschauung to describe a particular perspective on reality, demonstrating that worldviews are "cultural entities which people in a given geographical location and historical context are dependent upon, subordinate to and products of."[6] Nietzsche uses this definition of worldview as a way to show that authority for believing in a certain reality can come simply from the established convention of a particular culture or language. For Nietzsche, no ultimate universal reality exists.

While countless other philosophers and writers contributed to the use and abuse of weltanschauung and worldview in its development, they rarely deviated from the uses that are briefly sketched out here. However, just as important as the philological and conceptual development of worldview is the socio-politico-economic development that was happening in Europe and the rest of the world at the time. It is not surprising that a term like worldview would come into fashion during a time when Europe was solidifying its colonial holdings throughout the world. The worldview of Europe was challenged with each colonial conquest as the realities of other worlds came back to the European homelands in the form of wealth, commerce, and narrative tales of the other. The eurowestern colonial gaze consumed the other and justified the ideology of white supremacy. This white supremacy would be the ideological formulation for a logic of hierarchy that justifies the means by which the wealth of the world was stolen from Indigenous peoples and lands. Unfortunately, the relativist trajectory of worldview that is described above was not attached to a moral or ethical lesson where the Indigenous peoples of the world were allowed to live their own lives. The assumed superiority of whiteness and Christianity was imposed as a universal in the justification of the theft of wealth and lands, and the relativist positions posited by Dilthey and Nietzsche that offered a possibility of understanding the Indigenous perspective on land and life would have to wait for postmodern thinkers to again take up their ideas.

The Evangelicals

A school of thought has been developing among evangelical academics that uses worldview as a concept for understanding Christianity as an all-encompassing cultural entity. I will be looking particularly at three authors, David Naugle, James Sire, and Paul Hiebert. While there are other authors who are also writing on the topic, these three represent some of the titles that most directly speak on the topic of worldview.[7] Their project is the exposition of a particularly Christian worldview, usually described in contrast and in conflict with a secular world. While their project is different from my own, their use and misuse of the concept of worldview will help to sharpen my own definition and use of the concept.

While Naugle's brief descriptions of the varied uses of worldview as a concept are useful for neophytes along with his bibliography, his project suffers from two problems. First, the cultural difference that he is attempting to describe is actually between two different ideologies, Christianity and secular culture. This limits the depth of Naugle's engagement with the concept of worldview as it allows him to stop his analysis at the level of ideology and renders his engagement with deep cultural differences dead on arrival. However, far more troubling to the usefulness of Naugle's deployment of the concept is the esoteric use and definition that he comes up with.

After eight chapters covering the history of the use of the term worldview, Naugle makes a curious move in his own definition. Rather than drawing from the trajectory of western thought that he just exposed, he turns instead to very specific Christian formulations of the importance of the "heart." He sets up his definition by stating that "all human cultures are under the jurisdiction of a particular sign or set of signs" and that these are "traceable to a series of world-interpreting narratives that provide the individual's 'bottom line' as well as the primary cultural 'given.'"[8] He then moves on to give his definition of worldview as a "semiotic system of narrative signs that creates the definitive symbolic universe which is responsible in the main for the shape of a variety of life-determining, human practices."[9] On the positive side, he does help to give credence to the powerful nature of the "world interpreting narratives," or origin narratives that help to give conscious shape to the worldview; but these are not the worldview itself. Origin narratives are an important element in the cultural expression of worldview, but there is something deeper. Furthermore, Naugle's description of worldview as a "semiotic system of narrative signs" does not effectively distinguish between the conscious ideological formulation of those signs and the deep cultural foundations that give rise to the making of those signs. His definition and use of worldview is not useful for getting to the foundational cultural elements that this project seeks.

Another evangelical author explicitly writing about worldview as a concept is James Sire. His book *Naming the Elephant: Worldview as a Concept* is an attempt to refine his working definition from his other book on worldview, *The Universe Next Door*. In positing his definition for worldview in his introduction, Sire follows

Naugle by stating that worldview is "a fundamental orientation of the heart," and then adding that "at the deepest root of a worldview is its commitment to and understanding the 'really real' . . . [there is] a consideration of behavior in the determination of what one's own or another's worldview really is . . . and a broader understanding of how worldviews are grasped by story."[10] His desire to get at the deeper nature of worldview is commendable, but as we shall see, he too falls short when his definition is further explained.

In addition to confusing ideology and worldview like Naugle, Sire demonstrates another problem with his exposition of worldview as an application of the concept when it comes to the human individual. According to Sire, in describing the function of worldview in his daily life, "there will be no other worldview in the universe that is identical to my own."[11] Here he breaks with his desire to describe the deep cultural components of worldview and exposes the surface nature of his definition. However, on the positive side, Sire does take seriously the ways in which "our worldview is not precisely what we may state it to be. It is what is actualized in our behavior."[12] This move to show worldview as a lived experience will become helpful when it comes to holding people accountable to their stated worldview and ideology. Considering the powerful effects that capitalist economic systems have on all our lives in the present, the question as to the lived experience of worldview will become a valuable analytical tool when it comes to social change. It also is important because it helps us demonstrate the ways in which our worldview is at play in everyday life.

While Naugle and Sire have chosen a primarily western philosophical trajectory in their definitional understanding of worldview, another evangelical, Paul Hiebert, has chosen a different path. Hiebert is trained as a cultural anthropologist, so his definition and analysis of worldview takes on a different flavor. He defines worldview as the "fundamental cognitive, affective, and evaluative presuppositions a group of people make about the nature of things, and which they use to order their lives."[13] While vaguely written, when he puts this definition into practice, it too offers some potential for exposing the deep cultural nature of worldviews as well as some problems.

By drawing from a different disciplinary trajectory, Hiebert is able to emphasize some different aspects to worldview that Naugle and Sire do not. While philosophy has been primarily interested in the cognitive element of worldview, anthropologists have focused more heavily on the behavior of individuals and groups, and their connections to their material environment. This anthropological trajectory allows

Hiebert to comment that for some cultures, "space is more important than time. Time separates past from present. Space brings them together."[14] This reference to time and space helps to provide distinction between worldview and ideology and focuses the discourse on the logics associated with culture. However, Hiebert then shifts gears and agrees with Morris Opler that "conflicts and power struggles are endemic to all societies, and that different segments of a society seek to oppress the others for their own advantage. It makes us aware, too, that worldviews are often ideologies that those in power use to keep others in subjection."[15] This is problematic on two levels. Not only is he conflating worldview and ideology like Naugle and Sire, he universalizes the power struggles of the eurowest as though they occur in all places and all times. This type of universalizing of the data can only cause confusion and misunderstanding when we apply this type of study to other cultures.

For a brief summary of the evangelicals that have just been discussed, I can say that there are some parts of their discussions of worldview that are helpful. From Naugle we have the emphasis on "myth" or origin narratives as a close descriptor of worldview, and from Sire we have the concept of worldview as acted out in human behavior. From Hiebert we can glean some of the deep cultural questions about time and space that are an important element of worldview. However, I believe that there are some serious limitations in their studies because of their goals. For both Naugle and Sire, their goal is to attempt to legitimize "Christian" scholarship as an academic enterprise. While Naugle's bibliography and breadth of study is helpful, to end up with a concept of worldview being a part of the "human heart" as undefined seriously undermines the efficacy of his study. There is also a significant amount of projecting specific western categories, especially the Manichean dualism of good and evil. Naugle spends an entire chapter discussing the Christian worldview as "spiritual warfare" and the necessity for the forces of Christian discipleship to defeat Satan and his cosmic army of evil.[16] While Sire is not as explicit in his elaboration of cosmic Christian domination, he also relies too heavily on concepts of good and evil in his exposition on worldview. However, Hiebert's project is even scarier than that. He elaborates the deep cultural elements of worldview as a means "to transform them. Too often conversion [to Christianity] takes place at the surface levels of behavior and beliefs; but if worldviews are not transformed, the gospel is interpreted in terms of pagan worldviews, and the result is Christo-paganism."[17] Even though Hiebert and others may have the "best intentions" in mind, their project is simply the continuation of a long history of missionary cultural genocide, wreaking cultural and physical violence throughout the entire world as part of a project of colonial domination.[18]

Social and Political Theory

Another discipline where worldview has been used as an analytical lens is in the field of social and political theory. Mike Hawkins, in his book *Social Darwinism in European and American Thought, 1860–1945*, attempts to use worldview as a lens for understanding the rise and use of social Darwinism on the social and political landscape. This work is helpful for two reasons. First he attempts to define worldview particularly, and at the same time he also defines ideology as separate from worldview. He defines worldview as a "set of assumptions about the order of nature and of the place of humanity within it, and how this order relates to and is affected by the passage of time."[19] He goes on to explain that worldview "usually contains a view of social reality" and shows how this social reality "fits into the overall configuration of nature, human nature and time."[20] Hawkins then moves on to explain how ideology "comprises a theory of human interactions and how these are mediated by institutions."[21] He further explains that "the ideological aspect of a theory thus contains both descriptive and evaluative features which often makes difficult the separation of the empirical and normative claims that are being made."[22] While his attempts at particular definitions are commendable, when we see how they play out in his work, they leave a lot to be desired. Hawkins goes on to state that "Social Darwinism is not, in itself, a social or political theory. Rather, it consists of a series of connected assumptions and propositions about nature, time and how humanity is situated within both."[23] According to Hawkins, because social Darwinism does not give specific elements to human social and mental development or elaborate on "optimal conditions" for human social existence, it lacks the "ideological component" necessary to label it as an ideology.[24] So following Hawkins's logic, since social Darwinism lacks the necessary components to meet his definition of ideology, it must be labeled something else in his scheme of things that is a worldview.[25]

While Hawkins's attempts at defining worldview and ideology fall short for our present purposes, his analysis does offer a deeper look at the concept of time as an element of worldview. Within the eurowestern thought process there is a deep cultural reliance upon the notion of time as a linear progression, and I think Vine Deloria Jr.'s analysis sums it up best as naming it the sin-salvation-eschaton trajectory.[26] This overwhelming reliance on sin-salvation-eschaton can be most readily seen with the philosopher John Fiske. As a social Darwinist, he believed that progress was the law of history. In short, he followed the traditional Darwinian progressional chart from primitive status where war was the rule of the day (sin), which was elevated to civilization when egoism was supplanted by altruism (salvation), and finally there would be (eschaton) "a future in which individuals existed in perfect harmony with their fellows, united in a World Federation."[27] This was all supposed to be due to the power of natural selection. But, as Hawkins asks, "What form, then, would natural selection take in this period of peace and mutual harmony, and how would progress continue?"[28] Hawkins suggests,

> Here, once again, we encounter the dilemma which the determinism and universalism of Social Darwinism posed for thinkers like Fiske who believed in moral progress and the triumph of civilization. These could be shown to be the work of natural laws such as the struggle for existence. But the complete realization of these ideals implied a future state in which the laws of nature were no longer applicable to humans. And unless these laws were suspended, the harmonious ideal appeared unrealizable.[29]

While this is a good analysis of the situation, I believe Hawkins misses a chance at a deeper analysis of worldview because he fails to recognize the ways in which these largely non-Christian people (or at least marginally Christian) continue to demonstrate an inherently Christian ideal of linear time.[30] Because the concept of the linear progression of time is a deeply held belief at the level of worldview, it is difficult to think of other methods of organizing time, or in the case of Fiske, it is difficult to recognize when your thought process becomes logically inconsistent. The sin-salvation-eschaton conceptual schema is so deeply engrained at the level of worldview that thinkers like Fiske were unable to see the failings of their own ideological formulations of social Darwinism.

Weltansicht and Linguistics

There is also a trajectory of thought that discusses worldview in the field of linguistics that can be traced to Wilhelm von Humboldt. In the early nineteenth century he coined a term similar to weltanschauung, using *weltansicht* to describe the "capacity which language bestows upon us to form the concepts with which we think and which we need in order to communicate."[31] Humboldt's use of weltansicht, which James Underhill translates as worldview, is concerned with the way that language "shapes the perspective and conception we have of the world and to a large extent shapes the way we negotiate our way through the course of life on a day-to-day basis as we converse with others."[32] Here we can see an early association of language and culture in the development of the idea of worldview. James Underhill demonstrates that Humboldt's ideas have been glossed over in the English-speaking world, representing a missed opportunity to consider the medium of language as an important analytical aspect of worldview.[33]

While there is little evidence of the direct connection from Humboldt to twentieth-century linguistics, the notion that language is intimately involved in the concept of worldview is discussed early in the century.[34] The ethnographic work of Franz Boas represents the early stages of these developments, which were negotiating the "confrontation with the very different cultures and languages of North America that forced linguists (used to working within the frameworks of Indo-European languages) to reevaluate some of their fundamental premises about language."[35] This confrontation of cultures, which in the early twentieth century meant the intended destruction of Indigenous peoples, helped to call into question the presumption of eurowestern universality. Edward Sapir helped to sharpen some of this discourse on language and culture, working towards a better articulation of the relationship between language and culture. He negotiated the complexity of language as associated with culture, differentiating that "culture may be defined as what a society does and thinks. Language is a particular how of thought."[36] However, according to Underhill, Sapir's work leads towards a contradiction in that "language, as the product of human usage, governs thought, but then [he] rejects the seemingly implicit consequence that thought will condition the culture we create."[37] Sapir's research, while pushing boundaries of linguistics, was not a clear articulation by the time of his death. A student of Sapir, Benjamin Whorf, took this work and extended it to connect language and culture to everyday behavior. Whorf used a comparative analysis of English and Hopi languages to negotiate the relationships between language, thought, and culture. In relation to worldview, he provided evidence of particular cognitive orientations for each language and culture "by describing specific, observable patterns of behavior in the two associated cultures."[38] This connection to lived experience is a useful trajectory as it provides concrete manifestations of the conceptualizations associated with language and thought. However, in part because of the untimely deaths of both Sapir and Whorf, it seems their research was not able to reach maturity and rid itself of some of the internal contradictions.[39] Hence, as this linguistic work was taken up among other theorists, it would eventually be reduced to the Sapir-Whorf hypothesis. This reduction would come to rest with the notion that Sapir and Whorf are suggesting that language determines thought and culture. The discourse of much of linguistics and linguistic anthropology would then be about proving or disproving the hypothesis of linguistic and cultural relativity.

The rest of the twentieth century would see this discourse on relativity split into two primary camps of anthropology and cognitive linguistics. On the anthropological side there is a discussion of the extent to which language affects worldviews, and on the cognitive side the "dispute was whether a series of facts about linguistic differences necessarily entailed 'incommensurable' conceptual structures."[40] While it may seem that these lines of discourse would be beneficial to a theory of worldview, there are three problems. First, following the discourse of modern linguistics has meant overly emphasizing the technical minutia of language and concepts, losing the connections to larger cultural issues. For worldview to be a useful category to demonstrate cultural difference, it must be related to more than language. Secondly, this failure to get at the depths of cultural difference in the discourse stems from a problematic starting place. The bulk of linguistic studies use the Sapir-Whorf relativity hypothesis as a jumping-off place and work to prove or disprove its tenets. These theoretical and methodological approaches limit the scope of the studies, and they fail to speak to the many problems facing Indigenous communities. Lastly, this emphasis on language tends to overly determine the relationship to worldview, often equating language and worldview. This precludes the possibility of different languages, say Indigenous languages, sharing the same or a very similar worldview. While the discourse has helped to push back against some of the universalizing tendencies of colonialism, it still lacks the depth of analysis to reach the questions that are guiding this development of worldview as an analytical lens. This problem can be seen in the work of James Underhill in his example of the difference between weltansicht and weltanschauung. In trying to elaborate Humboldt's position about weltansicht, or "worldview as the configuration of concepts which allow conceptual thought," he uses an example of capitalist and communist worldviews as occupying different weltanshauungs (ideology and metaphysics) within the same language.[41] This example helps to demonstrate that his negotiation of cultural difference, in my own terms, stops at the level of ideology and does not take into consideration further depths of cultural difference. This begs the question, if capitalism and communism are the same worldview, then how do we talk about the differences between capitalism, communism, and Indigenous cultures? What word do we use to conceptualize these deeper differences? If we allow worldview to conceptualize all of these differences, it works to erase the particularities of Indigenous cultures by presuming an equal footing with the ideological nuances inherent in eurowestern political discourse.

Cultural Anthropology

For Indigenous peoples, there is a distrust and sometimes contempt for the discipline of anthropology. Anthropologists have taken the torch from missionaries and travelers in their attempts to "explain" Indigenous culture, which really means they have used a slightly different eurowestern framework of thought to catalog, explain away, and sanitize the ongoing genocide of Indigenous people. This shift in thought constitutes a shift from missionary justifications of the work of Christ bringing new souls to the Lord (as eurowestern nation states laid waste to native populations) to the "scientific" explanations of the progress of western expansion and assumed superiority over the "primitive races" of Indigenous peoples (as the eurowestern nations continue to lay waste to native lands and populations). As the fight over frameworks of power between science and religion was played out in the nineteenth and twentieth centuries, the "scientific" explanations of progress used studies of Indigenous peoples as "primitive" to develop their framework of linear progress, "demonstrating" the evolutionary shift of societies from "primitive" to religious to scientific. By playing off of the already pernicious linear thinking in eurowestern cultures, they were able to anoint themselves as the best and the brightest of the "superior" race, and naturalize their rise to and exercise of power as an evolutionary process that not only cannot be stopped, it should be exalted and promoted as the crowning achievement of not only eurowestern culture, but of the entire world.[42]

With that sort of trajectory of anthropological thought, it may sound counterintuitive that this discipline that helped to continually justify its definition of the "dying races" of Indigenous people would also help to develop the thought around worldview. Being confronted by very different cultures had the effect of causing anthropologists to scramble for methods of understanding peoples that were fundamentally different from their own. This confrontation with difference caused them to ask some basic questions about how we as humans negotiate our lives within the environment. While the development of a theory of worldview has a number of the same shortfalls among anthropologists as it does among other disciplines, it does begin to take more seriously some of the fundamental deep cultural differences that shape the ways in which we negotiate our daily lives.

While a number of anthropologists have used the term worldview to describe various elements of culture, I would suggest that it was the work of Robert Redfield at the University of Chicago that helped to shift the discourse around worldview. According to Redfield, the concept of worldview is "in short, a man's idea of the universe. It is that organization of ideas which answers to a man the questions: Where am I? Among what do I move? What are my relations to these things?"[43] While these questions could be answered in a concrete way, instead Redfield continues on a line of abstraction suggesting that "'World view' may be used to include forms of thought and the most comprehensive attitudes towards life . . . [worldview] can hardly be conceived without some dimension in time, some idea of past and of future."[44] While his abstractions leave a lot to be desired in providing a concise definition with concrete examples, his questions do offer a new direction to study. In this set of questions we can begin to see the possibility of further theoretical development in that he is naming space, time, and relationships as primary understandings of the concept of worldview. However, Redfield himself recognizes the limits of his own study, lamenting that although he believes that worldviews are universal, there is not much to guide an attempt at naming these universals, as "Concepts about world view are hardly developed, and comparative studies are barely begun. So any suggestions now put forward are almost random and are highly tentative."[45] The further development of worldview in the field of anthropology would have to wait for other theorists.

Another cultural anthropologist who is worth mentioning is Clifford Geertz. While his work on worldview was only minor in his published work, he did help to make some important connections that others have followed. Geertz's main contribution to the study of worldview is his recognition of the necessity to connect the "thick description" of ethnographic work to a more comprehensive analytical framework in cultural theory. According to Geertz, cultural theory "is unseverable from the immediacies thick description presents, its freedom to shape itself in terms of its internal logic is rather limited."[46] The job of cultural theory is to "provide a vocabulary in which what symbolic action has to say about itself—that is, about the role of culture in human life—can be expressed."[47] This is an important move as it attempts to connect the worldview of a people and understand it as connected to and consistent with their lived experience. To connect lived experience with a more comprehensive understanding of culture, Geertz employed two associated concepts that were common in anthropological parlance in the mid-twentieth century, worldview and ethos. He described ethos as the "tone, character, and quality of their life, its moral and aesthetic style and mood," and worldview as the "picture they have of the way things in sheer actuality are, their most comprehensive ideas of order."[48] For Geertz, these two aspects of culture were held together by religion, which helps the social values of a culture to be "coercive." To keep a society intact, "sacred rituals and myths are portrayed not as subjective human preferences but as the imposed conditions for life implicit in a world with a particular structure."[49] Religion provides the narratives necessary to make the structure of society meaningful and compels the members of that society to reproduce the same behaviors and meanings.

While the connection of worldview to the lived behavioral experience (the thick descriptions) of the ethnographer's study is a step in the right direction, Geertz's analysis still suffers from two major shortcomings. First, his definition of worldview as "the picture of the way things in sheer actuality are" is far too abstract to be helpful in making a direct connection between a worldview and a lived experience. He does give several examples of what he means, but it is in these examples that we can see the second problem, the euroforming of Indigenous and other cultures. For example, he quotes a passage from a Lakota informant, discussing the concept of a stone as sacred, then immediately puts this concept of stone in a particular eurowestern framework of thought by stating, "Here is a subtle formulation of the relation between good and evil, and of their grounding in the very nature of reality."[50] Apparently impossible to Geertz, among the rest of the anthropological field, is that the Manichean concepts of good and evil are eurowestern cultural particulars, and they do not apply, like religion, to Indigenous and many other cultures. This preponderance of euroforming the cultures that they study causes their analysis to fall far short of anything other than simply observation and conjecture. Geertz himself recognizes that his work is a very small beginning, calling the concepts of worldview and ethos a "prototheory, forerunners it is hoped, of a more adequate analytical framework."[51] While his work misses the mark in its abstraction and projection of assumed universal cultural categories, it does push the concept of worldview a little further towards a useful analytical lens.

While there was some academic work around worldview in the mid-twentieth century among anthropologists, as recently as 1980, Michael Kearney still commented that for a term as important as worldview is to cultural anthropology, "no comprehensive model of it has been formulated prior to this effort."[52] He, like Redfield and Geertz before him, suggests that his work towards this comprehensive model of worldview is "a preliminary attempt," and he does make some modest gains in helping to flesh out a more comprehensive model of worldview. In his 1984 book *World View*, Kearney follows Redfield's and Geertz's lead in attempting to connect worldview as an organizational structure in culture with the lived experience of that culture. In this line of thought, Kearney describes worldview as a "dynamic logico-structurally integrated system of knowledge."[53] He begins with five worldview universals of the self and other, relationship, classification, causality, and space and time. According to Kearney, these questions need to be addressed by all societies, but they can and do respond to the questions in different ways. However, what is most important for Kearney is that the response to these universals within a culture is interrelated, therefore a system: "World view is itself ordered by the dynamic interrelationships among its elements, which are the images and assumptions that form the contents of the various worldview universals. These interrelationships are what I have been calling a logico-structural integration."[54] This move is important because it helps to both recognize and begin to decipher some of the complex relationships within a worldview and demonstrate how they are usually logically consistent.

Another question that helps to drive Kearney's interest in worldview is: how are worldviews formed? His answer to this question is another area of modest advancement in the anthropological study of worldview. Kearney recognizes a dynamic relationship between the environmental conditions that a group of people live in, and their images of that world that form their worldview. Kearney explains,

> A world view is linked to reality in two ways: first by regarding it, by forming more or less accurate images of it, images that mirror the world; and second, by testing these images through using them to guide action. By being put into action faulty images are corrected and brought more into line with the external world.[55]

In this model, Kearney helps to explain not only the dynamic formation of world-view and lived behavior, but also the possibility of social change. While this model is a step forward in the study of worldview, it needs to be stated that he gets to this model through Marxist notions of historical materialism. This reliance on Marxist thought is a double-edged sword. On the positive side it allows him to break with what he calls the "idealist" camp of Boas and Redfield, who, according to him, have continued the service of anthropology in liberal bourgeoisie interests and demonstrate the "bias of the intellectual who, secure in his study, analyzes human knowledge apart from the so-called real world in which common human knowledge arises."[56] This idealist model does not take seriously enough the historical materialist environment that the worldview arises in dynamic relationship with. In this sense, Kearney's analysis is helpful. The downside is that, like other anthropologists, his analysis imposes Eurocentric categories of cognition like historicism and peasant, and only understands ideology in its hierarchical imposition of a mode of thought used to coerce subjects into obedience. While his modest advancements in the study of worldview are helpful, his model lacks the linguistic, conceptual sophistication to fully understand the depth of difference between some cultures, such as the differences between Indigenous peoples and the eurowest.[57]

A final anthropologist worthy of note is A. Irving Hallowell. While his work lacks a concise definition of worldview, it is important for two reasons. First, his studies are primarily of Anishinaabeg in Anishinaabe Akiing, so his analysis speaks directly to my project. Second, his method of investigation is far different than most other anthropologists directly speaking to worldview, because he takes very seriously a linguistic conceptual analysis of Anishinaabemowin. It is this emphasis on the structure of language and its meaning in the lived experience of a people that sets Hallowell's study apart. In his own words,

> It may be argued, in fact, that a thoroughgoing "objective" approach to the study of cultures cannot be achieved solely by projecting upon those cultures categorical abstractions derived from Western thought. For, in a broad sense, the latter are a reflection of *our* cultural subjectivity. A higher order of objectivity may be sought by adopting a perspective which includes an analysis of the outlook of the people themselves as a complementary procedure.[58]

By taking the conceptual world of Anishinaabeg seriously, Hallowell was able to break down some of the eurowestern projections that had until that time inhibited anthropological work towards a meaningful deployment of worldview.

As part of this process of conceptual decolonization of anthropological work, Hallowell focused on the animate/inanimate linguistic distinction that is part of Anishinaabemowin. He began with the basic question "what is the meaning of animate in Ojibwa thinking?"[59] For non-Anishinaabemowin speakers, the animate/

inanimate distinction causes a lot of confusion. Usually it is assumed that animate means "alive" in a eurowestern sense and inanimate means "not alive." However, upon investigation, this imposed dualism breaks down when applied to words like *sin*, or stone, which is grammatically animate. Hallowell explains by giving an anecdote from one of his informants, who when asked if all stones were alive, replied, "No! But *some* are."[60] He goes on to suggest that Anishinaabeg do not consider stones as animate (living) more than eurowesterners, but the differences lie in the "cognitive set" that grammatically *sin* is a part of. There is an important origin narrative involving Flint, an important character in Anishinaabe thought who is made from stone and helped to form the world. Furthermore, some stones in Anishinaabe Akiing do manifest animate properties of motion. Hallowell correctly asserts, "The crucial test is experience. Is there any personal testimony available?"[61] To answer this question he gives several examples of informants answering in the affirmative to their own experiences of *sin* moving and demonstrating other animate properties like speaking and keeping implements for people.[62] This foray into the linguistic-conceptual world of the Anishinaabeg helps to demonstrate both the lack of a dogmatic formulation of animate and inanimate in our conceptual world, and the efficacy of demonstrating a much more authentic experience of Anishinaabe culture with his chosen methodology. This example speaks to the hyper-empirical nature of Anishinaabe thought and culture. What is believed to be true and is considered to be true by Anishinaabeg ultimately depends upon the experience of the people.

Another subject within Anishinaabe thought where Hallowell deploys this linguistic conceptual methodology is in the recognition of what "person" can represent. He suggests that "person" in Anishinaabemowin is a much larger category than within eurowestern culture. To understand "person" in Anishinaabe thought, we have to talk about our relationships to entities like *giizis*, or the sun. *Giizis* is not thought of as an object as in eurowestern thought, it is a relative; or as Hallowell puts it, "the sun is a 'person' of the other-than-human class."[63] This "other-than-human class" of person, or *manidoog* in Anishinaabemowin, is an important turn in the work on worldview as it begins to take seriously the web of relatedness that we as Indigenous people live in. Our ancestors, the characters of our origin narratives like Sky Woman, Flint, and the many *manidoog* are all our relatives of this "other-than-human" variety. Hallowell presses the point using the example of "grandfathers." Within a eurowestern construction, only human persons could be called grandfather in its eurowestern usage. However, in Anishinaabe thought, the four directions and numerous animals who were here when Sky Woman fell from the sky are also considered to be "grandfathers." Anthropologists studying Anishinaabeg and other Indigenous peoples have long imposed this eurowestern framework on us, and hence euroformed our cultures, creating dualisms where none exist. But, as Hallowell points out, "if we adopt a world view perspective no dualization appears. In this perspective 'grandfather' is a term applicable to certain 'person objects,' without any distinction between human persons and those of an other-than-human class."[64] Furthermore, he points out that other anthropologists have often relied upon a natural/supernatural dualism to explain Indigenous thought, with natural meaning human "grandfathers," and supernatural being applied to the characters of the origin narratives and other *manidoog*. However, as Hallowell explains, to apply natural/supernatural to Ojibwa characters "is completely misleading, if for no other reason than the fact that the concept of 'supernatural' presupposes a concept of the 'natural.' The latter is not present in Ojibwa thought."[65] These dualisms like natural/supernatural are a good example of the euroforming of our cultures in anthropological literature, and Hallowell helps us to root out some of these eurowestern imposed categories. By projecting these eurowestern dualisms onto Indigenous cultures, anthropologists have done more to misunderstand and misrepresent our cultures than they have done to create understanding. While Hallowell's work is far from flawless, as he too imposes some eurowestern categories like religion, his work does take more seriously what Indigenous cultures can communicate when we take their linguistic conceptual fields and knowledge more seriously.

Indigenous Philosophy

The final group of authors bring us closer to both an effective methodological approach and conceptual analysis that will help develop a useful definition and theory of worldview. Like cultural anthropologists, Indigenous authors by necessity have to deal with two (or more) very different cultures, both in their theoretical work and possibly in their daily lives. This negotiation of different worlds necessitates a deep understanding of the linguistic and conceptual processes in play. Failure to negotiate this cultural divide successfully will usually mean a confusion of Indigenous thought in eurowestern terms, or as Kwasi Wiredu puts it, "the outcome is likely to do violence (though not premeditatedly) to [our] indigenous categories of thought."[66] Unfortunately, because of the ongoing colonization of Indigenous cultures by eurowestern powers, many of us have participated in these acts of cultural violence against our own peoples, and this demonstrates the need for our own conceptual decolonization. Both Vine Deloria Jr. and Kwasi Wiredu have done groundbreaking work in the realm of conceptual decolonization, and while neither of them have explicitly worked to precisely define worldview as a concept, their work exemplifies the deep cultural analysis that the concept of worldview is suited for.[67]

While Wiredu rarely uses the term worldview to describe his analytical work, his methods of conceptual decolonization consistently speak to some of the fundamental differences between his Akan culture in Ghana and the eurowest. His work is helpful in demonstrating some of the ways spatiality is thought of differently in the Akan language and culture in comparison to the eurowest.[68] In one exposition, Wiredu takes on the concept of "nature," suggesting that "the way in which the Akans conceptualise that which others conceptualise through the term 'nature' is so different from the latter as not to be susceptible to an equivalent verbalization."[69] Wiredu begins with a brief elucidation of the term nature in the eurowest, showing that it is "the concept of the realm of all those material phenomena (things, events, and processes) that conform to the kind of laws which exist in commonsense thinking as crudely perceived regularities and receive their rigorous and sophisticated formulation in science."[70] He further illustrates that in the eurowest there are two basic camps in regard to this formulation of nature, where naturalists believe that this concept is a full elaboration of nature, and the non-naturalists deny this. While there is not necessarily agreement as to the parameters of the existence of nature between the naturalists and non-naturalists, they do both assume that there is an intelligible distinction between the material and the nonmaterial, the natural and the non-natural, and the natural and the supernatural. But according to Wiredu, "None of these contrasts is intelligible within Akan thought."[71] To get at the unintelligibility of the material/nonmaterial distinctions in Akan, Wiredu returns to Akan origin narratives and to their concepts of their "supreme being." Again, utilizing the Akan language, he shows that while they have many names for the supreme being, when they speak of the creative aspects of this being they use "Borebore" or "Obooade." Both of these terms speak of "hewing out, making, manufacturing, fashioning out," so their name for the supreme being is translated best as "the maker of things."[72] The significance of this formulation cannot be underestimated because it shows that "the notion of ex-nihilo creation (creation out of nothing) cannot be coherently expressed in

Akan . . . since the word for 'create' presupposes raw materials."[73] Furthermore, Wiredu shows how in Akan, even the concept of nothing can only be expressed as "the absence of something *in a given place*."[74] Similarly, the concept of existence in Akan is "wo ho," which translated properly means "to be at some place."[75] Hence, what we see here in the Akan worldview is a fundamental orientation to space as indicated in their linguistic structure, origin narrative, and conceptual framework. This is a radically different orientation to space than in the eurowest, where the concept of space is given a secondary relation to time.[76]

Another way that Wiredu gets at the fundamental differences between his traditional Akan thought and the eurowest is in an examination of the intelligibility/unintelligibility of the Cartesian dualism of material/spiritual. For the Akan, there is only one universe "of many strata wherein God, the ancestors, humans, animals, plants and all the rest of the furniture of the world have their being."[77] The point here is that the concept of the supreme being is spatially configured so that it cannot be effectively described by what eurowesterns usually impose as a "supernatural" concept. So if the natural/supernatural dualism does not work, how are we to conceptualize an important entity like the ancestors in Akan thought? Wiredu suggests that the material/spiritual dualism here is also unintelligible because of its inability to understand spatiality, not to mention the problem of having no intelligible definition in its own right. Instead, he suggests that a better way of thinking about ancestors or other "unseen" conceptualizations is to think of them as partially material, or "quasi-material."[78] This allows for a spatial conceptualization of these entities, and still allows for their understanding within the Akan spatially configured worldview because the ancestors are thought of living around them in their space. Wiredu then moves to show that if we are to understand the concept of "spiritual," then we would have to have an intelligible definition of that concept as well. However, upon further reflection, no such definition exists. Usually a negative definition is given, where the spiritual is that which is nonmaterial, but this is really unhelpful. As Wiredu asks, "How are we to differentiate between the spiritual and the void?"[79] Others will move to define spiritual as the unseen, or the invisible. But this too is far too broad to be helpful because this description could also be used for something like gravity.[80]

In addition to the lack of a useful definition that would make the material/spiritual dualism intelligible within the eurowest, Wiredu expounds on the lack of internal coherence of the natural/supernatural dualism. In the eurowest, the idea of nature has its own set of concepts that help to bring an understanding of their worldview, including the idea that there are laws of nature that are immutable. The idea of supernatural has been applied when those laws of nature have been transcended in some way. As Wiredu explains,

> a supernatural event is one whose occurrence is contrary to the laws of nature. But if the event actually happens, then any law that fails to reckon with its possibility is inaccurate and is in need of some modifications, at least. However, if the law is suitably amended, even if only by means of an exceptive rider, the event is no longer contrary to natural law. Hence no event can be consistently described as supernatural.[81]

Not only is the dualism of natural/supernatural not applicable to the Akan conceptual framework, it is not internally coherent as a way of explaining phenomena in the eurowest. Therefore we can see that the natural/non-natural, material/spiritual, and the natural/supernatural dualisms that are consistently used in the western academy to describe both the eurowest and other cultures are "not a universal feature of human thinking, since the Akans, at least, do not use it. And in any case, its coherence is questionable."[82]

While Wiredu may only rarely use the term worldview to describe the types of differences he is explaining, his analysis is consistent with Indigenous conceptualizations of culture, space, and the distinctions between our Indigenous cultures and the eurowest. However, considering that Wiredu is Akan, and writing about lands and languages that are different from those here in North America, we also have to demonstrate that these ideas are in play here.

I have already mentioned some of Vine Deloria Jr.'s thinking about spatiality and worldview in the introduction, discussing the lands for American Indian people as "having the highest possible meaning."[83] While this statement certainly is true, we are now in a position to take it a step further. To demonstrate the fundamental place in which land functions in an Indigenous worldview, we can show how this relationship helps to organize our cultures. Deloria helps us to think about an Indigenous worldview, as Michael Kearney suggests, as a "dynamic logico-structurally integrated system of knowledge" where several worldview components all work together to create a systemic cultural whole.[84] Deloria points out, largely stating the obvious, that there is an inherent relationship between space and time. However, contrary to eurowestern culture, it is not time that helps to understand space, but "Space generates time."[85] Space, our land, is the basic building block of a cultural whole, and our living in these specific places gives an understanding of cyclical time. While there are understandings of time as linear, as we grow older and experience more throughout our lives, both communally and individually, these linear understandings are a distant second to the importance of cyclical time, and all are generated by the primacy of the land. *Giizis*, the sun, moves through the sky on a daily run from east to west, *dibiki giizis*, the "night sun," has her own twenty-eight-day cycle by which we mark time, and we move throughout the year to the rhythms of the changing seasons, all to start over again in cyclical fashion the next cycle.

From these two components of a worldview, space and time, Deloria then also elaborates how spatial thinking is connected to two other elements of an Indigenous worldview. As we gain our sustenance, we must inevitably participate in acts of violence against our other living relatives so that we can eat and live. A good portion of our ceremonial life has to do with keeping the balance of creation intact as we provide food for our communities. In this way of living, "spatial thinking requires that ethical systems be related directly to the physical world and real human situations."[86] Here, Deloria helps us to make the connection between spatiality and the rest of life with which we share a particular space. As we live in a web of relatedness in our space, and we have to participate in acts of violence to survive, we must participate in a ceremonial life that helps to restore a sense of balance with our relatives with whom we share that space. As a number of our narratives tell us, if we fail to follow through these ceremonies and the wishes of our relatives, then they may no longer be around to provide us sustenance. From these four "logico-structurally integrated" elements of an Indigenous worldview (intimate relationship to space, cyclical time, living in a web of relatedness, and the balance of those relationships), we can see the primary importance that space (land) plays in Indigenous life. Our ethical systems "must relate to the land, *and it must dominate and structure culture.* It must not be separated from a particular piece of land and a particular community, and it must not be determined by culture."[87] The space in which we live is the basic building block of our worldview. Our entire culture stems from the space that we occupy and our relationship to the rest of life with which we share that space. If removed from the land, we cease to exist in the same way that we had. This represents the gap in communication between the Indigenous people, who are trying to protect their essential relationships to the land, and the United States Government, which fails to recognize that relationship to land for Indigenous peoples. When removed from the land, we simply do not have the same relationships that we once had. We do not have an ontology that is temporally located, that primarily exists in a discursive history of events, assumed to be universal. Ontologically we are intimately related to our places, and cutting us off from those places, whether that is removal to distant lands, physical destruction of those lands from mining and lumber industries, or the occupation of those lands by recreational interests, all constitute acts of cultural genocide.

Worldview: A Definition

From this Indigenous genealogy of worldview as a concept, we can see an emphasis on certain topics that can help give direction for a definition. From recent evangelical developments (Naugle) we can see a consistent use of origin narratives as a way of understanding worldview. Also from an evangelical viewpoint (Sire) as well as anthropology (Geertz and Kearney) we get a theoretical desire to connect lived experience to a deeper cultural theory. From most everyone involved there is recognition of the importance of worldview helping to orient humans to space and time, including Vine Deloria Jr. Hawkins helps in his attempts to separate worldview and ideology. Finally, methodologically Hallowell and Wiredu develop a linguistic-conceptual analysis that allows us to ground the concept of worldview in a particular system of thought.

Thus far, there is a lack of a cogent definition of worldview that can be utilized as a method for cross-cultural analysis. This lack of a critical definition continually allows for the term worldview to be used by many people with differing, usually undefined, meanings and applied in a variety of ways ranging from deep cultural organization to individual "outlooks" on the world. With this lack of critical refinement, the term worldview could remain an ineffective conceptual tool. However, this long and sordid journey of weltanshauung to worldview across time and numerous academic disciplines also suggests a deeply held desire to develop a useful, critically accurate method of investigating cultural differences. Considering that there is at present a lack of critical concepts useful in demonstrating cultural differences, I am developing this definition and theory of worldview to fill that void. By coming to a more precise definition and useable theory, more accurate cross-cultural translations can be attained in the field of Indigenous studies. Furthermore, it can yield more accurate descriptions of our cultural traditions, and hopefully, better understanding for the project of protecting our lands and our relationships to those lands.

An accurate depiction of Anishinaabeg culture using a theory of worldview will begin with a precise definition of worldview. I define worldview as an interrelated set of cultural logics that fundamentally orient a culture to space, time, the rest of life, and provides a methodological prescription for relating to that life. In this definition there is a brief description of what a worldview is (interrelated set of cultural logics) and four components to which those logics associate (relationships to space, time, the rest of life, and a methodological prescription to relate to life). With this definition I am positing that each culture has a set of logics that allows its constituents to negotiate the world. These logics orient the culture to a consistent trajectory of thought organized around relationships that must be addressed to be able to build a meaningful life. Each culture must have some type of relationship to the lands that they occupy, to time, to the rest of life, to be able to live in the everyday.

The four logics that relate culture to space, time, life, and prescribe how to relate to that life, work together to give a footing to the culture. That is, they are a "dynamic logico-structurally integrated system of knowledge."[88] Since we have to negotiate our life on the earth, there has to be a conceptualization of what that space is like and a prescription for negotiating that space. Spatiality, as defined by Vine Deloria Jr., is the land on which we live. For Indigenous people it is not land in a general sense, but an *intimate relationship with a localized space*. Furthermore, it is this space, which allows for life to exist, that gives rise to time. To negotiate life on earth necessitates learning and memory, which presumes time. Cyclical and linear conceptualization of time are the two primary logics that help to structure culture. Both Indigenous and eurowestern cultures use cyclical and linear time. It becomes a worldview logic when it structures thought and culture. Another logic of worldview that is associated with space is a relationship to life. We are obviously not alone in this world, so we have to figure out a way to relate to the life with which we share our space. This structure of relatedness for Indigenous people means living in a web of relatedness where all of life is interconnected. For example, since we rely on our other-than-human relatives for food, we have to find a way of keeping those relationships intact. Minding our relationships to the rest of life, especially those whom we rely on for food, leads us to our fourth component of worldview, the methodological prescription for relating to life. Our relationships to our relatives, both human and other-than-human, must be kept in balance. Balance is how we understand life to function, and it is this concept that drives much of our behaviors, such as offering tobacco and performing ceremony for hunting, planting, and harvesting.

With this brief definition in mind, worldview is a framework for organizing culture. It is a mooring for culture, which keeps it organized along a consistent path. A worldview logic prescribes a parameter of responses to living on this earth that gives direction for daily activities. While worldview is an essential building block, it is important to also describe the limits of worldview. The conscious narratives that we tell each other, such as origin narratives that give voice to the worldview, are no longer the worldview itself. Origin narratives begin the conscious building of culture from its worldview foundation along the particular trajectories that the orientating logics have to offer. Once we enter the realm of the conscious, we leave the arena of worldview.

Worldview and a Theory of Culture

Thus far, most theories of worldview only take into account what a worldview is, and rarely make the necessary move to describe how worldview is related to other structural elements of culture, such as ideology, institutions, and everyday lived experience. While Geertz and Kearney have pointed to a relationship between worldview and behavior, it is yet to be a developed theory and one that will help bring clarity to both worldview and cultural theory. By defining worldview as an integrated set of cultural logics, it will be essential to demonstrate how a particular set of logics, like that of Indigenous peoples, can structure that specific culture. This elaboration of worldview as structuring cultural theory will help to clarify how the four interrelated logics of worldview orient a group to space, time, life, and prescribe how to negotiate the relationships to that life, and work as an integrated system that gives shape and direction to the ideology, institutions, and daily behavior of people in that culture.

In developing a clearer understanding of the place of worldview in a larger cultural theory comprising the ideology, institutions, and daily experiences of a people, we will have to further define these three other cultural components. First, ideology is not to be considered solely in its political form of domination, but also in its social and philosophical form as a necessary body of ideas that allow a group of people to make sense of their world. Ideology then, as I am defining it here, is "a body of ideas that reflects the beliefs and interests of a nation, political system, etc. and underlies political action" and "the set of beliefs by which a group or society orders reality so as to render it intelligible."[89] For example, in American culture this would render capitalism and Christianity as ideologies. They are sets of narratives that give direction for the structure of daily living, but they are neither the foundational logics of culture, nor are they the particular norms, customs, or laws that govern behavior. In Anishinaabe culture we can think of the origin narratives around Sky Woman as an ideology. It is a conscious rendering that gives voice to the worldview of the people, but as in the American context, they do not specify the particular customs or rules of institutions or daily behavior. This definition of ideology can be differentiated from worldview in that the former is the conscious articulation of narratives and ideas that give shape to their understanding of their surroundings, whereas the latter is the set of logics that gives the ideology grounding. The worldview provides the parameters within which an ideology can take shape. If we think of a home as a metaphor, the worldview is the foundation buried deep in the ground, giving support, but which cannot be seen. The walls and roof are the ideology, giving shape to the culture within the local environment.

From this basis of a worldview providing a framework for a system of narratives that give a conscious shaping of a culture, we can now move to more specific manifestations of that culture in the form of institutions. An institution is a subcategory of an ideology that gives more specific shape to culture, and can be defined both in its organizational and sociological forms as "an organization or establishment founded for a specific purpose, such as a hospital, church, company or college" and "an established custom, law, or relationship in a society or community."[90] While this definition is self-explanatory, some examples can help to make clearer how institutions function within a larger theory of culture. In the American cultural context we can point to capitalism and Christianity as having institutional apparatus as well. Capitalism is specifically regulated through a number of key institutions like banks, legally through the courts, while simultaneously in a sociological function as the norms around gifting during holidays. Christianity as an ideology has the church as its primary institution, though its actions are also regulated through the courts as well as customs around the liturgical calendar. In Anishinaabe culture we would think about the institutions of *doodemag*, or clans, which help to provide customs and norms for where one lives, how they obtain food, how they are related to other people, and other-than-human people as well. The Midewiwin Society would also be considered an institution, helping to keep balance within society and the world as a whole as keepers of cultural memory and narratives, as well as healing people when they are sick.[91] In the metaphor of the house, the institutions could be thought of as the inside walls that partition off the house and create different rooms under the ideological roof.

Finally, we come to the everyday lived experience of a group of people, as organized and codified by worldview, ideology, and institutions. This is where the customs, laws, and norms are experienced on a daily basis, and by experiencing them, we reify the ideological and institutional norms on a daily basis. In American culture, capitalism is lived out in a myriad of ways as we purchase goods like food and housing so that we can live from day to day. Capitalism is also lived out in the daily work that everyone does so that they can make the money to purchase what they need and want in the everyday. Christianity as a lived experience is a bit more complex in that the primary behavior involved, going to church, is done on a weekly schedule. However, individuals may participate in daily activities such as prayer or other rituals.[92] For Anishinaabeg, we would perform our *doodem* in a number of ways, from the markings on our clothing; the particular rituals we may partake in, like a morning song or thank you ritual; to the type of food we eat and how we relate to the others in our community. We as Anishinaabeg experience balance in the ceremonies we partake in, the food offerings to *manidoog*, and the manner in which we conduct ourselves in daily interactions with others. In this way, our everyday lived experience has the power to elucidate our ideological manifestations, or it also has the ability to call those ideological and institutional customs and norms into question. The lived experience of the culture is the particulars of the house in the metaphor, the colors of the walls, decorations, and furnishings that we interact with on a daily basis.

With this brief sketch of worldview as part of a cultural theory that also includes ideology, institutions, and everyday experiences, we can move to describe the dynamic interrelatedness of these four components. As presented here, the house metaphor helps to understand the building of a culture, but only in one direction. The worldview provides the foundation, on which the conscious ideologies are built, like the walls and roof of the house. The institutions section off the house into rooms for different purposes. Finally, their everyday experiences provide the color of the rooms, the flooring on which they step, and the décor and furnishings of their culture. While this idea of building the culture from the ground up does work metaphorically and helps to understand the relatedness of the worldview to ideology, to institution, and to everyday experiences, this relatedness is not a one-way street. Each of the four components of this cultural theory also helps

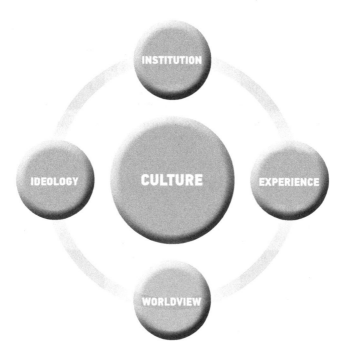

FIGURE. This figure demonstrates the interconnected nature of the four components of culture. Together they constitute the dynamic interplay that allows for social change, for better or for worse.

either to reify the preceding component and its categories, or perhaps to call it into question. This dynamic, multidirectional flow of energy provides for the possibility of social change, as everyday experiences can become burdensome, which can allow for the questioning of institutions and even ideologies if enough people are so inclined (see figure). Red Power and other social change movements demonstrate this phenomenon well.

While everyday experiences and institutions can change relatively easily, that is not the case for worldviews. Ideologies do change, usually with quite a bit of resistance, but the conscious articulation of a culture can shift. Again, think about the decolonization of the 1960s around the world, and the many examples of larger national narratives shifting to include more people, or to resist European influence. However, the logics of relationships to land, time, and the rest of life rarely do change. A shift at the level of worldview can happen, but it takes much longer. The worldview of Anishinaabe *ogimaag* signing the 1836 Treaty of Washington is very much the same as that of the Anishinaabe who still occupy the same lands. While some of the everyday experiences have shifted, as have many of the institutions, Anishinaabeg are still speaking the narratives that hold the ideologies and their embedded knowledge. This project is an attempt to elucidate the Anishinaabe worldview for the ongoing flourishing of life in Anishinaabe Akiing.

CHAPTER 2

Space

T reaties, or agreements between two or more groups of people to settle disputes or to make alliances, are nothing new to Indigenous peoples. Long before Europeans came to these lands we were already practiced at relationship building between communities of people. These negotiations were often held between peoples as a means of developing trade relationships, or much less often, for the purpose of ending a conflict. These intra-Indigenous councils, while no doubt sometimes conflictual, were between peoples who had very similar outlooks and understandings of the world. In short, they were negotiations between people with the same worldview. These intra-worldview councils were often longstanding because the parties involved shared a common conceptualization of the land.[1] Throughout the Indigenous Northeast, Algonquian, Haudenosaunee, and other Indigenous peoples held a common understanding of the land as a common pot, or the bowl with one spoon. This concept helps to bring a common understanding that the resources that *Mazikaamikwe* provides for us are shared between peoples.[2] However, with the coming of Europeans came some significant cultural changes, not only in the form of rapid population loss due to disease, warfare, and cultural dislocation, but also from the engagement with a very different culture from our own. No longer were the treaties between two parties who understood the land of Turtle Island in the same way. The treaties between Indigenous peoples and the newcomers to this land took on a very different tone.

For the Anishinaabeg, our treaty relationships began with the French, and then were transferred to the English after the "French and Indian War" and the Royal Proclamation of 1763. While our treaties with the French had been largely about trade agreements and did not give much thought to the relationship to the land, that all changed in 1763 with the end of the hostilities between the French and the British.[3] This Royal Proclamation gave voice to what was already evident in the eyes of Anishinaabeg, that the encroachment into our lands by the English would continue to happen.[4] This treaty was only in effect as long as the English held onto control of their American holdings. After the American Revolutionary War, the "right of conquest" once again changed hands. Only thirty-two years after the Royal Proclamation we got another drastic change with the Treaty of Greenville in 1795.[5] This treaty marked the first negotiations with the new American government and their desire for more land, soon to be followed by more treaties in 1807, 1817, 1820, 1821, 1828, 1833, 1836, 1855, and 1864. These treaties were the buildup to more and more eurowestern occupancy of our lands and the desire for Michigan statehood.[6]

What is important to note for this project is the language used in the treaties. Very little information is actually recorded in the text, except for the precise boundaries that are being ceded for money, goods, and services. While this should come as no surprise, as the record of the treaties are recorded in English and written by the colonial government, the lack of information about the Anishinaabeg understandings of the treaties provides us with an opportunity to ask the question, just what did the Anishinaabeg who signed the treaties understand was taking place? Here I am not suggesting a simple naiveté on the part of the Indigenous peoples, but I am asking a deeper linguistic-conceptual question. For people who had little experience of land ownership in the sense of eurowestern property, a different concept of a nation of people, and a very different relationship to the land, just what did signing a treaty that describes a transaction of a territory as an exchange for money, goods, and services mean?[7]

Like many interactions between the U.S. Government and Indigenous peoples throughout North America, the interactions with Anishinaabeg during the period of colonial expansion provide for a thorough questioning of the colonial hegemony evident in the proceedings. The 1836 Treaty of Washington provides one of these opportunities. In Article 13 of this treaty, it states, "The Indians stipulate for the right of hunting on the lands ceded, with the other usual privileges of occupancy, until the land is required for settlement."[8] In the buildup for Michigan statehood, this large tract of land, constituting approximately one-third of the overall land mass that would become the State of Michigan, was ceded to the United States Government for the usual list of money and provisions. However, the above passage demands further examination to be fully understood. From the U.S. position, this passage can be explained with legal language that distinguishes between fee simple ownership and usufructory rights. In short, fee simple land rights refer to the ownership of the land in total, the ability to sell it and have full say on how the land is to be used, and who can and cannot be on the property. This type of ownership is what the U.S. Government was "purchasing" during these treaties. Usufructory rights are the rights of usage on property that is not in use for other purposes. Parks and recreational areas exemplify this class of land rights. The public can use the parks and open space areas, but the government holds a fee simple title to those lands. From the perspective of the United States Government, the Anishinaabeg would hold usufructory rights over the ceded territory, *"until the land is required for settlement."*[9]

However, from the perspective of the Anishinaabeg involved in the treaty negotiations as well as those who stayed in their respective communities, these particular legal codes were not in their linguistic-conceptual understanding. That is not to say that they were ignorant of what was going on; the Anishinaabeg certainly understood that more white colonists were coming, and by engaging in these treaty negotiations that a certain amount of agency was being diminished in their broader surroundings. However, when it comes to the passage outlining the *"right of hunting on the lands ceded, with the other usual privileges of occupancy,"* there are other concepts and meanings we have to take into consideration in an Anishinaabeg context. For example, to have the rights to hunt, fish, and gather other living necessities, including medicines, would fall well within the Indigenous understanding of the land as shared in common by all of its inhabitants, understood as the common pot.[10] This Indigenous concept understands all of the land and its inhabitants as coequal partners in the full bounty that *Mazikaamikwe* has to offer. Even though there were experiences of greed and exclusion at the hands of American colonists by some Anishinaabeg, this concept of the common pot, as well as other Indigenous concepts, would have guided their thinking about any ceding of land. It would be unthinkable that the generosity of Earth Mother would be denied them or any other inhabitants of the land. Non-Anishinaabeg peoples have selectively forgotten the Anishinaabeg linguistic conceptual experiences of this treaty as understood and practiced by the communities in Anishinaabe Akiing. The dialogically related language, concepts, and worldview as present in that treaty signing are still available for those who can understand the complex sets of relationships embedded in Anishinaabemowin.

This and other treaty negotiations are useful tools in elucidating the deeper understandings of land that are evident from two very different worldviews. In the above example, it is "understood" from the perspective of the U.S. Government that they held dominion over the land, and that the treaty specified the boundaries within which they could exercise their dominion. From the perspective of the Anishinaabeg, it was "understood" that they were sharing the land with the colonizers, and while there were some particular places where Americans would have jurisdiction over the land, that the common pot was there for all to partake.[11] However, as we now know, a conceptualization of a treaty is only as good as what you can enforce. In the case of the 1836 Treaty of Washington, it would be the dominion of the United States Government that would be enforced throughout the nineteenth and most of the twentieth centuries. A challenge to United States and State of Michigan enforcement, or lack thereof, of this treaty would have to wait until the closing decades of the twentieth century. This and other examples beg the question, just what were the concepts of land that the Anishinaabeg were using when engaging in the ceding of the territory that would become Michigan? In this chapter I will work towards providing a deeper comprehension of that and other questions with reference to an Anishinaabeg worldview as an intimate relationship to a localized space. For Anishinaabeg, the concepts for land are very different from the eurowestern colonizer, and those conceptual differences are indicative of very different experiences with the land.

The Narratives

Sharing Anishinaabeg origin narratives is a task that is fraught with a number of difficulties. First of all, there are multiple versions to choose from since Anishinaabeg communities are spread out over a very large area of what is now called the United States and Canada. Furthermore, as a culture there is no centralized authority that demands allegiance to a particular narrative; hence there is no energy attempting to impose a "single ideological horizon" of thought.[12] There is no "right" or "correct" version, and each community tells its own versions of the narratives a little bit differently. So in sharing this excerpt from Anishinaabe tradition, there is no claim to some undefined central authority that does not exist. This narrative simply helps to provide an important starting point from where the worldview of the Anishinaabeg can be fully understood. It provides the literal grounding for the people to understand their own reality. Secondly, this narrative was chosen because it has already been put into print. These narratives are central to the culture, and there have been numerous attempts over the last century to lay claim to, or to take ownership of, these narratives, our culture, and our very identity by missionaries, anthropologists, and New Age seekers. Therefore, it is a form of cultural preservation, or defense, to utilize narratives that are already in print so that we do not inadvertently put more of ourselves out in public than what is necessary. Furthermore, it must be stated that due to the colonization over the last two centuries, a significant amount of colonial influence has worked to undermine the culture and identity, and those influences have infected the thinking of a number of Anishinaabeg and their communities. This has caused a lot of confusion in the frameworks of thought in which these narratives function. For example, it is easy to look for Anishinaabe "creation" stories because there are a significant number of them in print. However, many of these narratives are an example of colonial thinking in that they use eurowestern colonial frameworks and language superimposed on Anishinaabe concepts. Quite often, they are Indigenous people rewording the first and second chapters of Genesis with more Indian-sounding words like "Creator," "Great Spirit" or sometimes even "God." Obviously, these examples of thinking with a colonized mind are vain attempts to force-fit the culture into a prescribed eurowestern framework of thought. However, as this project will demonstrate, Anishinaabeg categories of thought are significantly different from those in eurowestern culture. Using the Anishinaabeg origin narrative as a starting place will help to give an authentic description of our worldview, as it begins the analysis well within the cultural tradition.[13]

As Anishinaabeg linguist and scholar Basil Johnston helps us to remember, the world was filled with many animals, plants, birds, fish, and other *manidoog*, but this world was flooded.

> But while the earth was under water and life was coming to an end, a new life was beginning in the skies, and she conceived.
>
> The surviving animals and birds observed the changes taking place in Sky

Woman's condition as they clung to life on the surface of the flood waters. They set aside whatever concerns they might have had about their own fates and asked one of their fellow survivors, the Giant Turtle, to offer his back as a place of rest for Sky Woman, who they invited to come down.

Upon settling on the turtle's back, Sky Woman asked for a moiety of soil. Only muskrat, the least of the animals, was able to retrieve the soil from beneath the flood waters, and Sky Woman took the pawfull of soil and etched it around the rim of the turtle's back. She then breathed the breath of life, growth, and abundance into the soil and infused into the soil and earth the attributes of womanhood and motherhood, that of giving life, nourishment, shelter, instruction, and inspiration for the heart, mind, and spirit. Only after she had done these things did Sky Woman give birth to twins, whose descendants took the name *Anishinaubaek*, meaning the Good Beings.[14]

From this narrative, a deeper understanding of the Anishinaabeg concepts of, and relatedness to, the land can be gleaned. Again, the narratives are not the worldview themselves. A worldview is the cultural framework of interrelated logics that establish a relationship to land, time, the rest of life, and a methodological prescription for interacting with that life. The origin narratives simply give us the closest look at the associated worldview by giving voice to the ideological foundations of culture. Here with the Sky Woman narrative, the literal beginnings of the human relationships to land can be seen.

While this is a helpful jumping-off point to discuss the linguistic-conceptual world of the Anishinaabeg, to fully engage this methodology I will have to demonstrate these concepts in Anishinaabemowin. We can begin with the word *aki*, or land.[15] This is a rather straightforward translation as *aki* refers to land, earth, soil, topography, or country. Anishinaabemowin is a complex language using numerous prefixes and suffixes, so other variations on this word would be *akiing* as a specific location, as in Anishinaabe Akiing, the Anishinaabe homeland of the upper Great Lakes.[16] Another word for land would be *kamig*. This also refers to the nature or quality of land or soil.[17] These particular words are nouns, and it is interesting to note that they are in the *maanda* class of nouns. Anishinaabemowin makes a distinction between two classes of nouns, *maaba* and *maanda*. These two categories themselves are difficult to translate, as there is no direct eurowestern linguistic comparison. This classification of nouns has been assumed to align with the eurowestern animate and inanimate; however, when one looks deeper, the eurowestern conceptualizations of animacy do not align with Anishinaabeg concepts.[18] This distinction has often been misunderstood as differentiating living things from nonliving things. However, under closer scrutiny, this meaning breaks down.

In the eurowest the assumption of linguistic animacy is that there is life involved, where inanimacy would be used to describe things that are considered nonliving. However, as A. Irving Hallowell has demonstrated, what is considered living within Anishinaabeg culture is very different from eurowestern concepts. According to Hallowell, the difference between the two cultures can be best understood as the difference between what constitutes a person in each culture. In the eurowest, only living humans would be considered a "person" conceptually. However, for Anishinaabeg, persons as a concept includes many other living things such as animals, but also nonliving things such as rocks, thunder, ancestors, and mythic persons such as Sky Woman and *Nanapush*. This difficulty in cultural translation caused Hallowell to coin the phrase "other-than-human person," which helps to incorporate a much larger realm of what constitutes a person. To understand the *maaba/maanda* differences, one has to think within the dialogically related concepts of Anishinaabeg culture and experience. Here, Hallowell was able to correctly state that

> The Ojibwa are not animists in the sense that they dogmatically attribute living souls to inanimate objects such as stones. The hypothesis which suggests itself to me is that the allocation of stones to an animate grammatical category is part of a culturally constituted cognitive "set." It does not involve a consciously formulated theory about the nature of stones. It leaves a door open that our orientation on dogmatic grounds keeps shut tight. Whereas we should never expect a stone to manifest animate properties of any kind under any circumstances, the Ojibwa recognize, *a priori*, potentialities for animation in certain classes of objects under certain circumstances. The Ojibwa do not perceive stones, in general, as animate, any more than we do. The crucial test is experience.[19]

Hallowell gave numerous examples of personal experience from his informants where rocks had behaved with animate properties, including moving on their own.[20] He also gives an example of the *maaba* quality of rocks in the narratives of Flint, grandson of Sky Woman, as a living person in their narratives. All of these examples demonstrate that from within Anishinaabeg culture, *maaba*, or animacy, is a much larger concept and category of thought than it is in the eurowest. Again, it is necessary to take into consideration the worldview of the Anishinaabeg that considers rocks and thunder to be *maaba*, to truly understand how *maaba* and *maanda* are structured in their thought. While no hard and fast rules can be applied to Anishinaabemowin and the *maaba/maanda* categories, there are two important points to make here. First, while generally speaking there is a greater sense of the possibility of power available in *maaba* nouns, this does not always hold true. In Anishinaabemowin, verbs take precedent and can affect the nouns associated with them when speaking, so while a noun like *aki* is generally *maanda*, there are instances where it could be *maaba*. This example demonstrates the second point, which is that there is fluidity in Anishinaabemowin and Anishinaabe thought. While it is interesting to note the general classification of the nouns *aki* and *kamig* as *maanda*, because of the fluidity inherent in the language, no conclusions can be drawn from the inclusion in the *maanda* class of nouns in and of itself.

While the previous discussion can help to give us a basis for understanding Anishinaabeg conceptualizations of land, definitions of *aki* and *kamig* are not enough to demonstrate our relationships to space. *Aki* and *kamig* are simply referents used to designate land as a general concept, and within the Anishinaabeg linguistic-conceptual world these words do not denote the relational aspects of the land. A concept that does provide understanding of the Anishinaabeg conceptualizations of land is *Mazikaamikwe*, or Earth Mother.[21] *Mazikaamikwe* as a concept helps us to understand kinship with our land as it places us in a familial relationship that corresponds to our daily lives. *Mazikaamik* (earth) and *kwe* (woman) places us as Anishinaabeg as children to a mother and demonstrates a relationship of dependence on the earth as a provider of sustenance. According to Basil Johnston, "By breathing the breath of life into the clutch of soil that Geezhigo-quae [Sky Woman] had etched around the rim of the Giant Turtle's shell, causing it to swell and grow into a continent, she infused into the earth the attributes of motherhood: nourishment, clothing, shelter, healing, teaching and instilling a sense of beauty and goodness."[22] In ceremony, we may thank *Mazikaamikwe* for providing food, shelter, clothing, and medicine for all of us. Since our sustenance comes at the expense of our relatives, we are also thanking them in this invocation. In this way, *Mazikaamikwe* as a concept helps to prescribe behavior in the land. Since the people are dependent upon her for our sustenance, that relationship demands a reverence similar to what we owe our own mothers. Here a dialogical relationship is set up whereby our relationships to our own mothers as individuals are mirrored by our relationship to *Mazikaamikwe*, which continually inform each other. *Mazikaamikwe*, when added to the concepts of *aki* and *kamig*, helps to give a deeper understanding of Anishinaabeg relationships to the land as a kinship system.

It is also essential to understand the process of land regeneration in this origin narrative. Often these narratives are misunderstood as "creation" narratives and are written about as though they are equivalents to the Genesis creation stories from the Christian Bible. However, by analyzing the language, we can see that Anishinaabeg narratives are actually quite different. When we work with a translation of the Sky Woman narrative, the concepts involved need careful consideration, lest we fall into the trap of "thinking with a colonized mind," as Wiredu puts it. To fully understand the relationship to land embodied in the *Giizhigokwe* narratives, it is important to carefully choose our words to test the translations so that we do not do harm to the narrative.[23] While there are a number of options to say "to create" in Anishinaabemowin, that only makes our task of choosing the best option all the more important.

There are two verbs to choose from to translate Sky Woman's actions in this flood narrative. The first one would be *zhitoon*, which means to make or create. However, when this verb is used it denotes an agency over the item being made by the maker. In technical terms, *zhitoon* as a verb is a transitive inanimate, meaning that the thing being made, in our narrative the land mass that would become North America, would be part of the *maanda* linguistic category. Since the narrative from Johnston describes Sky Woman giving the land the attributes of "giving life," this verb and translation would be a poor choice. It is interesting to note in this colonial contest of thought and action that is continually played out in the relationship between the Anishinaabeg and the eurowest, the verb *zhitoon* has been used in the imposition of eurowestern thought. In the early nineteenth century a young Anishinaabeg named Peter Jones was educated in a eurowestern school and later became a Methodist missionary and preacher among the Anishinaabeg and Haudenosaunee around the east end of Lake Ontario. Jones went as far as translating the Bible into Anishinaabemowin so as to make it more accessible both for his community and for other missionaries working among Anishinaabeg communities. In his translation of Genesis 1:1 (In the beginning God created the heaven and the earth), Jones translates this passage as "Wayashkud Keshamunedoo ooge oozhetoon ewh ishpeming kiya ewh ahkeh."[24] While there are a number of issues to take up on this passage, for the topic at hand we have the verb *oozhetoon* (*zhitoon* in a double-vowel orthography) and *ahkeh* (*aki*). I would suggest that this is an accurate use of *zhitoon* in that within the eurowestern worldview, God creates heaven and earth, and as a creator, has a hierarchy of power set up over both of them. Here *zhitoon* is only problematic in the sense that in this form it does not convey that what is being created is from nothingness, as in the biblical narrative. While I would suggest that this translation by Jones effectively communicates the biblical narrative in Anishinaabemowin, the use of *zhitoon* would clearly be inappropriate for the Sky Woman narrative in that there is no hierarchy or power over the land as in the Genesis narrative.

Another verb that could be used is *ondaadad* which means "to come from a certain place, originate in a certain place."[25] This is the root verb, which communicates childbirth, as in *ondaadiziike*. On the positive side, *ondaadiziike* does denote the subject of the *maaba* class of nouns; however, at least in contemporary terms, it is used mostly to describe the birthing process as a eurowestern medical procedure. It would be a stretch to suggest that *Giizhigokwe* gave birth in this sense as she helped to make what would become the North American continent. Another form of the verb *ondaadad* that makes more sense in our *Giizhigokwe* narrative would be *ondaa'aagan*. This form of the verb means "to stir or mix elements together."[26] This form of *ondaadad* is helpful in our translation as it is dialogically related to other Anishinaabe cultural elements. First, the Anishinaabeg live in a land surrounded by and saturated with water.[27] Clearly, for a group of people to not only survive, but to thrive in such a place necessitates a deeply held reverence for water. For the Anishinaabeg, that means an important ceremonial relationship with this part of their environment. This important relationship to water is primarily held by the Anishinaabekwe of our communities, the women. Women are tasked with keeping this important relationship strong by singing the water songs in ceremony, among many other responsibilities. So for a translation of the *Giizhigokwe* narrative, we may say "Giizhigokwe ondaa'aagan aki," translated as Sky Woman regenerated (mixed together the water and the pawful of soil) the land. This translation is grounded in the integrity of both the linguistic structure of Anishinaabemowin as well as in the cultural understandings integral to thriving on the land in which we live. It is important to press the point that in this translation of the *Giizhigokwe* narrative, nowhere is there a mention of this being "creation" in the sense that prior to Sky Woman there was no land, water, or earth. Clearly all of these elements are already in existence. The question of ultimate origins as in the biblical narratives in Genesis is driven by the worldview that is structured by a linear progression of time. The Anishinaabeg are not encumbered by such questions of a linear beginning. What the *Giizhigokwe* narrative helps the Anishinaabeg understand is the land, our space. The use of the verb *ondaadad* describes that "coming from a certain place," which is on the Great Turtle's back. For the Anishinaabeg, the *Giizhigokwe* narrative provides an understanding of how land came to be, and begins to give shape to a prescriptive trajectory for how we are supposed to negotiate our lives in that land.

In the linguistic-conceptual analysis given thus far, it is important to point out the differences between Indigenous languages and those of the eurowest. Indigenous languages have been identified as structured around the use of verbs. This is important to name as it helps to demonstrate the vast differences between Anishinaabemowin and the English language. Again, while the noun *aki* and the suffix *-kamig* are helpful to the discussion, if one only looked at these words, the vast differences between the cultures could easily be missed. This linguistic-conceptual analysis takes into consideration the importance of verbs and action within Anishinaabeg thought and helps to provide better translations of language and culture. Here we can make clearer distinctions between verbs like *zhitoon* and *ondaadiziike* when it comes to translating between the two languages. This clarity then allows us to take on a much more thorough and authentic analysis of the topic at hand.

Worldview and Cultural Theory

With the depth of the analysis above, we can now begin to look at the interrelatedness of these concepts of land from the Anishinaabe culture with integrity. As Wiredu reminds us, each of these concepts comes with its own "doctrinal history," and we can now turn to that field of knowledge.[28] Within Anishinaabe thought, there is a large part of cultural narratives devoted to land and the importance of particular places. When taken as a whole, this cultural complex of narratives constitutes what Bakhtin describes as a "socio-ideological horizon." These narratives provide lessons and examples for living in the particular lands of the upper Great Lakes and provide the necessary cultural trajectory to make a living. When we compare these narratives of spatiality with a eurowestern set of narratives that provide a framework of knowledge to think about land, we can see that the "socio-ideological horizons" of these two systems of thought do not meet. The eurowestern logic of domination originated well within the cultural complex of Europe and was only superimposed during the colonial project as a means of universalizing the European experience as the normative standard for the rest of the world. This colonial imposition set out to erase the Indigenous ways of knowing, negotiating, and thinking about the land of the Anishinaabeg. They were not successful. When the cultural logic of the Anishinaabeg worldview is described by these interrelated sets of narratives, a very different relationship to the land can be seen.

For the Anishinaabeg, the orientation to land can be best described as an intimate relationship to a localized space. As will be seen, this type of relationship to space at the level of worldview will have certain ramifications as we follow this cultural logic through the four interrelated elements of the cultural theory mentioned earlier. Also, because the worldview is the cultural framework of the Anishinaabeg themselves, it is difficult to describe it alone. However, since it is manifest in each of the other three elements of this cultural theory, we can better describe worldview by elucidating its manifestation as ideology, institution, and everyday experience.

The ideological manifestations of the Anishinaabegs' intimate relationship to localized space can best be seen in the *Giizhigokwe* narratives. From these interrelated narratives about the *ondaa'aagan* of the water and soil on the back of *Makinak*, the Great Turtle, we can see the formation of a basis for the relationship of the Anishinaabeg to their physical surroundings. To reiterate, *Giizhigokwe* fell from the sky to a place covered by water. She was brought down to *Makinak*, the Great Turtle, who offered his shell as a resting place for this new creature. With the help of the elder relatives already in existence in this place, *Giizhigokwe ondaa'aagan* mixed together the soil and water and formed a place for her and her unborn twins to live. So when we think of an ideology as a "set of beliefs by which a group or society orders reality so as to render it intelligible," there are four main points that we can make about this. First, the earth as a totality was already in existence, complete with water, soil, and other animals. This is important as it helps us to be particular about the verb choice of *ondaa'aagan* in *Giizhigokwe*'s actions in forming the land. This point is essential as it does not describe a creation from nothing as in a eurowestern creation narrative.[29] Secondly, associated with the first point is that there were already animals on the earth who then took it upon themselves to take care of *Giizhigokwe*. This sets up a dynamic of relatedness where these animals, already in existence, become elder siblings to the Anishinaabeg. From them we will learn how to negotiate our lives in this world in a good way. To press the point further, there are already relationships between animals in place, and they already have a good idea of how to relate to each other. Therefore it is the job of the newcomers to this place to learn these ways already in existence to get along with the elder brothers and sisters. Thirdly, the particular place where *Giizhigokwe* is set down to form a new land is on *Makinak*, the Great Turtle. It is one of the oldest living creatures in existence who offers his back to reform the land. This narrative of North America being Turtle Island is one that permeates much of eastern North America. It is a very old and common tradition; however, it is not a universal narrative. It is not meant to encompass the entire earth. So when Europeans come with other narratives explaining origins of land and peoples, in and of themselves they are not offensive nor do they challenge core Anishinaabeg beliefs. Those other narratives are for other people. It is only when those European narratives get imposed as a universal for all people that the friction of those competing ideologies begins. Finally, the widespread nature of the Turtle Island narratives would provide a common theme for many of the peoples of the Indigenous Northeast to find methods of cooperation and trade with each other. It provides a common orientation to the places many peoples of this part of the world call home.[30]

When we move from the ideological to the institutional manifestations of the Anishinaabeg worldview, we get a clearer picture of how the intimate relationship to localized space is manifest among these peoples. An institutional manifestation of this worldview in relationship to land can be seen in the sociopolitical-economic life of the Anishinaabeg village. To make sense of this facet of Anishinaabeg life and its relationship to worldview, I will have to make three preliminary distinctions about this site of Anishinaabeg life as it differs significantly from the assumed eurowestern norm. First, the village is the primary site of Anishinaabeg identity, both socially and politically. Socially, the village is the site of relationships to their respective *doodemag*, or clans. This part of Anishinaabeg identity is of the utmost importance as it is a guiding narrative for the relationship of the people to the rest of life.[31] Each village is led by a particular *doodem*. For example Makinak, the village, is led by the *Makinak doodem*, or Turtle clan. Bahweting (now Sault Ste. Marie, Michigan), a political center for that part of Anishinaabe Akiing, is led by the *Chejak doodem*, or Crane clan. This *doodem* structure helps to bring order to the relationships both within the village and with other surrounding villages. The extended family structure of the village provides a method of social organization that allows the people to successfully negotiate their lives with the rest of life in their particular places. Politically this village structure with its *doodem* leadership in a council is the primary site of the settlement of local conflicts, the organization of the village ceremonies, and the decision-making capacity in relationship to other villages. It is important to name here that this localized social and political structure is where traditionally all Anishinaabeg lived their entire lives, and that this localized life was absent an overarching national identity. While there was recognition that each village was related to other villages in a linguistic and cultural identity as Anishinaabeg, this national identity was a distant second in importance as compared to the local village/*doodem* relationship.[32] Secondly, the local village was also the primary site of food and other resource acquisition. It is within this intimate relationship to localized space where the people would grow their food, both in gardens near the villages and by improving the land with selective cultivation and fire technology to keep the surrounding areas healthy for the edible flora like blueberries and for the native fauna. Furthermore, the economics of space are also dependent upon the political structure of the local village to set boundaries for particular extended families to hunt, fish, and grow and cultivate foods and medicines. The acquisition of food and medicine is also dependent upon the familial relationship of the local village for distribution. Food and medicine are distributed to the community along these *doodemag* kinship lines. Finally, the life of the Anishinaabeg in this complex sociopolitical-economic milieu is primarily communal. That is to say, that the individual is so enmeshed within this complex web of relatedness to both human and other-than-human persons that the individual is of secondary importance when compared to the community. Here the primary social unit is the community, which is much different than the social unit of possessive individualism that the eurowest places as primary in their culture. As Tink Tinker states, "American Indian indigenous cultures are communitarian by nature and do not share the euro-west's capitulation to the priority of the individual over against community."[33] This communal structure of the local village provides the material and social sustenance for the individual, and each individual has a responsibility to the larger community, both human and other-than-human, to act in ways that help to promote the flourishing of all members of that local community. This is the institutional structure of the *doodemag*, which prescribes the actions of the Anishinaabeg to live in an intimate relationship to the localized space of the village.[34]

As with many societies, the act of naming a location in which they live is important to the Anishinaabeg. As I have already mentioned, the name of the village Makinakong (also known as M'chi Makinakong, or the largest possible or most important turtle) is closely associated with the *Giizhigokwe* narratives and places a significant amount of importance on that particular place. The naming of this location came from early contact with the Anishinaabeg during a westward migration from the east coast.[35] Before the Anishinaabeg were living in the Great Lakes area, they were living somewhere around the meeting of the St. Lawrence

River and the Atlantic Ocean. But there came a great time of suffering when the ancestors of the Anishinaabeg decided to remove themselves from that place. They migrated westward until they reached a place that came to be known as Bahweting, the place of the rapids. There some Anishinaabeg stayed, and others moved along the divergent lakeshores around what is now known as the Upper Peninsula of Michigan. Along the southern route, where the two peninsulas come close to meeting, other Anishinaabeg made camp and decided to stay there. No doubt, as part of that founding, the appearance of the relative *Makinak* must have showed himself, and the name was given to that place.

While the naming of Makinakong is relatively straightforward, more needs to be said about Bahweting. *Bahwetigo idjiwan* is how one would say "rapids," as in rapids of a river. However, *bahwetigo* (rapids in a river) can be changed into a locative with the suffix *-ng*. Therefore, when the Anishinaabeg named the stopping place among the rapids at the east end of Lake Superior, it becomes Bahweting. This locative function of naming places is consistent, as in Ishpeming (the place above, on the north side of the Upper Peninsula).[36] This naming of places is directly related to a particular feature of the land, or sometimes of the particular flora or fauna associated with that place, like Chi-asining (the place of the big rock, now Anglicized as Chesaning, a village in the Saginaw valley of mid-lower Michigan) or Moningwanay kaning (Island of the Golden-Breasted Woodpecker, an important political center on the western side of Kitchi-game). These examples all help to demonstrate the intimate Anishinaabeg relationship to a localized space. Within this naming process, the land, topography, quality, and structure of the space was taken into consideration. It can be said that the land itself had agency in the naming process; it helped to decide how it would be called by its features (Bahweting and Chi-asining), its spatial location (Ishpeming), or a quality (Makinakong and Moningwanay kaning). This is not to say that the land could only be called one thing but that the land was taken into consideration in the process of naming these particular places. This dialogical communication with the land in the naming process is an example of their intimate relationship to a localized space.

Spatial Ontology

While these arguments help to give a general picture of Anishinaabeg concepts of spatiality and their relationships to land, they do not yet give a depth to the subject. To deepen the linguistic-conceptual analysis, we now turn to translations of ontology. Once again, philosophical formulations by African philosophers about the Cartesian cogito (I think, therefore I am) can help to elucidate the linguistic-conceptual differences between Indigenous language and thought, and that of the eurowest. The cogito has been a focal point for African philosophers and theologians to demonstrate cultural difference in the twentieth century as a process of their own decolonization movements. This fascination of the cogito has become an effective method of demonstrating not only cultural difference in general, but the different conceptualizations of space, time, being, and existence between the eurowest and Indigenous cultures.

Alexis Kagame, a Rwandan philosopher and theologian, offers a compelling argument for cultural difference when he directs his analysis towards the cogito. In studying the Bantu culture and the possible translation of the cogito, Kagame demonstrates the unintelligibility of the cogito as "the verb 'to be' is always followed by an attribute or an adjunct of place: I am good, big etc., I am in such and such a place, etc. Thus the utterance '. . . therefore, I am' would prompt the question 'You are . . . what . . . where?"[37] In this critique, Kagame points to a very different concept of being among the Bantu. For this Indigenous people, there is no intelligible form of existence as separated from place or some sort of description of how the person was feeling or doing. Kwasi Wiredu furthers this line of inquiry on the cogito in his native Akan language and culture. His inquiry strengthens Kagame's analysis by adding to it a more potent linguistic component, and a demonstration that the concept of existence for the Akan is necessarily spatial. According to Wiredu, "'Wo ho' is the Akan rendition of 'exist'. Without the 'ho', which means 'there', in other words, 'some place', all meaning is lost. 'Wo', standing alone, does not in any way correspond to the existential sense of the verb 'to be', which has no place in the Akan syntax or semantics."[38] When the cogito is translated into the Akan language, what gets transmitted is that "I am there, at some place; which means that spatial location is essential to the idea of my existence."[39] Clearly, this is a very different understanding of existence than what is communicated in the cogito. Wiredu continues, "As far as he [Descartes] is concerned, the alleged fact that one can doubt all spatial existences and yet at the same time be absolutely certain of one's existence under the dispensation of the *Cogito* implied that the 'I', the ego, exists as a spiritual, nonspatial, immaterial entity."[40] The linguistic and conceptual necessity of the spatiality of existence in the Akan culture makes a strong suggestion for a very different relationship to the land as exists in the colonial eurowest. As Kagame and Wiredu demonstrate, the necessity of a spatial existence in the translation of the verb "to be" suggests a much more intimate relationship to those spaces that they inhabit. This intimate relationship to space, as demonstrated in the linguistic-conceptual world of the Bantu and the Akan, is significantly different than the "spiritual, nonspatial, immaterial" belief in existence that is encapsulated in the cogito. It is to this necessity of spatial location as understood within the Anishinaabeg linguistic-conceptual world that we now turn.

Into Anishinaabemowin, the cogito would translate as *n'maaminonendam indawaaj n'ayaa*. Following Wiredu's method of checking the validity of translations with symmetry, we get a return translation back into English as "I am thinking, therefore I exist." On the surface this symmetry would suggest a good translation, and from a purely semantic point of view it is. However, when we dig deeper into the meaning of the words and the structure of Anishinaabe thought, that assumed symmetry breaks down. Similar to the critique of the cogito by Kagame, the verb "to be," *ayaa*, is always followed by "an attribute or an adjunct of place."[41] In Anishinaabemowin, the verb *ayaa*, when applied to an attribute, changes with the prefix *izhi-*, which signals that the following words have a particularized meaning. So if one is going to "be" in a certain way, which is necessary to be linguistically and conceptually correct, the proper translation would be *izhi-ayaa*.[42] This addition obviously negates the presumed symmetry of the above translation of the cogito, as *izhi-ayaa* would have to be followed by a descriptive attribute. More specifically, according to John D. Nichols and Earl Nyholm, who have established the preeminent Anishinaabemowin dictionary, the verb *ayaa* does not just translate as "to be" or "to exist," but assumes a locative quality. That is, *ayaa*, "to be" in Anishinaabemowin, can only mean to be *in a certain place*.[43] This follows Wiredu's point that for the Akan, the linguistic-conceptual structure of the language and culture intimately tie existence to a specific location. There is no such a thing as existence as "spiritual, nonspatial, immaterial entity," and for the Anishinaabeg, like the Akan, "spatial location is essential to the idea of my [our] existence."[44] This more thorough linguistic-conceptual analysis of Anishinaabemowin and thought helps to bring into focus the extraordinary importance of the institution of the village as that certain place which grounds the people in their daily lives. The linguistic-conceptual field of the Anishinaabeg helps to demonstrate that their orientation to land is one of an intimate relationship to a localized space.

We can now move to the fourth component of a theory of culture by naming the Anishinaabeg worldview of land as connected to a lived everyday experience.

It is within a lived communal experience that we can see, touch, taste, and smell the manifestation of a worldview of land as an intimate relationship to a localized space. As the cultural logic of an intimate relationship to a localized space from worldview to everyday experience is followed, we consistently find the narratives of *Giizhigokwe* as foundational to Anishinaabeg daily actions. From these narratives, we can see a consistent theme of humans as newcomers to this land who are dependent upon the other animals already in existence. These elders have role-modeled the form of a council, the economics of gifting, and the ceremonial lives necessary to keep a balance among the living beings in their particular place.

An effective political council is necessary to organize and settle conflicts about the acquisition of food, boundaries for hunting, and agricultural spaces. They also provide the decision-making capacities to send emissaries to other villages when there are disputes about adjoining lands and waterways, as well as to larger regional councils that help decide international issues.[45] In this way, the political aspect of the councils is about the organization and facilitation of the acquisition of food, shelter, clothing, and medicine for the people. From the councils held to decide the fate of *Giizhigokwe*, we understand the purpose of these actions. We are told that *Giizhigokwe* and her twins "depended upon the care and goodwill of the animals. The bears, wolves, foxes, deer and beaver brought food and drink; the squirrels, weasels, raccoons, and cats offered toys and games; the robins, sparrows, chickadees, and loons sang and danced in the air; the butterflies, bees and dragonflies made the children smile."[46] However, the first winter was harsh and the plant food that was brought to the Anishinaabeg was scarce, so "bear, fearing the death of the infants, offered himself that they might live."[47] This narrative describes the dependence that we as humans have on the rest of life, and helps to guide our daily actions when we go about the acquisition of food, clothing, shelter, and medicine. To honor the plants and animals that give their lives so that we may live, it is necessary to do ceremony to help keep a sense of balance in the world. These ceremonies may be a simple offering of *asema* (tobacco) and a few words to tell the plant and animal that the person is sorry for killing them and what they will do with their life. There could also be much more elaborate cleansing rituals and series of songs and dances for entire communities, such as ceremonies preparing for the planting or harvesting of corn, or preparations for hunting.[48] By participating in these rituals, which were given by the elder brothers and sisters, they may continue to offer themselves for our sustenance. If we fail to abide by the customs of taking care of animal bones, or take for granted the generosity of the plants and animals, their gifts may no longer be available to us. There are numerous narratives that teach how to take care of the plants and animals when they are killed. Each of these can be taken not just as a constructed narrative to teach, but as connected to a place where the Anishinaabeg failed to take care of certain plants or animals and the ensuing difficulty in relearning how to be in proper relationship with them.[49] These narratives then are about the memory of learning how to properly relate to the elder plants and animals, told in story form.

Once again, in the relationship to the land we see the primacy of action in Anishinaabemowin as the animating factor that connects the people to the land. As a language, Anishinaabemowin demonstrates a great wealth of verbs to help people relate to the land on a daily basis. While the daily economic activities of hunting, fishing, agriculture, and the associated ceremonies demonstrate this intimate relationship to localized space, there is another term unrelated to food acquisition that helps to elucidate this intimate relationship to land. The term, *nametoo*, is difficult to translate into English, but also points towards the nature of the intimacy of the Anishinaabeg relationship to land. *Nametoo* roughly translates as "to leave signs of one's presence."[50] However, more needs to be said to effectively demonstrate the meaning of *nametoo* within the heteroglossia of Anishinaabemowin and thought. If one were to come across this word and read "leave signs of one's presence," that could easily be misunderstood as leaving a footprint in the mud or breaking a branch as one walks through the woods. However, *nametoo* has a much deeper meaning when the worldview of the intimate relationship to a localized space is taken into account. When someone is born into a society where the narratives of *Giizhigokwe* are told and retold while they are participating in a complex daily and annual ceremonial cycle to provide balance for sustenance, what constitutes "leaving one's presence" has a much deeper meaning. Within the Anishinaabeg worldview, it is understood that the rest of life has its own agency, its own being, and its own energy that are not dependent upon humans at all. Within this world where the trees, plants, and other animals of the woods and prairie have their own forms of knowledge and energy, these places in the land have an energy and an agency all their own. This consciousness or life energy in the land, with its own agency, interacts with us as we go about our activities on the land. This concept of the life energy of the land can be described as *manidoo*.

This concept, *manidoo*, is also difficult to translate, yet it is necessary to go deeper into this word as it helps to demonstrate not only the dialogical relationship to particular spaces, but also the dire need for conceptual decolonization. The most common definition of *manidoo* is "spirit," and sometimes to that is added "god" or "God," as well as "essence, substance, mystery … [or] the unseen."[51] While a number of Anishinaabeg and non-Anishinaabeg alike allow for this translation, there are three problems that must be discussed. First, for "spirit" to be an intelligible translation, it must itself have a knowable and agreed-upon meaning. As Kwasi Wiredu has demonstrated, the concept of spirit or spiritual has little to no grounding that can give it an intelligible meaning. From Cartesian sources, the definition "is that the spiritual is that which is nonmaterial. But definition by pure negation, such as this, brings little enlightenment."[52] Another definition, from Saint Paul, that of spiritual being the "unseen," falls into another trap, that "it is so broad as to make gravity, for example, spiritual."[53] So a definition of "spirit" for *manidoo* does nothing to help describe what it actually is.

Secondly, spirit as a concept is grounded in its eurowestern cultural particulars of the material/spirit dualism that is not part of an Anishinaabeg conceptual world. As demonstrated above, the Anishinaabeg ontology is entirely spatially located, so existence, human or other-than-human, as a "spiritual, nonspatial, immaterial entity" is unintelligible.[54] Since "spirit" has the capability of existing completely separated from a particular place, it cannot effectively define *manidoo*, which can only exist as spatially located within the Anishinaabeg conceptual world.[55] To allow for this translation to "spirit" is representative of "thinking with a colonized mind." This colonization of a nonspatial entity imposed on a spatially configured cultural concept does violence to the relationship to land and life for the Anishinaabeg.

Thirdly, that the commonly held translation for *manidoo* is spirit, a concept that neither has an intelligible definition itself, nor is intelligible within Anishinaabeg spatially grounded thought, demonstrates a dire need for the conceptual decolonization. It should come as no surprise that because of the ongoing colonization of Anishinaabeg, land and thought, more often than not we think and act in English. As Wiredu helps us to understand:

> The problem is that thinking *about* them in English almost inevitably becomes thinking *in* English about them. It is just an obvious fact, in philosophy at least, that one thinks most naturally in the language of one's education and occupation. But in our case this means thinking along the lines of conceptual frameworks which may be significantly different from those embedded in our indigenous languages. By virtue of this phenomenon, we are constantly in danger of involuntary

mental de-Africanization, unless we consciously and deliberately resort to our own languages (and culture).[56]

Basil Johnston pushes the decolonization of *manidoo* with the recognition that anytime *manidoo*, in any form, was uttered, that it automatically meant spirit. According to Johnston, if someone uttered "*manitouwun* to refer to some curative or healing property in a tree or plant, they took it to mean spirit. When a person said the word *manitouwut* to refer to the sacrosanct mood or atmosphere of a place, they assumed it meant spirit."[57] His analysis helps to demonstrate the colonization of *manidoo* as a concept, but his attempt at decolonization unfortunately stops there. He too capitulates to the eurowestern framework of a material/spirit dualism, and even promotes the definition of *manidoo* as "spirit(s)" or "God."[58] It is essential to use our knowledge of eurochristian particularities of concepts to continue the work of decolonization.

When one takes into consideration the dialogically related conceptual world of both the Anishinaabeg and the eurowest, it becomes clear that translating philosophical ideas that come with their own doctrinal histories is a challenging task. In devising a definition for *manidoo*, the demands of an entirely spatially configured conceptual world comes into play. Therefore, to do justice to a translation for *manidoo*, one must take into consideration the spatial existence of those entities. Once again, Wiredu provides a methodological template as he describes the dialogically related spatial world of the Akan. To deal with the spatial location of the ancestors and those recently dead who are traveling to the *place* of the dead, Wiredu uses "the term 'quasi-material' to refer to any being or entity conceived as spatial but lacking some of the properties of material objects."[59] Here Wiredu refuses to give in to the Cartesian dualism of material/spirit and forges a new concept that allows for both the spatiality of Akan thinking and the lack of consistent visibility to most of the population. The ancestors are still near to them spatially, though they are only readily identifiable to a person with a gift or with sensory training.[60] This concept of "quasi-material" is incredibly helpful as it provides an intelligible translation for what have been considered nonmaterial items.

So to attempt a decolonized definition of *manidoo*, taking into consideration the spatial necessity of Anishinaabe thought and culture, it is a quasi-material life energy. It is quasi-material in that it can be located in space, and life energy to demonstrate a dynamic, knowable power with which one can have a relationship. I would like to add some cognitive traction to this notion of "quasi-material" to provide a better understanding. Here I think a push into quantum physics is a helpful exercise. When we think of "quasi-material," it is useful to understand *manidoo* by thinking about wave-particle duality in the theories of light. In short, wave-particle duality refers to light having qualities both of waves and of particles.[61] While neither theory can fully explain what light is, wave-particle duality recognizes these two theories of light as working together to provide a better understanding. Since light must be located in space, it satisfies our need for spatial location. This is useful for the definition of *manidoo* for three reasons. First, in Anishinaabemowin the best conceptualizations of *giizis*, the sun, understand it as providing quantum energy in both heat and light. This association of both quantum energy and light make the shift into physics a useful transition. Secondly, *manidoo*—in particular *gitchi manidoo*—has strong connections to *giizis* in visual representation. Again, this closely associates *manidoo* with the most powerful source of light in the Anishinaabe world. Thirdly, when Anishinaabeg and other Indigenous peoples speak about experiencing *manidoo*, they often communicate this as seeing lights or sparks. Again, *manidoog* as perceived are closely associated with the presence of light, often in a very dark place.[62] When we further define "quasi-material" as similar to the qualities of light that have both wave and particle properties, we can closely associate the definition with the light often associated with *manidoog*, while also still keeping it spatially located with the particle properties.[63] This definition, which associates *manidoog* with light and the wave-particle duality, helps to demonstrate the possibility of a relationship with the land as a power or life energy since it is energy and can be spatially located.

So as one passes through the land, one can leave a presence, or knowledge of self with the land. The person or community can recognize that in the memory of the sights, smells, or sounds of those particular places, but those memories only recognize a one-way transaction. If one says *n'nametoo*, it is recognized that the land remembers them as well; a relationship is formed.[64] Like all relationships, they have to be honored to continue. So while the memory may last for a person walking through the land, unless they go back regularly, the dialogical bond with that land may no longer be there. Or if the trees are clear-cut, if a large open pit mine is established, or recreationists continually take from and pollute that land, then the *manidoog*, the life energy in that place, could cease to exist or go somewhere else. To experience the land in an intimate way comes with relational attachments that must be continually regenerated with participation and ceremony. The concept of *nametoo*, understood within a larger Anishinaabeg logic of land as an intimate relationship to localized space, helps to recognize a dialogical relationship to the land, and the power inherent within the land as recognized by the people. Only when one takes into consideration the larger cultural complex of the Anishinaabeg, their narratives (ideology), their villages and communities (institutions), and their daily ritual and ceremonial lives (everyday experience) can one begin to fully appreciate and understand the intimacy that is involved when *nametoo* is uttered.

Eurowestern Comparison

To demonstrate the significant cultural difference that is embodied in this logic of an intimate relationship to a localized space of the Anishinaabeg, this analytical gaze will now be directed towards the eurowestern culture that imposed itself upon the Indigenous peoples of North America. It is used as a means of shedding light on the rarely thought-about relationship to space that for most people living in North America is taken for granted. By juxtaposing these two very different cultures and their relationships to land, the reality of both the cultural difference and the inherent violence in the colonizing process of imposing these eurowestern conceptualizations of land onto the whole of Indigenous North America can be brought into full view.

The worldview of the eurowestern colonizers of Indigenous North America can best be described as a logic of dominion over the land and all of the life contained within it. This logic can be seen in the origin narratives of the Christian Bible. After God creates all of the living creatures in Genesis 1:20–25, verse 26 provides the ideological organization of the relationships of humans to the rest of life as "God said, 'Let us make humankind in our image, according to our likeness; and let them have dominion over the fish of the sea, and over the birds of the air, and over the cattle, and over all the wild animals of the earth, and over every creeping thing that creeps upon the earth.'"[65] In 1:28, God furthers this command by saying, "Be fruitful and multiply, and fill the earth and subdue it; and have dominion over the fish of the sea and over the birds of the air and over every living thing that moves upon the earth."[66] This is not to say that since it is written in the Bible to have dominion over the earth and to subdue it, then that is the only way that Christian followers could have acted. But it is to suggest that the "word of God" has held a lot of weight within the eurowestern historical trajectory, particularly in the process of colonization. These passages, among others, would become powerful justifications for the colonization of Indigenous North America, and throughout the rest of the globe. As evidenced by the present state of ecological degradation, species loss, and the presence of Christianity and capitalism in every corner of the globe, clearly the message of having dominion and subduing the earth was not lost on eurowestern peoples.

From this Christian narrative, there are two important points to make that differentiate the eurowestern creation narratives from that of the Anishinaabeg. This is a narrative of an all-powerful god creating the universe ex nihilo, out of nothing. As noted above, this concept of the creation out of nothingness is unintelligible to the spatially configured Anishinaabeg culture without colonizing Anishinaabeg thought and language. Secondly, there are actually two creation narratives in the first two chapters of Genesis that differ in their order of creation. In chapter 1, God creates the flora and fauna first, then creates humans. In chapter 2, man is created first, then the flora and fauna, then "the rib that the Lord God had taken from the man he made into a woman and brought to her the man."[67] While it is common to have multiple narratives covering the origins of a people, these two parallel narratives are curious in that the order of creation is significantly different. It is interesting to note that the creation narrative in the first chapter of Genesis is similar to the Anishinaabeg one in that the rest of creation was already in existence before humans. However, that did not lead to a reverence for the rest of life as it did among the Anishinaabeg. This passage, rather than establishing a commonality between forms of life, establishes humans as godlike in both their image as well as in their control over the rest of creation. The cultural logic of this hierarchy of humans over the land and the rest of the created order establishes an ideological precedent for the possibility for the manipulation of land and life with very little ethical consideration for the wellbeing of any other form of life.

When we shift the analysis to the institutional level of eurowestern culture, it demonstrates some significant differences in conceptualizations around the primary site of social, political, and economic life. The early colonial period in the Americas was an interesting place of the negotiation and establishment of what would become the new political ideas of democracy, the transition of economics from late mercantilism to early capitalism, as well as the shift from communal identities to the establishment of the individual as the primary social unit. The colonizers lived out their ideological dominion in the "New Israel" as they further developed legal methods of controlling land as property, and used that property as a means of creating individual and national wealth from land sales, farming, mining, furbearing animals, lumber, recreational pursuits, and the beginnings of industry.[68] The nation became the ideological and institutional apparatus that provided the colonizers with the means for legitimizing the experience of dominion, and for the ongoing theft and destruction of Indigenous North America. While the daily experiences of the colonizers were in the local villages, it was the nation to which these villages would belong that provided the coalescing of legal arguments, statutes, laws, and the necessary raising of national militias to implement these ideas against the will of the Indigenous peoples. What became the United States and Canada are top-down federal organizations that negotiated the boundaries between themselves and Indigenous North America and used the monies made from those land sales to finance the ongoing colonization and destruction of new lands further west.[69] The ideology of Manifest Destiny provided further justification to repeat this process of imposing the colonial will onto the land, fundamentally changing the web of relatedness and ecological balance in the land through the destruction of many species for the profit of a small number of people. The logic of dominion is manifest in the ideological, institutional, and everyday experiences of the colonial newcomers to this land, at the expense of the Indigenous inhabitants of that land.

The logic of dominion is also evident in the naming of the places where they lived. As mentioned above, among the Anishinaabeg, the naming of particular villages and places was done with a sense of dialogical communication with the land. In a brief glance at a map of the United States, in particular the east coast, we can see the lack of agency in the land with place names like New England, New Hampshire, New Jersey, and New York. The colonial ritual of naming is indicative of a larger phenomenon of claiming power over the places to which they went. This naming ritual was relied upon by eurowestern colonizers in the transformation of the lands of Indigenous North America into the dominion of property by the colonizing nation-states. This seemingly benign ritual functioned as a gross act of power that worked to legitimize and sanitize the colonial actions.[70] Renaming the landscape in their own image was a manifestation of the ideological mandate of subduing the earth.

A closer look at the original charters helps to get at the economic impetus for colonization. As Albert Memmi reminds us, "Colonization is, above all, economic and political exploitation."[71] These colonial charters not only established the land base of the colonies with no interactions with the Indigenous inhabitants, but maybe more importantly were economic charters in that the original colonists were supposed to make money for the private investors who funded the colonies.

Hence, in Jamestown tobacco was grown to sell to the home country for a profit. However, this tobacco was grown with eurowestern monocropping techniques that quickly depleted the land of its nutrients. Tobacco, while it does provide some pest control benefits for companion planting in agriculture, is destructive to soil in large quantities because it requires an enormous nutrient input from the soil.[72] So as the tobacco market grew in Europe, more and more land was put into tobacco production and was also quickly depleted. Thus, more and more land needed to be cleared, both of trees and of the Indigenous inhabitants who lived there, for tobacco fields.[73] The same process can be seen in the fur trade further north. As the colonies in New England and near Montreal got themselves deeper and deeper into the fur trade to satisfy the European appetite for furs, the local streams, rivers, and lakes were depleted of the furbearing animals on which the trade depended. Rather than developing a practice of sustainability where the use of furs could match the reproduction rates of the affected species, the colonists moved further west to exploit newer streams, rivers, and lakes, only to deplete them as well.[74] Therefore, the ideological command to "subdue" the earth played out as economic exploitation and radically altered the Indigenous landscape of North America. In this sense, Manifest Destiny had as much to do with the economic necessity of moving to new resource-rich areas because of the practice of depleting the natural resources as it did with the realization of a racialized cultural mandate.

Conclusion

From the above sketch, a clearer picture of the vast differences in the relationship to space between the Anishinaabeg and the eurowest can be brought into focus. From the European side, the logic of human dominion over the land and the rest of life is clearly indicated in the ideology of the Christian Bible in Genesis. This ideology has spawned numerous social, political, and economic institutions that facilitate this cultural logic in the conceptualizations of land as property, and the economic transactions of buying and selling that property, which necessitate the legal codes and statutes that protect those transactions. These economic and legal institutions then work to structure the everyday experiences of the people of the nation that live out this relationship to land in the extractions, manipulations, and destructions of the land and the other life forms that share this space. Within this anthropocentric cultural logic, the culture has developed no effective ethical constraints that would demand different ideological, institutional experiences from the people.[75] While it is possible for individuals to think differently about this cultural trajectory of dominion, that thinking does not constitute a different worldview. A worldview has the full complement of ideological, institutional, and everyday experiences as a dynamic dialogical world to facilitate the lives and thought of people. Again, individuals can think outside of this semiclosed system, and they can act contrary to what the culture suggests; but they too live in the worldview of dominion.

An Anishinaabeg cultural trajectory exemplifies a very different relationship to land. The Anishinaabeg logic of an intimate relationship to localized space is ideologically manifest in the *Giizhigokwe* narratives with her regeneration of the land base for Indigenous North America. This ideological formation demonstrates the proper relationship of humans to the land (as children to *Mazikamikwe*), and to the rest of life (as younger siblings). These narratives help to guide the Anishinaabeg to develop institutional apparatuses of ceremony to keep balance in this space. They also establish the local village as the primary site of social, political, and economic life as well as their identity in relationship to their *doodem*. The everyday experiences that arise from these institutions recognize the rest of life as coequal partners in the ongoing regenerative processes that guide their seasonal lives in the Northern Great Lakes, Anishinaabe Akiing. The cultural logic set forth in the *Giizhigokwe* narratives demonstrates a reverence for the rest of life in which the ceremonies reproduce the balance that the community of life in Anishinaabe Akiing demands. The ethical constraints codified in the origin narratives of *Giizhigokwe* function to promote the flourishing of the Anishinaabeg and the rest of life with whom they share their space. The daily experiences that facilitate the flourishing of life not only demonstrate a lived experience of *Giizhigokwe*, but also help to strengthen those narratives as they are retold in the wintertime.[76]

With the differences of these two worldviews brought into conversation with one another, the problems of understanding Article 13 in the Treaty of Washington in 1836 can be better analyzed. Again, it is no surprise that the bulk of the treaty language is about property boundaries and the goods and services exchanged for the land. And Article 13 of that treaty should also come as no surprise now that "The Indians stipulate for the right of hunting on the lands ceded, with the other usual privileges of occupancy, until the land is required for settlement."[77] The ongoing relationship to the spaces in which they live, and which immediately surround their villages, was defended in this treaty. Here I am suggesting that in the language of this treaty negotiation, the Anishinaabeg meaning behind this brief and cryptic comment is that the common pot, the community of life with whom they share their space, was being written into this treaty. Even though it was recorded in "rights" language and described as hunting, the act of hunting within the cultural logic associated with land for the Anishinaabeg presumes that the balance of life in those communities will stay intact. The logic of an intimate relationship to a localized space was being invoked in this treaty, and Article 13 must be understood not just as a right for hunting, but for the dialogically complex relationships that hunting is associated with in Anishinaabemowin and Anishinaabe thought. This provision in the treaty is an attempt to defend the social, political, and economic lifeways associated with the logic of an intimate relationship to localized space.

Unfortunately, this attempt at defending Anishinaabe Akiing in Article 13 was not successful, as the conquest and genocide have continued to take place throughout the nineteenth and twentieth centuries, and on into the twenty-first. The vastly different lifeways represented by the encroaching eurowestern political and economic systems overwhelmed the Anishinaabeg and others in Indigenous North America. As the old-growth forests were destroyed for building projects, as huge swaths of land were strip-mined for ores, and as *t'chi gumeeng* (the Great Lakes) were polluted with industrial waste, the ability to live out this logic came under attack. When one thinks deeply and critically about the worldview represented here within the linguistic-conceptual world of the Anishinaabeg, the necessity for very different cultural experiences associated with this worldview become clear. When one is enveloped within a spatially configured world, with the prospects of being removed from your homeland and being denied the ability to live in relationship to those places, then the acts of eurowestern conquest can be correctly named as acts of genocide. The eurowestern conquest of Anishinaabe Akiing, with the destruction of the land and the imposition of nonmaterial categories of thought, has radically altered our ability to be Anishinaabeg, the good people.

From this place of radical environmental degradation, we have the task of continually reproducing Anishinaabeg praxis in our lands. In this process, it is essential that we develop methodologies of engagement that help to provide a solid mooring for our sociopolitical-economic activities. Religious language and the promise of protection can no longer be relied upon. As has been codified in the United States' legal system, "Even assuming that the Government's actions here will virtually destroy the Indians' ability to practice their religion, the Constitution simply does not supply a principle that could justify upholding respondent's legal claims."[78] However, radical engagements with our relatives in our homelands can provide regenerative power. From *Giizhigokwe* we know that we have had to engage in numerous rebuilding projects in our lands. With this process of critically retranslating Anishinaabeg concepts of spatiality, it is possible that fresh thinking about relationships to the land can be regenerated and new methods of defending Anishinaabe Akiing can be pursued.

CHAPTER 3

Time

Anthropologists and social scientists have long recognized the concepts of time and space as important to understanding diverse cultures. Consistently, these two concepts are covered in academic treatises on worldview and the ethnographic discussions of people. However, rarely have these discussions helped to enlarge "the universe of human discourse."[1] For example, Michael Kearney has discussed the relationship to space and time in his book *World View*. In this treatment of space and time, Kearney works toward enriching the discussion, suggesting that "whereas perception of spatial relations is dependent upon immediately sensed information (object location, body position, motion, etc.), time as a percept is not so directly tied to objects."[2] This is helpful as it points towards a primacy of space as generating the possibility of a temporal relationship. However, this analysis then falls flat as he moves to the examples of "temporal prepositions and particles in many languages [that] are marked forms of spatial locatives."[3] While this analysis does suggest a relationship between space and time, it fails to get at a deeper understanding that can elucidate Indigenous understandings and concepts of this complex relationship. This failure is largely due to the lack of an authentic Indigenous starting place in concepts of space, and the relationships to the rest of life that are necessary in those spaces. With a more thorough understanding of Anishinaabeg space at hand, we can now delve into an Anishinaabeg logic of time.

For all cultures, there are limits to both space and time. As Vine Deloria Jr. suggests, "Space has limitations that are primarily geographical," which can be contrasted with the limits of time that "must begin and end at some real points, or it must be conceived as cyclical in nature, endlessly allowing the repetition of patterns of possibilities."[4] Previously we have seen the Anishinaabeg logic of space as an intimate relationship to a localized space. There were geographical boundaries of roughly the northern Great Lakes and surrounding tributaries, and more localized boundaries that are the spaces around the village where most people negotiate their lives. However, when that Indigenous concept of space is contrasted with a eurowestern conceptualization of space as land to be dominated, it is easy to see how the geographic limitation of that eurowestern space can be transcended to incorporate larger boundaries since there is no sense of ethical restraint built into that relationship. In the colonial contest of Indigenous North America we have seen these differing conceptualizations of space play out over and over again. However, this contest over space is also affected by the relationship of that space to time. The desire to dominate all space by the eurowestern peoples is closely associated with an understanding of time as linear progress. There is a strong past-present-future concept of time where the colonizers consider themselves to be ordained by god to fulfill their manifest destiny of ruling all of North America, and later the entire world. This myth of linear progress can be sharply contrasted with an Indigenous understanding of time as primarily cyclical in nature, repeating a continuous cycle of days, moons (months), and seasons. The importance of these differing concepts of time is that they represent very different cultural logics for a society to follow, and there are far-reaching consequences for these differences. As Deloria quips, "When one group is concerned with the philosophical problem of space and the other with the philosophical problem of time, then the statements of either group do not make much sense when transferred from one context to the other without the proper consideration of what is taking place."[5]

These radically different logics of time clashed in the colonial contest of Indigenous North America. The eurowestern emphasis on linear time and the Indigenous emphasis on cyclical time can again be seen in the treaty literature. The cultural differences evident in treaty proceedings can be easily overlooked without a trained eye, both because the treaty literature is short and it is written in a eurowestern language. Time as a component of worldview is often taken for granted by people, and as such, the particularities of cultural differences can be easily overlooked. However, the cultural conceptualization of time as cyclical for the Anishinaabeg and linear for the eurowestern colonizers is evident within the treaty literature and the actions surrounding the treaties themselves.

Robert Williams Jr., a Lumbee legal scholar, has written extensively about the treaty literature and the difficulties inherent in studying such material. In *Linking Arms Together*, Williams addresses the early colonial period (before 1800) to demonstrate the ways in which American Indian nations held a significant amount of power to shape treaty relationships and negotiations. These treaty negotiations practiced Indigenous customs, so that in the early colonial period, "Indians can be witnessed inviting Europeans to make known the 'good thoughts' of peace, to smoke the sacred pipe, to clear the path, to bury the hatchet, to link arms together and unite as one people, to eat out of the same bowl together."[6] These Indigenous concepts all helped to guide both the ceremonies and the relationships that resulted from those meetings throughout this period. One of these Indigenous concepts that guided early treaty relationships is that of renewal. This concept is significant as it is grounded in Indigenous relationships to cyclical time. This meant that upon entering into a treaty relationship, there were expectations of annual meetings to renew and strengthen these bonds created in the treaty ceremony. As Williams explains, "Renewal, in fact, was regarded as a continuing constitutional obligation of treaty partners."[7] The cyclical concept of time functioned as a cultural logic that helped to form the relationship of treaty partners to annual renewals of that relationship. The Indigenous peoples and the eurowestern participants both negotiated these treaties from an understanding that the relationship would be renewed each year. In this early colonial period, it was the cyclical time of Indigenous North America that would drive the temporal understanding of these treaty relationships.

Among the Anishinaabeg, this emphasis on cyclical concepts of time and the obligation for renewal in treaties can be seen as late as the Treaty of Greenville in 1795. This treaty, which negotiated the end of hostilities between the U.S. Government and the "Wyandots, Delawares, Shawanoes, Ottawas, Chipewas, Putawatimes, Miamis, Eel-River, Weeas, Kickapoos, Piankashaws, and Kaskaskias," demonstrates an emphasis on cyclical time.[8] Article 1 states that "peace is hereby established, and shall be perpetual," and Article 4 describes the goods to be delivered as payment "henceforward every year forever."[9] While there are clearly both cyclical and linear concepts of time evident here, with "every year" as cyclical and "forever" and "perpetual" representing continuity over time, there is no discussion of end points of time or descriptions of these payments going on for specific periods. With the cycle of payments (read gifting from the Indigenous point of view) being "annually delivered," the concept of annual treaty renewal suggested by Williams is evident here.[10] However, when the Treaty of Washington in 1836 is revisited, there is a noticeable shift in the treaty language. The descriptions of time in this treaty forego the concepts of continuity written as "perpetual" and "forever" in 1795, and instead use terminal language of specific periods of time. Article 3 of this 1836 treaty ceded the reserved tracts of land "for the term of five years from the date of the ratification of this treaty, and no longer, unless the United States shall grant them permission to remain on said lands for a longer period."[11] Curiously enough, the payments for these land cessions were to be paid "per annum, in specie, for twenty years," and payments supporting education would be "contined [sic] twenty years and as long thereafter as Congress may appropriate for the object."[12] If these different periods for living on land and receiving payments were not confusing enough, Article 13 states that "The Indians stipulate for the right of hunting on the lands ceded, with the other usual privileges of occupancy, until the land is required for settlement."[13] Clearly there is a significant shift in discourse evident in the comparison of these two treaties regarding the conceptualizations of time.

The reason that these treaties represent such different notions of time, even though they are only forty-one years apart, is suggested in the Treaty of Washington. Article 8 states that "It is agreed, that as soon as the said Indians desire it, a deputation shall be sent to the southwest of the Missouri River, there to select a suitable place for the final settlement of said Indians."[14] Not only were the United States government officials, represented here by Henry Schoolcraft, hurried to establish firm boundaries and title to the land of Michigan for statehood, in 1836 the Indian Removal Act was being enforced upon numerous Indian peoples who were still east of the Mississippi River. Evident in the Treaty of Washington is this emphasis on removal, and hence the linear time periods with a built-in terminus. Furthermore, after the War of 1812, the United States entered treaties with American Indian peoples with an emboldened sense of exceptionalism as they became the preeminent European power in North America. With this new sense of power, the United States no longer had to negotiate with Indigenous peoples as equals, but shifted to a greater sense of conquest in their mannerisms.[15] Tink Tinker quips upon this shift in power in negotiating treaties with the United States, suggesting that "'Permanent,' it turns out, means in english 'a few years,' since we were forced to sign a series of treaties over about six decades, almost always ceding new pieces of territory."[16] The shift in power away from the Indigenous peoples in North America is represented in this shift in language on time as well as the loss of Indigenous protocols of treaty making.

The colonial contest between Indigenous North Americans and the eurowestern colonizers as demonstrated in the treaty language and protocols elucidates a larger difficulty in translating not only language, but the cultures that are represented by those languages. In the diplomacy around treaties, Williams suggests that "Europeans were confronted with a much different way of thinking about the world and the way in which relationships between peoples were to be structured in it."[17] What has been recorded for us in these treaties is helpful to point out the different worldviews that are represented. However, the written records we have are from the point of view of the colonizer, which only tell part of the story. A further elaboration of the Indigenous thought represented in these treaty proceedings waits for a deeper engagement with the language and culture of a particular group.

Narratives

Once again, the *Giizhigokwe* narratives help us to get started with the translations of Anishinaabeg time. By beginning here, we can see the logic of cyclical time in a number of complex ways that guide the establishment of institutions and everyday experiences. While all cultures understand and use both cyclical and linear conceptualizations of time, for the Anishinaabeg it is the cyclical understandings of time that provide the cultural logic for the organization of our culture.

In the *Giizhigokwe* narratives, one of the most striking features is that they are almost void of references to time. There is already life in existence before *Giizhigokwe* falls from the sky. Therefore, this narrative is not an account of "creation," but of regeneration. The world leading up to the flood was destroyed, and the narrative of *Giizhigokwe* signals a renewal, which now includes humans. The concept of regeneration and not creation is incredibly important because it embodies a constant cycle of rebirth, growth, senescence, purity, and subsequent regeneration that is indicative of cyclical concepts of time.[18] Here I use senescence instead of death because as a biological concept it does a much better job of describing the planned aging and decay as part of a cycle of life. Death, in its eurowestern form, is a linear conceptualization as a finality of life. The concept of creation, as understood in the eurowestern narrative of the Bible, establishes a clear starting point for a linearity to develop. The concepts of creation and death function as bookends to linear conceptualizations of life, do not make a connection from death to rebirth, and offer a poor translation for an Indigenous understanding of ongoing cycles of time and life.

The *Giizhigokwe* narratives belong to a group of stories called *aadizookaanag*.[19] Hallowell translates this term as "myth," though I believe this to be misleading as myth can sometimes mean something that is simply not true.[20] This is a mistake, as the point of these narratives is not to articulate a "true" or "historically accurate" narrative, but to teach people how to relate to each other and the land. As a set of narratives the *aadizookaanag* happen *mewinzha*, in the long, long ago.[21] In this category of time, humans and other-than-humans interacted and communicated more freely, and the ability to change physical form was more prevalent for all forms of life. The animals had council together, *Giizhigokwe* regenerated land on the back of *Makinak*, and the ordering of relationships between humans and other-than-humans would be worked out in a series of events held in the narratives.[22] This set of narratives gives the Anishinaabeg a rendering of their origins as a people, how they are to be relatives with those peoples they share their space with, lessons on how to avoid difficulty, as well as methods to get themselves out of difficulty if they find themselves there. These narratives also give an account of the origins of *doodem* relationships, medicine societies, and foods. So the *aadizookaanag* can be thought of as a reservoir of cultural knowledge that gets told and retold throughout the life of the village to reproduce the culture.[23]

Linguistically, *aadizookaan* belongs to the *maaba* class of nouns. This is important as it signifies that the narratives and the characters of the narratives have a certain amount of power attached to them. The characters and stories themselves are living ancestors worthy of significant respect. This is why the *aadizookaanag* are only told in the wintertime. It is considered disrespectful to tell them out of that season and allows for the possibility of retribution by the *aadizookaanag* (characters) in the form of frogs and toads crawling up your clothing.[24] Considering that these *aadizookaanag* are part of a spatially configured cultural complex, they are located in that space, in Anishinaabe Akiing. The *aadizookaanag* are accessible through the narratives as strength to draw on to help guide everyday situations that the people have to negotiate. While the narratives are only told during the winter season, the knowledge that they impart can be recalled throughout the year to help the people make decisions that will affect the lives of the entire community.

Another type of narrative that also has a teaching function is the *dibaaji-mowinan*, which differs from the *aadizookaanag*. According to Hallowell, the *dibaajimowinan* are defined as "'News or tidings' . . . i.e., anecdotes, or stories relating to events in the lives of human beings."[25] William Berens told Hallowell at least twenty-six narratives of this variety, which tell of his experiences and people whom he has known in their own exploits, often involving a dream as an important part of the narrative. For example, five of these *dibaajimowinan* discuss experiences of Berens from important dreams that he has had; four others discuss experiences of *wiindigo*, and another gives an account of a *waabano* ceremony.[26] This last narrative is a cautionary tale of the importance of treating animals respectfully. In this ceremony a hunter was asking for help to kill animals for food, because he was unable to find any animals to kill. In this *waabano*, the voices of the moose leader and the wolf leader were heard telling him that he had to stop leaving animals lying in the bush without using their meat.[27] Berens explains, "Not supposed to kill animals and leave them in the bush. If you kill a moose make use of him, his meat, dry it and you'll have luck—then if you starve you'll know it did not come from there [that reason]. Seems to me the animals know when they are not used right."[28] The *dibaajimowinan* also deliberately give lessons for living, "even if their messages are understated or left implicit."[29] This class of narratives is important in that they are an effective teaching tool, even if they do not match the power of the *aadizookaanag*.

From an analytic point of view, there are three primary distinctions between the *dibaajimowinan* and the *aadizookaanag*. First, from a linguistic perspective, *dibaajimowinan* is of the *maanda* class of nouns; therefore these narratives as a category do not carry the same weight as do the *aadizookaanag*. Secondly, since the *dibaajimowinan* do not carry the same power as the *aadizookaanag*, they do not come with customary restrictions of seasonal telling and can be recited at any time of the year. Thirdly, the subject matter primarily concerns daily life of the Anishinaabeg, including the narrators themselves. The *dibaajimowinan* then can be thought of as giving empirical evidence in the lives of the people in their contact and communication with other-than-human persons. In this way they are a learning tool where the lives as experienced by the Anishinaabeg can live in the same narrative space as the *aadizookaanag*. The time of *mewinzha* can be collapsed in Anishinaabe Akiing, and the people can experience a life similar to their ancestors' in their space. For example, *Makinak*, the Great Turtle of the *Giizhigokwe* narratives, speaks in the *waabano* ceremonies as an ancestor who is still communicating with Anishinaabeg. Also, in the *dibaajimowinan* related by Berens, we can think of the communication from the moose and the wolf as the elder siblings giving counsel to this person asking for help, as well as the rest of the people who were in attendance.[30] Once again, the importance of an entirely spatial existence (no spirit) is essential in understanding the power in these narratives. The ancestors are not separated by time or space; they are available for council through ceremony and through the retelling of the narratives themselves. There is no chronological distance to travel to be in conversation with the ancestors; we share the same space and they are available for counsel. In this sense the retelling of these narratives functions to reproduce the culture for each generation as they are told and retold. The *aadizookaanag* (characters) of the narratives are kept in communication in two ways. First, with the telling of their adventures and misadventures, they continually impart knowledge to the Anishinaabeg in attendance. Secondly, they can be summoned in ceremony to offer advice and help those who are willing to ask for it. Stated in another way, the *aadizookaanag* (characters) participated in events of land regeneration *mewinzha*, but they live continually in Anishinaabe Akiing, and are available to give counsel in ceremony.

Relationships to Time

The previous discussion of narratives raises as many questions as it answers. While it is helpful to discuss the general relationship of narratives to time as it begins to establish an Anishinaabeg worldview, it does little to elucidate the deeper philosophical understanding of time. In a chapter titled "Temporal Orientation in Western Civilization and in a Preliterate Society," Hallowell makes a comparison between a Western conceptualization of time and the "Saulteaux." In one aspect of comparison, Hallowell suggests a similarity in the method of recalling time by individuals in both cultures when they recall events and place them in relationship to each other as a means of recalling temporal references. This is a method of "human reference" where events "in the life history of individuals—birth, marriage, or other significant occurrences—are constantly evoked to which other events may be related. Even in Western civilization, despite the fact that the logics provide us with the alternative of employing exact dates for all such events, similar unformalized reference points are in use."[31] Hallowell uses this comparison as a means of demonstrating certain, if "unformalized," methods of understanding the passing of time through events. While he is able to shed some light on the temporal concepts as "culturally constituted" frames of reference, his elaborations do not go deep enough to describe the relationship of human events to time.

In a similar reckoning of temporal conceptualizations in the Akan culture, Kwame Gyekye follows a trajectory much like Hallowell's, though he extends his analysis deeper to describe time as a metaphysical concept. Gyekye is responding to John Mbiti's assertion that African languages do not "generate a concept of an infinite future."[32] In his critique, Gyekye elaborates on an Akan understanding of the "human reference" of time as noted by Hallowell, suggesting that the sequencing of events in the life of a people "implies the presupposition of the existence of time."[33] While it is correct that in Africa the referencing of time is done with the connection to events, "this fact cannot be taken to mean that time itself is composed of events. If the events were not taking place within time, they could not be reckoned temporally, nor could people in Akan communities speak of the Adai festival coming *before* or *after* the Ohum festival."[34] Therefore, the human events that are referenced are not time itself. Instead, time "is held to have an objective metaphysical existence, so that even if there were no changes, processes, and events time would still be real."[35] This separation of events from the metaphysical concept of time is essential for two reasons. First, it undermines an anthropocentric notion of time where human events generate time. This anthropocentrism is unintelligible in Anishinaabeg culture as other animals were here long before us. Secondly, recognizing time in its metaphysical existence demands that a deep cultural relationship to time must be established for humans to be able to live in a community. Without time there is no memory, no learning, and no community. Time as a metaphysical concept demonstrates the necessity of its inclusion in the realm of worldview. It is an essential building block for human community to exist.

With the above analysis in hand, a more thorough rendering of the relationship of Anishinaabeg to time in the narratives can be considered. With time as an independent metaphysical entity, we can now understand that the events of both the *aadizookaanag* and the *dibaajimowinan* are taking place within time, where the *aadizookaanag* happened *mewinzha*, and the *dibaajimowinan* have taken place more recently. To get a thorough grasp on the conceptualizations of time used by the Anishinaabeg, it is important to push the connection of space to time here. The *aadizookaanag* are events that happened *mewinzha*, in the long ago. However, they also happened here, in Anishinaabe Akiing. The *aadizookaanag* as characters share in Anishinaabe Akiing, not in a past tense, but continually from long ago into the present context. The events of *aadizookaanag* happened, but the characters as other-than-human persons live on and hence are accessible to the Anishinaabeg in ceremony. Therefore, *Makinak* can come into a *waabano* ceremony along with the *moozoog* (moose) and *ma'iingan* (wolf) to give counsel to an individual seeking help and guidance. So in this sense, the *aadizookaanag* as narratives offer guidance on how to live in a good way in their oral retelling in the wintertime, and the *aadizookaanag* as characters are available to continually give guidance in ceremony. In this way, the distance across time of *mewinzha* is collapsed in Anishinaabe Akiing, as the events of long ago are continually made present in the Anishinaabeg villages, homes, and ceremonies.[36] The events of the Anishinaabeg continually happen in time and are continually (cyclically) made relevant with the retelling of the *aadizookaanag* and *dibaajimowinan*. The characters of the narratives continually live and are accessible in ceremony, dreams, and the daily lives of the Anishinaabeg.

Time in Anishinaabemowin

One of the basic units of time for the Anishinaabeg is *giizhigad*, or day. This unit of time has two meanings. First, *giizhigad* means "during the day," or when the sun is up. Secondly, it can also be used to designate a day as a 24-hour period, as in *giizhig*, or simply "day."[37] The day does have certain subdivisions, though they take on environmental particularities and do not function in the same uniform way that eurowestern hours do. First, the day, *giizhig* (24 hours) has two units, *giizhigad* (day) and *dibikad* (night).[38] Living above the forty-fifth parallel, these two units of time vary during the year according to the position of the sun. The etymology of these two words demonstrates the importance of celestial bodies in the relationship to time. Not surprisingly, *giizis* is "sun" and *dibiki giizis* is "moon," or more literally, "night sun."[39] However, I will say more about these concepts, as there is not a direct, one-to-one translation between these Anishinaabemowin and English words. We have to delve deeper into the dialogical experiences of these utterances as each has its own culturally specific cognitive set of meanings. Within the word *giizis* is knowledge of this entity in the sky that lights our days and gives us heat as a source of quantum lifegiving energy.[40] This is important as it describes a deeper relationship to, and understanding of, this ball of energy in the sky than what is often afforded to Indigenous peoples. Accordingly, *dibiki giizis* literally translates as "night sun," and also comes with the knowledge of the moon as a giver of quantum lifegiving energy.

More needs to be said regarding the translations of *giizis* and *dibiki giizis*. If I stopped at this part of the translation, it could be assumed that the concepts of *giizis* and *dibiki giizis* match the eurowestern concepts of sun and moon respectively. However, while there are some basic similarities in the meanings of these words, there are also some significant differences that need to be noted. First, in Anishinaabemowin there are familial relationships that are associated with these concepts that help to conceptualize Anishinaabe Akiing as a large extended family. *Giizis* is thought of as *giinwiisayeny*, older brother.[41] Thanks is offered to *giinwiisayeny* for every day running his path from east to west and providing energy, light, and heat along the way. *Dibiki giizis* is also *g'okomis*, or "our grandmother." She is given thanks for offering light at night and watching over us while we sleep. There is a clear function of gendered balancing with these two celestial bodies being termed male and female. These gendered and familial relationships to *giizis* and *dibiki giizis* are part of the cognitive set of knowledge regarding these two temporal entities, information that is not existent with the concepts of sun and moon.

So the *giizhig* (24 hours) is split between *giizhigad* (day) and *dibikad* (night). When a group of people negotiate their lives without electricity and only have the light of fires and *dibiki giizis* to negotiate their way through the woods and waterways of the northern Great Lakes, this splitting of the 24-hour period of *giizhig* takes on a lot of significance. Hallowell quips that "This pattern of returning to one's own camp before nightfall is so well established even among the Indians at the mouth of the river that, on several occasions, the family with whom I lived thought that I must be lost in the bush when I did not show up at the expected time."[42] The consistent cycle of returning to camp at nightfall provides an effective structure for the conceptualization of the 24-hour day. Most of the morning activities of village life for people who hunt and fish are very important. Therefore these waking hours can have more defined subdivisions. Among the people of Berens River, Hallowell discusses six temporal divisions from dawn until the "tops of trees when hangs (the) sun."[43] In comparison, six more references to temporal divisions are recorded by Hallowell to account for the rest of the day, three of which describe the last few minutes of the sun going below the tree tops to dusk.[44] In this method of temporal division, we can see several meaningful differences. First, the times of the day when there is a lot of activity around hunting and fishing coincide with smaller temporal divisions. This should come as no surprise to anyone who has spent time hunting, fishing, or camping. The activities of fish and game animals are entirely dependent upon cycles of day and night in combination with atmospheric and seasonal changes, particularly in the dawn and dusk periods. To successfully negotiate this life of weather patterns and cycles of days and seasons, a uniform measurement of time is unnecessary. The people move primarily when the fish and game move. Secondly, no arbitrary method of timekeeping needs to be developed in this lifestyle. *Giizis*, running his path across the sky, provides all the necessary reference points to make a good living for the community. Precision, to the point of inventing small, uniform units of measurement, is unnecessary, and hence never developed among the Anishinaabeg.

The *giizhig* are not numbered, there are no particular names for the days, and there is no sequencing of days that resembles anything like a week. These are all particularly eurowestern temporal phenomena. This difference between the two cultures can be explained in two ways. First, considering the economic activities of the Anishinaabeg, each *giizhig* is very similar. There is food to cook and seasonally dependent food acquisition like sugarbushing, fishing, gardening, or hunting. There is no necessary regimentation outside of what the seasons and weather offer. Secondly, the weekly seven-day cycle is a particular temporal category stemming from the first chapter in Genesis. God made the universe in six days and rests on the seventh; therefore Christians follow that cycle. No such temporal cycle between the *giizhig* and moon cycles became necessary until the missionaries showed up. Then, Anishinaabeg were coerced into living lives regimented by a Gregorian calendar split up by months and weeks. Among eastern Anishinaabeg, it was the Jesuits who first came, so the Anishinaabeg names of days reflect specific Catholic influences. For people around Bahweting and Makinakong, Sunday became *name giizhigak*, or prayer day.[45] Given that the missionaries were desperately working to bring "civilization" to the Anishinaabeg, they imposed these foreign temporal cycles onto the people. Each *giizhig* then became numbered in a sequence from *bezhig* (one) to *nisimdana shi bezhig* (thirty-one). The early missionaries kept a foreign relationship to time in Anishinaabe Akiing with the ringing of their church bells on Sunday, and their teaching of numbers to their not-so-willing students. When the missionaries were few, their effect was minimal, and while some Anishinaabeg learned these ways and kept their own calendars, very little about the rest of their lives changed.[46] However, as disease, warfare, and cultural dislocation reduced the power of the Indigenous population, the effects of these new temporal cycles began to eat away at the fabric of Anishinaabeg culture. This process of temporal reorientation became a powerful form of cultural dislocation as the rhythms of days, moons, and seasons gave way to weeks, months, and years. Over generations, these temporal changes have continually pushed the Anishinaabeg and other groups away from their Indigenous temporal relationships based on repeating cycles in favor of eurowestern cycles oriented around the linear progress of time.[47] This temporal reorientation constitutes a significant problem for the cultural regeneration of many Indigenous peoples.

The female relationship of *dibiki giizis* as *g'okomis* has already been mentioned, but this is only one aspect of the female association with the moon. As in many other cultures, *dibiki giizis* has a strong female orientation in its twenty-eight-day cycle, which has the same temporal consistency and duration of the twenty-eight-day menstrual or moon cycle of women. This connection of women to the moon was not lost on the Anishinaabekwe (Anishinaabeg women) as they, along with other Indigenous women, have kept a close relationship to *dibiki giizis* for guidance in conceiving children.[48] There is also a close relationship of agricultural planting and harvesting to cycles of the moon. Here, in addition to the femininity of the moon and Anishinaabekwe was added the power of *Mazikaamikwe*, Earth Mother. These powerful female relationships are evident in the realm of female economic relationships and their responsibility to plant and gather food. There is no conceptual difference among Anishinaabeg between planted crops like corn, beans, and squash, and the more naturally occurring *miinan* (blueberries) or *asasaweminan* (chokecherries). These "wild" plants were cultivated, fertilized with controlled burns to provide needed potash, and looked after during the year.

This female power as a relationship between *dibiki giizis* as *g'okomis* and *Mazikaamikwe* is also represented in the naming of moons. In a lunar cycle there are thirteen moons for each year, and for the Anishinaabeg these names are directly associated with the seasonal activities of the local flora and fauna that help to economically sustain the people.[49] These economic activities represent the reliance upon *Mazikaamikwe* for sustenance. In the naming of the moons, we can also see a strong female connection with the *Makwa Giizis*, a temporal signal for returning to *Ziigwan*, or spring. This roughly correlates with February and is when the mother bears give birth to the cubs in their dens. Often a few warm days will occur as *giizis* gets higher in the sky with longer days, and this signals a move towards the end of the cold season of winter and to the regenerative power of *Ziigwan*.[50] Next is *Onabadin Giizis*, or Snow Crust Moon, which correlates with March. With the warmer days above freezing, the snow can get a firm crust on top, which can make it easier to walk across. Moving towards April, there is *Ziisbakadake Giizis*, Sugar Making Moon. This is when Anishinaabeg break their winter camps and move to the sugar bush with their extended families to make maple sugar.[51] *Namebine Giizis*, or Suckerfish Moon, is when the suckers run from the lakes into the streams in large numbers, so they gather around these streams to stock up on an important food source in April/May. *Baashkaabigonii Giizis* marks the time when the flowers begin to bloom, hence the name, Blooming Moon. This is parallel to June. *Miin Giizis* comes next, when the berries begin to come into season and the people spend time picking and drying the berries (and of course eating a lot of them while they pick). This roughly correlates with July. Next the wild rice stands on the lakes become ripe, so the people camp at their ricing fields for *Manoominike Giizis*, Wild Rice Moon. This happens towards the end of summer, around August. Then the weather begins to turn colder during the nights and the days get shorter. This movement towards autumn in September is known as *Waabaagbagaa Giizis*, or Leaves Turning Moon. After the leaves turn color, they fall off during *Binakwe Giizis*, or Falling Leaves Moon. This happens in this part of Anishinaabe Akiing in October. Then the weather turns cold, and the snow begins to come around November, which is known as *Baashkakodin Giizis*, or Freezing Moon. This places the Anishinaabeg into winter, which comes into full force during *Manidoo-Giizisoons*, or Little Manidoo Moon.[52] This correlates to December/January. Then the deepest part of the winter is under *Manidoo Giizis*, or Manidoo Moon. This moon returns the Anishinaabeg from the resting silence of winter back towards spring with the regeneration of *makoons*, or the bear cubs in the dens in *Makwa Giizis*.[53]

There is a long gap of time between *giizhig* and *dibiki giizis*, which, if not filled, could make community planning a challenge. While there is no concept of a "week" present in Anishinaabemowin, there are subdivisions of the lunar periods that can function as time periods shorter than a moon and longer than a day. The full lunar cycle begins with *michaabikizi*, the full moon. In the waning period of the moon getting smaller it can be *aabitawaabikizi*, or half full, followed by the *oshkagoojin*, or new moon. In the ensuing waxing period again the *dibiki giizis* will go to *aabitawaabikizi* and finally back to *michaabikizi*.[54] In a twenty-eight-day period, then, these three subdivisions break the lunar cycle into approximately seven-day increments. This is useful as it allows for community planning of ceremony and moving to places like sugar bush or fish runs in longer temporal periods than a few days and fewer than the twenty-eight.[55]

So *dibiki giizis* plays an important part in the temporal organization of the

Anishinaabeg. This female celestial being brings light in the night, can be used as a guide for conceiving a child and planting and harvesting food, is associated with different cycles of economic and seasonal activities during the year, and helps to organize community life. This longer explanation of *dibiki giizis* is important as it evokes the larger cognitive set of cultural information that is associated with the temporal cycles of what is often translated as moon. It is important to point out that in the case of *dibiki giizis* there is no concept of linearity involved. Hallowell correctly points out that "As in the case of the day, a 'moon' is not a division of continuous time, it is a recurring event."[56] There is not a successive buildup to any end point in this temporal system; each moon is its own cycle.[57] As *dibiki giizis* repeats its twenty-eight-day cycle, the seasonal changes occur that prompt the Anishinaabeg to get food from different sources, move to new locations, and prepare themselves for the coming winter.

In moving to longer temporal orientations, seasons come in longer than *dibiki giizis* cycles. Seasons do not reflect any sort of precision in orienting to time, yet they are a significant part of Anishinaabeg thought. Hallowell comments that in Berens River, "In conversation that has reference to past events, seasonal names, too, appear to be more frequently employed than 'moon' names. Although less exact, these larger units are sufficiently precise and they function in much the same way among ourselves."[58] Both in recalling events and planning for coming activities, it is rarely necessary to be more accurate than describing what season the activity did or will happen in. Here the economy of language can be evoked; as the events recalled are understood as happening at a particular time, it is unnecessary to be more accurate than what season the event takes place in.[59] Here Hallowell makes a helpful parallel in suggesting a similarity in seasonal usage between the Anishinaabeg and eurowestern peoples.

Among the Anishinaabeg, four seasons are recognized. With a close relationship to other forms of life around them, *Ziigwan* recognizes the movement away from the cold, purifying silence of winter to the warmth of the sun, ice leaving the waterways, and green foliage returning all around them. The seasons do not specifically correlate to *dibiki giizis* cycles, but are more reliant upon weather and temperature indicators, as well as star knowledge. In Anishinaabe Akiing (northern Michigan specifically) the snow usually leaves during *Ziisbakadake Giizis* as the temperatures increase with the days lengthening and the sun higher in the sky. However, if the temperatures stay low and snow keeps falling into *Namebini Giizis*, then one may say that "winter is staying longer." Hence, there is a certain amount of variability in seasonal changes.[60] The flexibility of seasons is recognized in some *aadizookaanag* that speak of North Wind and South Wind fighting over who is more powerful, and another where northern animals go south and steal summer from the southern animals so they do not get to have it all the time.[61] Summer, or *Niibin* comes next, as the plants begin to flower and the berries come to be ripe. This season moves from the new growth of plants to the ripening of the berries in *Miin Giizis*. Next, *Dagwaagin*, or autumn, moves from the fruit of the berries to the fruit of the water as *manoomiin*, or wild rice, ripens. Also, as the days get shorter and the nights get colder, the leaves begin to turn color (*Waabaagbagaa Giizis*) and eventually fall off the trees (*Binakwe Giizis*). Finally, *Biboon* takes over and ice forms on the water (*Bashkaakodin Giizis*) and the snows begin to fall. In *Biboon*, the Anishinaabeg move to their winter hunting camps and the *aadizookaanag* are told to the people for their edification.

These seasonal movements between camps and economic activities are evident in the naming of *dibiki giizis*, but because of the shifting of moon cycles, they did not necessarily mark the times for movement. These seasonal movements were motivated by four seasonal constellations. By watching the bright northern sky, these seasonal movements could be more accurately predicted. According to Carl Gawboy, "The Ojibwe did use the sun as a daily marker and the moon as a monthly one, but for them it was the changing constellations, the figures they saw in the sky, that were of utmost importance."[62] The coming of *Ziigwan* is recognized with the rising in the southwestern sky of *Mishibizhii*, the great underwater panther.[63] As this constellation rises higher in the sky is it said to become more powerful, thereby pushing the Wintermaker out of the sky. *Mishibizhii* is associated with the power of water as *Ziigwan* is fraught with difficult travel and the potential for flooding. When *Mishibizhii* was reaching its highest point in the sky then it was time to move to the sugarbush camps. Next, the coming of *Niibin* was signaled by the appearance of *Nanapush* on the southeastern horizon, with his bow shooting an arrow at *Mishibizhii* to chase it out of the sky. This is a useful connection as one of the flood narratives involves Nanapush killing *Mishibizhii* and the Great Panther, creating a flood. Here, written in the stars we see a seasonal reenactment of that narrative.[64] The Anishinaabeg also move away from their sugarbush and spring fish-run camps to the larger communal towns used for summer ceremonies and gatherings. Towards the end of *Niibin*, we get the *Mooz* (moose) constellation "which dominates the night sky from late September through most of November. Moose hunting season."[65] In *Dagwaagin*, we get the movement to the hunting camps and the preparations for putting up venison for the long winter ahead. Finally, *Biboon* is signaled by the rising of the Wintermaker in the south. This constellation is welcomed with ceremony and feasting for the purification that it brings to *aki*, the land. Here we see the movement to the winter camps where smaller family units were gathered together to tell the narratives that could only be spoken during *Biboon*.[66] Here they would stay until *Mishibizhii* would once again return with warmer weather to chase the Wintermaker from the sky.[67]

I intentionally use the word "movement" here in describing the seasons as they are linguistically considered verbs in Anishinaabemowin. This is an important distinction as it emphasizes the action and movement of life that is happening during that temporal period. A verb-oriented language like Anishinaabemowin demonstrates the flow of energy from *giizis* and *dibiki giizis* through *Mazikamikwe* as the land and all of the forms of life absorb this life energy and combine it with the water and earth to grow, live, and reproduce. There is a beauty in the seasonal actions that take place in this yearly cycle of life. The stored energy in roots, seeds, wombs, and *wiigwams* from the previous cycle is put into growing action with the warmth of *Ziigwan*. That energy is amplified in *Niibin* into the flourishing of life in the heat and light. The life cycle continues in *Dagwaagin* with the harvesting of food while the seeds from that season of growth are set to store energy for the next growing season. Finally, *Biboon* sets in to purify *Mazikamikwe* with the snow and the cold so that in the next *Ziigwan*, the land is ready to flourish again. The seasons as verbs effectively describe this emphasis on the flow of quantum energy from *giizis* through life drawing sustenance from *Mazikaamikwe*. This movement is not a progress from year to year, but a cycle of rebirth, growth, senescence, and purification that continually repeats.[68]

Linear Time in Anishinaabemowin

With no linear concept of time providing a logic of progress to follow, the concept of the year in Anishinaabemowin, while present and translatable, is a very different concept. Like most Anishinaabeg concepts of time, the year is a cyclical process. Similar to other Indigenous peoples of the region, *Biboon*, or winter, was used as a marker of a year. Hallowell suggests a paradox in this temporal period in that "Such an interval was an integral part of the temporal concepts of the native Saulteaux but was of little practical importance."[69] *Biboon* is used as a marker of naming a quantity of years that has passed, such as *Niimdana n'daa ensa boonigiz* (forty winters I am) or "I am forty years old."[70] Hence to make sense of this paradox, one has to think about the usefulness of a year as a temporal period. When the concept of one year is invoked it is often in reference to a particular activity, so that season or moon would be invoked with the phrase "I hope this sugarbush is as good as last year." This utterance of the year is unnecessary because the temporal period is understood. The seasonal terms instead of the year were most often used to discuss future or past events.[71]

As stated above, another place of importance where *Biboon* as a marker of a year comes into play is often for the discussion of a person's age. This function of a temporal scheme makes the jump from cyclical to more linear conceptualizations of time. Hallowell quotes Cope on this subject, who suggests that regarding the use of *Biboon*, "this expression no doubt developed through contact with civilized people."[72] Here the two anthropologists are incorrect, as there are a number of reasons why keeping track of the age of children and adults would come into play. Parents keep track of the age of their children to help identify maturation goals, such as when it is appropriate to no longer keep them in their *dikinaagan*, or cradleboard, or when to perform their puberty rites.[73] It would also be useful to know how long a camp was kept on a particular spot of land, as the camps were moved every so often so as to let the land rest. This would also be true of Indigenous crop-rotation techniques in agriculture. While not used in the same way as in the eurowestern world, the ability to keep track of linear sequences of time were used to keep the health of the communities and their relationships to land in check.

However, Hallowell and Cope do recognize more frequently used references for the maturation of individuals in terms of their stages of development. Hallowell gives five categories of words that correspond to a child as a newborn (*abinoojiinh*), little boys and girls (*giiwizens* and *ikwezens*), young men and women who have reached puberty but are not married (*moozhabe* and *moozhikwe*), married men and women (*oshki-inini* and *oshkiniigikwe*), and old men and women (*akiwenzii* and *mindimooyenh*).[74] They are correct in asserting that these general stages of life are used far more often than a particular "winter count." Like other temporal durations mentioned above, the stages of life as a conceptualization of the linear movement of an individual through their life is plenty accurate to describe individuals.[75]

Anishinaabemowin provides another example of the ability to think in a linear conception of time. Sometimes it is necessary to distinguish between which *giizhig* and *dibiki giizis* an event happened or is going to happen. In Anishinaabemowin, the addition of the prefixes *gii* (past tense) and *gaa* (future tense) signify past and future events. There are also particular words to differentiate today (*noongwa*) from yesterday (*jiinaagwa*) from tomorrow (*waabang*).[76] So in Anishinaabemowin, one can say, *Jiinaagwa niizh waawaashkeshk n'gii waabamaa*, or "Yesterday I saw two deer." One can also designate a future event by saying, *Namewag n'gaa paa jiibakeaananig waabang*, or "I will cook the sturgeon tomorrow."[77] More than one day before or after *noongwa* is designated by the addition of the prefix *waas-*, as in *waasnoongwa* (two days ago) and *waaswaabang* (two days from now). Three days before and after *noongwa* is *ekwa-nisiganagak* (three days ago) and *kchiwaaswaabang* (three days from now).[78] These concepts demonstrate an ability to think in both past and future and allow Anishinaabeg to recall specific recent events and easily plan for activities in the near future. While there is a linear stream of thinking in these types of past-present-future linguistic configurations, the *giizhigag* like *dibiki giizis* are still "not a division of continuous time, [they are] a recurring event."[79] Therefore, it is still the logic of cyclical time that dominates Anishinaabeg thinking in time.

Finally, there are two more examples from Anishinaabeg culture that demonstrate the ability to think in linear terms over time, including an infinite future. First, Kwame Gyekye provides an example from Akan culture, describing the experience of time as "concrete change, growth, generation, and passing away of specific things."[80] This passage parallels the yearly cycle of rebirth, growth, senescence, and purification in *Biboon* as described in the seasonal changes of Anishinaabe Akiing. This cycle is clearly recognized in Anishinaabe thought. However, if we combine this thought of recognizing change and growth over time with the lifetime of an individual or community, then the recognition of elders as a wealth of community resources makes all the more sense. Elders are recognized as important to a community because they are the holders of accumulated knowledge over time. The elders embody the ability to take in, learn, and grow in knowledge for the purpose of helping your community live better lives. That youth are instructed to respect and listen to elders helps to demonstrate the ability to think in an infinite future, as the youth and younger adults are able to recognize that over time one can change and grow themselves. This social and political position of elder helps to demonstrate the ability to think in an infinite future for Anishinaabeg. Like the cycle of rebirth, growth, maturity, and senescence associated with the seasons, the lifetime of a person also has its own similar, if longer cycle that parallels this process.

Secondly, there are certain ceremonies that also help to demonstrate the ability to think across time in an infinite future. *Waabano*, or "tent shaking" ceremonies are performed so people in the community can ask for help. Sometimes this help is about the curing of sickness, and other times it may be about a community member asking about the whereabouts or the wellbeing of a loved one. In these instances the *waabano* practitioner can ask the *manidoog* about how someone is doing who is not present, or when they may return. A community may also inquire about outcomes in the future, such as how they may fare for the coming *Biboon*. Again, these examples help to demonstrate Anishinaabeg ability to think in an infinite future.[81]

Time in Cultural Theory

When Gyeke's assertion that time has "an objective metaphysical existence" is taken seriously, the relationship that peoples have to this metaphysical presence can be properly seen as its own cultural construction. This point will become important as the comparative analysis between the Anishinaabeg and the eurowest will come into play. This section, which elaborates the Anishinaabeg relationship to time as played out in the worldview, ideology, institutions, and everyday experiences demonstrates that it is a cyclical conceptualization of time that provides the cultural logic for the organization of our culture.

Considering the power embedded in the cultural narratives of the Anishinaabeg, they provide an important look at the concept of time. Again, the *Giizhigokwe* narratives provide a base knowledge that addresses a relationship to time as cyclical. The narratives build on an Indigenous theme of regeneration, where a previous world was destroyed and a new one was constructed with the remnants of soil and water from the previous world.[82] These narratives as *aadizookaanag* happened *mewinzha*, in the long ago. This period of time is set apart from the more contemporary *dibaajimowinan*, which happened within the memory of the Anishinaabeg communities. This separation of time helps to differentiate the actions of the *aadizookaanag* (characters) as capable of greater feats of strength, power, and metamorphosis, as the ancestors were not entirely human. The *dibaajimowinan* narratives also provide for fantastic efforts and feats, but they do not achieve the same power as do the *aadizookaanag*, except for a few medicine people who are able to call on certain *manidoo* helpers who can still perform certain types of communication and metamorphosis. However, it is important to note that the *aadizookaanag* (characters) are not completely cut off from contemporary interactions, as they still are able to communicate to Anishinaabeg communities in certain ceremonies. This is essential to understanding relationships to both space and time for the Anishinaabeg, as the *aadizookaanag* (characters) share the same space with the Anishinaabeg, they just have been around for a longer time. So the *mewinzha*, while it does represent a period in time when the *aadizookaanag* (characters) helped regenerate the land as the Anishinaabeg know it, does not function as a period of time that is distant from the present. As the narratives are told and retold to each generation, they are kept alive in the culture in the place in which the events occurred. There is no chronological distance that separates Anishinaabeg from the ancestors from our contemporary lives when the relationships to the land are primary and cyclical time structures thought. The "trickster" *Nanapush* is said to have commented on the relationship of the *aadizookaanag* to the Anishinaabeg: "We'll try to make everything to suit the Indians (änicinábek) as long as any of them exist, so that the Indians will never forget us and will always talk about us."[83]

The cultural logic of regeneration as manifest in the *aadizookaanag* can also be seen in the institutional relationships to time. In the villages, the ceremonies that give a rhythm to Anishinaabeg life all follow a cyclical pattern. For the many societies, these cycles in time necessarily follow a seasonal flow. The *Midewiwin* welcome in new members and help to renew the relationships of the people with a ceremony in the spring, after the sugarbush and spring fish runs. This ceremony initiates new members, processes members into higher orders, and attends to the health and wellbeing of the entire community.[84] The various rounds of planting and harvesting ceremonies obviously follow their seasonal rhythms, as do the *doodem* ceremonies. The political meetings of the village leadership also follow a seasonal pattern, taking advantage of the open waterways that make travel among the villages much easier. At the institutional level of the village and *doodem*, the relationship to time is largely kept at a seasonal level, which helps to organize the political, social, and economic functions of the community. Each spring when the people gather in their villages, the regeneration of life that is happening all around helps to dictate which activities need to take place for the flourishing of the community. Each year, village life then can best be thought of not as "a division of continuous time, [but as] a recurring event."[85] Like the regeneration of worlds and lives from the *aadizookaanag*, the spring is regenerated each year from the purifying powers of winter, and the cycle of rebirth, growth, senescence, and purification is followed each year. The cyclical conceptualization of time also follows this logic, each year following the same pattern of seasonal ceremonies that help the community to flourish.

While the community lives on a seasonal cycle of ceremonies, the daily life of an individual is largely oriented around the shorter temporal cycles of the *giizhig*. The rising of *giizis* in the morning and the setting in the evening provided the primary temporal orientation of the experiences of the people. With the light of the *giizis*, the daily activities of fishing, hunting, planting, cooking, and weaving would commence, to be followed throughout the daylight hours until it was dark and the people would return to their homes for rest. The daily activities would shift throughout the seasonal changes according to which economic and political activities were demanded by the community. For example, in the sugarbush the people would spend most of the day carrying containers of sap to the boiling place in the camp, haul wood, cook, eat, and put up the sugar and syrup into containers. In the spring fishing camps they would set their nets, bring them in, and dry the fish for storage.[86] The rising and setting of *giizis* would act as temporal bookmarks for daily activities that shifted throughout the year. Each season demanded different particular actions to gather enough food for the community. The rhythm of *giizis* and *dibiki giizis* provided the temporal structure for the people to live their lives in the short term. While these daily experiences worked themselves out, they interacted with a larger cycle of seasons and the year to orient the people to different activities as the economics of living close to the land demanded. Even though the particular daily activities shift throughout the seasons, it is still the conceptualization of repeating cycles that drives the daily activities. While there are concepts that demonstrate an understanding of linear time, such as age and growth over time, it is the cyclical conceptualizations of time that orient the Anishinaabeg to the metaphysical concept of time.

Eurowestern Conceptualizations of Time

In discussing the differences between Indigenous and eurowestern conceptualizations of space and time, Vine Deloria Jr. has commented that "Time has an unusual limitation. It must begin and end at some real points, or it must be conceived as cyclical in nature, endlessly allowing the repetition of patterns of possibilities."[87]

The Anishinaabeg cyclical conceptualizations of time have been discussed above, detailing the cultural logic associated with cyclical relationships to time. Those Indigenous relationships will now be compared to the linear formulations of the eurowest. The concept of the linear progress of time will be shown as the cultural logic that prescribes the ideological, institutional, and experiential aspects of eurowestern culture.

Once again, the ideological foundations for the eurowestern relationship to time can be found in the Bible. In the first chapter of Genesis, God creates the universe and humans.[88] This moment is important, but in and of itself does not necessitate a linear trajectory of time. However, in the third chapter, Eve and Adam eat from the forbidden tree.[89] For Christians, it is this act that "sets the scene for an understanding of the entrance of sin into the world."[90] This moment of sin sets "enmity" between humans and snakes, brings pain to childbearing, makes women subservient to men, and "curses the ground."[91] Such a violation in this mode of thought, then, requires an action to redeem it. This action would become the atonement for sin in the death and resurrection of Jesus. As Deloria elaborates, "The major thesis of the Christian religion is thus contained in its creation story, because it is for the redemption of man that the atonement of Jesus of Nazareth is considered to make sense."[92] This linear trajectory is given an endpoint with eschatological thought, where Christians wait for the second coming of Jesus, or the Apocalypse, depending on which tradition one subscribes to. Therefore, the linear trajectory of sin-salvation-eschaton in Christian thought is complete from beginning to end. It is this theological formulation that becomes the guiding logic for a relationship to time for the eurowest.

At the institutional level, the Christian church negotiates both the linear time of sin-salvation-eschaton and the cyclical liturgical calendar of Advent season to Pentecost.[93] While the emphasis of the activities of the church are geared towards the cyclical negotiation of the liturgical calendar, this ceremonial cycle is best seen as a "division of continuous time," since each cycle has its own marker as a numbered year, which differentiates each cycle from any other. It is this "division of continuous time" that best defines the differences between the cyclical temporal logic of the Anishinaabeg and the linear temporal logic of the eurowestern experience. Science also demonstrates an ability to negotiate both cyclical and linear concepts of time. Biology and physics have both been able to articulate with extreme precision the cyclical temporal events of the movement of the sun, earth and moon in orbit, its effects on the seasons, and the seasonal changes that take place in a solar cycle for life on the planet. These cyclical temporal events are understood very well within the context of eurowestern thought. However, part of that thought presumes a linear trajectory of time, so even though there is no evidence of a linear trajectory of these celestial and biological events, these cycles are still placed within a linear timeline and follow a very similar numerical ordering of the solar year.[94] Again, the solar, lunar, and life cycles are understood as a "division of continuous time." Capitalism also adds an institutional perspective here in its relationship with time. It too understands cyclical processes in its track of quarterly profits, comprehending the necessity to compare apples to apples, if you will, from year to year. However, capitalism also adds powerful language to the concept of linear time in its emphasis on progress and development. These ideological concepts are put into play at the institutional levels of corporations and governments in the assumptions that all nations and corporations must be developing along a singular linear trajectory to the pinnacle of free market democracy. Hence, Third World nations are termed developing nations, and if a business is not growing it is considered to be dying.[95] The ideology of progress and development then are acted out in the institutions as they provide for the ideological manifestation of what is best described as the myth of linear progress. The assumption that time can be understood as linear progress is deeply ingrained from the sin-salvation-eschaton trajectory of thought into the eurowestern conceptualization of time.

The actions of Americans in the everyday are also largely shaped by the temporal cycles of the sun. While electricity has recently allowed many to not have to rely upon the light of the sun to go about their daily business, most people still spend most of their waking time during daylight hours. There are also weekly and monthly cycles that function to organize eurowestern relationships to time. The week largely organizes the capitalist activities of work, and the month differentiates four-week cycles from each other and allows them to be associated with particular holidays and seasons. The seasons still function to affect behavior, but usually in type of dress and activities, not as a sense of shifting economic responsibilities. Work for most people is the same the year round. And of course, there is the concept of the year, which does a double duty of both conceptualizing the solar cycle of one trip of the earth around the sun (science) and providing a locus for counting the linear progressions of those years (Christianity).

For most Americans, their year can best be described by what I call the American Liturgical Calendar. This yearly cycle begins with the "new year" of January 1, and is followed by the Super Bowl, Easter, Memorial Day, Fourth of July, Labor Day,

Halloween, Thanksgiving, all of which lead towards the ultimate American experience, the great economic frenzy of Christmas. Designating this as the American Liturgical Calendar gives voice to the ways in which the Christian, scientific, and capitalist ideologies and institutions cooperate to function as a semi-united whole for the sake of reproducing American culture. While there are some small additions or subtractions depending upon the region and specific family, this is the yearly cycle that most Americans are accustomed to. However, while all of these temporal cycles function in parallel to one another from the day to the year, they are all part of a logic of linear time in which all events are placed. The eurowestern worldview of the linear progression of time is the primary relationship to the metaphysical entity of time. Again, if this metaphysical nature of time is thought of as a blank slate upon which conceptualizations of time are constructed, it is the belief in the linear progression of time that provides a cultural logic to follow. Hence, the temporal cycles play very little into the larger conceptualizations of eurowestern identity. As Vine Deloria Jr. has stated,

> The very essence of Western European identity involves the assumption that time proceeds in a linear fashion; further it assumes that at a particular point in the unraveling of this sequence, the peoples of Western Europe became the guardians of the world. The same ideology that sparked the Crusades, the Age of Exploration, the Age of Imperialism, and the recent crusade against Communism all involve the affirmation that time is peculiarly related to the destiny of the people of Western Europe. And later, of course, the United States.[96]

There are two important points to bring up regarding the manifestation of linear time in eurowestern culture. First, the measurement or justification given for these imperialistic endeavors has shifted over time. Early in the colonial period it was the call to Christianize the world that justified the colonization of foreign lands. That language was then secularized, and it was the goal to civilize the primitive masses. The civilization mantra then gave way to the ideas of progress and development throughout the twentieth century. While the language of progress and development continues, they are becoming more and more narrowly defined by technological development of electronic media in the American context and the development of resource extraction in the colonial lands of the Global South. Secondly, it needs to be noted that the development of this culturally constructed notion of the linear progression of time is not supported by any celestial phenomenon. There are no visible celestial phenomena that any group of people can experience that suggest a linear progression of time. Therefore, the development of the myth of linear progress can be seen in its proper place, as an entirely culturally constructed, extraterrestrial phenomenon. The myth of linear progress is, quite literally, not of this land, and it is not shared by any other known form of life.

Conclusion

From the above discussion of Anishinaabeg and eurowestern relationships to time, the differences between the two cultures can be brought into greater focus. Like all cultures, both have understandings of cyclical and linear concepts of time. However, when one considers how these two concepts of time function as a cultural logic, the similarities pale in comparison to the differences between the two cultures.

It is important to recognize the relationship of concepts of time to concepts of space. When we look at the eurowestern worldview, this relationship demonstrates that it is time as linear progress that provides the primary purpose of the culture. It is the narrative of the movement of people across time that generates the framework for understanding the world for eurowesterners. From the movement of Israelites out of Egypt to the movement of Christianity into Europe and eventually across the North American continent, it is the anthropocentric narrative of a chosen people moving across time that provides the eurowestern cultures with their primary understanding of the world. Space, the land, is simply understood as the place where these events play out. Even sacred places can be easily abstracted into sacred geography, and it is unnecessary to keep a physical relationship with this. The Holy Land is still Jerusalem, yet eurowesterners have not had a longstanding physical presence there, ever. Sacred geography, this relationship to land, is an abstract notion that is secondary in importance to the narrative of the movement of the chosen people across time, living out their divinely mandated history.

When the above analysis of the eurowestern worldview is compared to an Anishinaabeg worldview, the differences between the two cultures are significant. While Anishinaabeg can conceptualize the accumulation of knowledge, experiences, and relationships over time, can linguistically separate past from present and future, and recognize change and growth over longer periods of time, it is still the cyclical concepts that provide a logic to understand themselves in time. It is the repetition of *giizhig*, *dibiki giizis*, and annual seasons represented as the passing of one year told in the narratives in the stars that function as the primary logics of time that are followed. These three concepts provide a cognitive set representing the passing of time, familial relations, and the flow of quantum energy, which function as "recurring events" and not "divisions of continuous time." The Anishinaabeg culture is completely void of the fetishization of linear progress that is a core value in eurowestern cultures.

The telos of Anishinaabeg culture is not driven by narratives of a people across time, but by the narratives of praxis in relationship to place. In this way, Anishinaabeg concepts of time are driven by the primacy of the concepts of space. In the Anishinaabeg relationship of time and space, it is space that plays a primary role. It is the relationship of *Giizhigokwe* to *Makinak* and the rest of the elder animals that provides an ideology of the importance of space and cyclical time for us to follow. The cycle of rebirth, growth, senescence, and purification provides the grounding for our relationship to space. This cycle of life in Anishinaabe Akiing is the telos, or purpose of the community. It is our responsibility to participate in those sets of relationships in a good way. In this comparison, then, we can demonstrate that for the Anishinaabeg, Vine Deloria Jr. was correct in stating, "Space generates time."[97] It is the relationship to space and the life cycle of rebirth, growth, senescence, and purification that drives the primacy of cyclical time as compared to linear time. The cyclical time concepts of *giizhig*, *dibiki giizis*, and the four seasons both mirror and help us to stay in tune with the life cycles that the *aadizookaanag* describe for us.

With the above analysis of concepts of time, one can more easily understand the differences of time represented in the Treaty of Washington. While the previous treaties clearly represent Anishinaabeg conceptualizations of cyclical time and the responsibility of a yearly renewal, the Treaty of Washington shows an emphasis on both the imposition of colonial power with the desire for removal, and that shift in power allows for the overemphasis on the linear conceptualizations of time. After 1836, Anishinaabe Akiing would become part of the American narrative of Manifest Destiny and would provide the physical geography where colonialism would take hold. The presumed progress and development of America spread across the North American continent with its clearcutting of forests, digging of minerals from the earth, and the eventual poisoning of *Chi Gumeeng*, or the Great Lakes. Winona LaDuke recognized these differing views on development when she discussed an incident in July 1995 of high winds flattening about 100,000 acres of forest. This event was considered a "natural disaster"; however, "when lumber companies similarly vanquish the trees, it is commonly called 'progress.'"[98] The Treaty of Washington, and numerous treaties after that, would be the beginning of a very different and destructive relationship with the land. The Anishinaabeg logics of an intimate relationship to a localized space and the cyclical understanding of time would be supplanted by the logics of the eurowestern American culture, with its myth of linear progress and concepts of space to be dominated. Now that the environmental destruction resulting from that shift in power evident in the Treaty of Washington has come back to negatively affect all people living in Anishinaabe Akiing, different ideas are being sought out to restore and regenerate some of the environmental balance that was taken away. The Anishinaabeg have a longstanding relationship with this part of the earth and have developed effective methods of thinking about and acting in ways that promote the flourishing of life in this area. The logics of an intimate relationship to localized space and the cyclical conceptualizations of time are an effective grounding for that return to balance.

CHAPTER 4

Relationships to Life

ndigenous peoples live in a world saturated with relationships. These relationships form a large connected web of relatedness in which humans occupy a place of equity, not of privilege. To understand Indigenous peoples, one must comprehend the logic of living in a web of relatedness with the rest of life as a component of worldview. While the concept of relatedness is often brought up in discussions of Indigenous culture, it is rarely afforded the necessary depth that would render the cultures and actions more intelligible. This chapter will demonstrate that depth of understanding within Anishinaabe culture.

Treaties are nothing new to Indigenous peoples. Long before contact with western Europeans, we had longstanding treaties between groups of people that helped to define boundaries, keep peace between groups, and bind peoples into mutually interdependent relationships. When these treaties were negotiated between groups who shared a similar lifestyle and desire for peaceable relations, these treaties were much easier to negotiate. In *Linking Arms Together: American Indian Treaty Visions of Law and Peace, 1600–1800*, Robert Williams Jr. suggests that life for Eastern Woodland peoples was lived in a complex web of connective, reciprocating relationships. Connection to others improved the chances of overcoming some calamity or disaster that might befall the individual or group. Peaceful relations with other tribes could provide inestimable benefits: trade and subsistence goods that were unavailable or in short supply in the territory, [and] military alliances that extended power and influence.[1]

The benefits of peaceful, interdependent relationships significantly outweigh the prospects of war, so Indigenous peoples were practiced both at the art of treaty making and the maintenance of those agreements. These treaties involved annual rounds of gifting as part of the treaty process. It is in these annual meetings where the relationship between the two groups was continually solidified. The economics of gifting helped to keep the groups in a mutually interdependent relationship, and the annual meetings allowed for any grievances from the past year to be voiced and rectified. These annual treaty meetings are better thought of as rounds of gifting ceremonies where feasting and dancing are the center of the meetings. It is in this context of mutually beneficial ceremonial fun that Indigenous peoples are used to negotiating and maintaining treaty relationships. However, with the coming of Europeans, the context and content of treaty relationships shifted dramatically. When one negotiates a treaty with someone who has a very different conceptualization of relationships, the outcome of these agreements may be very difficult to maintain.

When the eurowestern newcomers entered these lands of Indigenous North America, there were already well-established treaty protocols, rituals, and ceremonies. In the early encounter treaty era, the colonizers had to adopt these protocols in treaty negotiations because the power manifest in the Indigenous communities greatly exceeded that of the newcomers. However, as the vicious cycle of disease, warfare, and cultural dislocation continued to destroy Indigenous communities on the borders of early colonial America, eventually the power imbalance began to tip in favor of the European population. Yet, even as late as the 1795 Treaty of Greenville, which helped the new American government enter into the theft of the Ohio Valley, the treaty negotiations were still ritually conducted with Indigenous protocols, including seating arrangements, requickening and mourning rituals, and a strong use of Indigenous narratives to make meaning out of the event.[2] Even after what is widely understood as a losing battle for the Ohio Alliance of Natives, these treaty protocols were all observed. Particularly in Indigenous eyes, place has power, and that these treaty protocols were observed in the Ohio Valley was important for their implementation.[3]

However, as the colonial war machine continued to move north and west, the power of place would be circumvented with the new practice of shipping Indigenous leaders to Washington, DC, for treaty negotiations and signing. These new protocols had two primary shifts of power. First, moving the place of negotiation limited the number of people who could attend the meetings, which allowed a much greater colonial influence on the Indigenous participants as they were no longer surrounded by their homelands and communities. Second, these new travel protocols were used as a demoralizing tactic as the "chiefs" were ushered around the growing industrial power centers on the east coast, complete with their large cities and buildings. These tactics represent a significant shift in the colonial power dynamics of the early nineteenth century, and the Treaty of Washington in 1836 is indicative of this shift in power. Not only did the treaty deliberations and signing take place in Washington, DC, they included only a small portion of the community leadership. In a very short forty-one-year period, the balance of power swung decidedly in favor of the United States Government for the deliberation of these treaties. Rather than signifying a reciprocal relationship of honor, gifting, and a method of continually staying in balance with one another, the Treaty of Washington represents the codification of a relationship of hierarchical power (no reciprocity), payment (not gifting), and no regular meetings to continue the relationship.[4]

The relationships that are written into the Treaty of Washington are entirely within the framework of understanding of the colonial government. Articles 1 through 4 discuss the boundaries of land between the peoples involved. Articles 4 through 7, and 9 through 12 discuss various forms of payment for the ceded lands. Article 8 discusses sending a group of Anishinaabeg to seek out reservation land west of the Mississippi River. Only Article 13 makes reference to "the rights of hunting on the land ceded with the other usual privileges of occupancy, until the land is required for settlement," which requires a deeper comprehension of Anishinaabe culture to understand.[5] It is this Thirteenth Article that gives us opportunity to discuss the vast differences between the two cultures in the ways relationships are organized in this nineteenth-century treaty. While the official written version of this treaty may look similar to previous treaties as to what is covered, this similarity belies a much deeper power difference represented in the treaty deliberations and implementation. Had the implementation of this treaty incorporated an annual meeting to gift and remember the positive relational aspects of the treaty, then it would have been possible to work out the problems with implementation. Instead, the Anishinaabeg were poorly compensated for land that was being taken under force with no meaningful reciprocity built in to address problems. As the nineteenth century gave way to the twentieth, more and more problems came to the fore with the deforestation and pollution of the ceded land and valuable waterways. This colonial destruction of land would greatly harm the Anishinaabeg ability to relate to the land and its inhabitants in ways that are culturally recognizable. The ability for Anishinaabeg and other Indigenous peoples to reproduce their worldview and respective ideologies became strained.

When we look at the shift of power represented in the Treaty of Greenville in 1795 and the Treaty of Washington in 1836, we can easily see a shift away from a web of relatedness in the treaties towards the imposition of a hierarchy with the eurowestern colonizers firmly on top. The negotiating power of Indigenous peoples waned with each successive wave of disease, warfare, and cultural dislocation, and this waning power is evident in the lack of Indigenous protocols used and the outcomes of the treaties. Even under the duress of going to Washington, DC, to negotiate the Treaty of Washington in 1836, Anishinaabeg leaders still insisted upon Article 13, and the "right of hunting on the lands ceded, with the other usual privileges of occupancy."[6] With so little in the treaty language itself about this article, it is important to discuss its implications in greater depth to be able to comprehend the complex Anishinaabeg kinship systems represented in this article. On the side of the U.S. Government, we can conclude that they thought the Anishinaabeg would be well across the Mississippi River within twenty years, so the allowance of this article probably carried little to no consequence. However, since most of the Anishinaabeg associated with this treaty stayed well within Anishinaabe Akiing, there are important implications for this treaty, and especially Article 13. The "right to hunt" and the "usual privileges of occupancy," when understood in an Anishinaabeg context, come with a whole cultural complex of relationships. For example, if we are going to have the right to hunt, that assumes we also have those animals that are hunted (deer, elk, rabbit, bear, etc.) along with the habitats that are associated with those animals. It is now commonly understood that these game animals are part of a wider ecological whole of which they are just one part. One can argue that it took eurowestern science several hundred years of development to finally catch up to an Indigenous perspective on the relatedness of individual animals to the species as a whole, and that species as part of a larger web of relatedness. For the Anishinaabeg, this web of relatedness was certainly understood for the signers of the Treaty of Washington in 1836 and has been passed down through generations to those of us who are still living in these ways. Therefore, it is essential for us to both remember the ways in which we conceptualize this web of relatedness and then live it out.

The "settlement" of Anishinaabeg lands that has happened since 1836 has called into question our right to hunt, as the ensuing environmental destruction has significantly reduced game populations and the habitat that they need. Eurowestern culture, and the hierarchies with which it negotiates relationships with the rest of life, has been an effective destroying machine. Until the recent articulation of ecological knowledge as part of a scientific ideology of eurowestern knowledge, the recognition that there is a meaningful relationship between species did not have an effective voice. This voicing of a worldview that articulates a web of relatedness is a longstanding tradition for Indigenous peoples. According to Vine Deloria Jr., "The task of the tribal religion, if such a religion can be said to have a task, is to determine the proper relationship that the people of the tribe must have with other living things and to develop the self-discipline within the tribal community so that man acts harmoniously with other creatures."[7] While I disagree with the use of the concept of religion to describe Indigenous cultures, I am taking up Deloria's suggested task in the examination of these relationships in the Anishinaabeg context.

Nature as a Cultural Particular

It would seem to be uncontroversial to suggest that there is an intimate relationship between culture and language. While the more relativist position of the Sapir-Whorf hypothesis has been softened by the recognition of the elasticity of language and meaning, it is clear that although it is possible to communicate between languages and cultures, there can also be concepts that do not translate well as each language and culture continues to respond to its particular environment over time.[8] The African literary theorist and philosopher Ngũgĩ wa Thiong'o has stated this relationship well: "The choice of language and the use to which language is put is central to a people's definition of themselves in relation to their natural and social environment, indeed in relation to the entire universe."[9] With this in mind, it is easy to see that a language like Anishinaabemowin, which has continued to adapt to its environment over time, would be very different from the English language, which adapted to a very different environment.

Kwasi Wiredu's work is also helpful in demonstrating the differences between cultures by using a sophisticated linguistic-conceptual methodology. In a 1985 colloquium paper titled "The Akan World-View," he begins with a bold statement: "A fundamental fact about the Akan worldview is that there is nothing in it that might be called a conception of nature."[10] He uses this statement as an entry point into discussing the differences between the Akan system of thought as related to their environment and the system of thought of the eurowest.[11] First he uses modern logic to establish that for each concept there is a distinction between the intension (meaning) and the extension (reference). Then he moves to the discussion of the concept of nature to show that "It cannot be assumed that the connotation or intension or meaning of the word 'nature' is the only possible option in conceptualizing that denotatum or referent."[12] While the referent, or the trees, land, water, rocks, and other life, may be the same or similar in two places, that does not suggest that the way people conceptualize those referents has to be identical. Wiredu pushes on to suggest that

> the way in which the Akans conceptualise that which others conceptualise through the term 'nature' is so different from the latter as not to be susceptible to an equivalent verbalisation. In other words, among Akan conceptions there is nothing equivalent to the basic connotation of 'nature,' but there, of course, are concepts which aim at the same denotatum as the term 'nature.'[13]

Next Wiredu shows how the basic concept of nature is framed by the naturalist and non-naturalist ways of viewing material phenomena, where the naturalists believe that all of existence conforms to the laws of science, whereas the non-naturalists do not believe this. While there are metaphysical differences between the naturalist and non-naturalist points of view, they do share a common framework for conceptualizing the relationship to nature. Wiredu continues, "Both the naturalists and their adversaries assume the intelligibility of the distinction between (a) the material and the nonmaterial, (b) the natural and the non-natural, and (c) the natural and the supernatural (which is a special case of (b))."[14] Then, returning to his initial point in the essay, he states, "None of these contrasts is intelligible within Akan thought."[15] He then goes through the lack of intelligibility within Akan thought of foundational eurowestern concepts related to nature, such as Creation, transcendence of God (Supreme Being), and the possibility of non-materiality, by demonstrating that the Akan worldview, as understood within its own linguistic-conceptual framework, is spatially configured in ways that do not translate into eurowestern concepts such as nature.[16] Hence, for the Akan, where spatial location is a concept embedded in the language and thought, there is no "equivalent verbalisation" for the eurowestern concept of nature.[17] This sophisticated essay provides theory and method for a specific demonstration of the differences between cultures and their respective languages that Ngũgĩ wa Thiong'o and others have espoused. In this essay, Wiredu helps us to delve into the particulars of cultural and linguistic difference that are necessary to decolonize our languages and thought. With an effective methodology, we can now return to Anishinaabeg relationships to space as understood within their own linguistic-conceptual horizon.

A. I. Hallowell has also called into question the accuracy of the translation of nature into Anishinaabe thought. In his article "The Role of Dreams in Ojibwa Culture," he describes his reasoning for coining the phrase "other-than-human persons." He states that he has "used this somewhat awkward term in order to avoid applying the label 'supernatural' to them. The concept of the 'natural,' ambiguous as it often is when used in Western culture, is certainly not indigenous to Ojibwa thought."[18] Then, considering the lack of applicability of "natural" to Anishinaabeg, the extension of the supernatural would also lack an accurate translation. In this case, Hallowell is correct in his suggestion that the natural/supernatural dichotomy does not apply to the Anishinaabeg.[19] Similar to the argument that Wiredu makes above, Anishinaabeg conceptualizations of that which eurowesterns term as nature are grounded in a spatially located world that functions as a unified whole. Therefore the dichotomy of natural/supernatural is unintelligible because there is nothing outside of the empirical conceptualizations of our environment. All that is experienced is part of the same world; there is nothing that is shunned because it does not fit. It seems that Hallowell stumbled upon a truth that he was unable to fully explain.

Thankfully, we do not have to rely upon anthropologists stumbling their way through our cultures to effectively communicate how we conceptualize our relationships to our environment. With an intact language, trained linguists, and elders who can communicate with an authentic Anishinaabeg voice, we can also negotiate the difficult task of linguistic-conceptual translation in a fashion similar to Wiredu. One such Anishinaabeg expert is Margaret Noodin. In her article "*Beshaabiiag G'gikenmaaigowag*: Comets of Knowledge" she is able to communicate some of these worldview differences between Anishinaabeg and eurowestern perspectives of the environment. She begins by describing some of the basic differences in linguistic structure, demonstrating that Anishinaabemowin is a verb-based language, where the addition of prefixes and suffixes to those verbs helps to provide meaning and emphasis. She suggests that

> These verbs and the way they can be woven together are an integral part of the *Anishinaabe* network of knowledge, a system of connections between language and conscious or subconscious beliefs. Connections lost in the translation to English are regained when read, and then written, in *Anishinaabemowin*.[20]

She gives an example of this difference between a noun-based language like English and a verb-based language like Anishinaabemowin, demonstrating that "no single noun equates with the concept 'nature.'"[21] Even though it is common to attribute the concept of an Earth Mother to Indigenous peoples, in Anishinaabe culture these images are rarely evoked. Interestingly enough, the concepts *Shkaakaamikwe* and *Mazikaamikwe*, which are used to communicate the notion of a "Mother Nature," do not contain the word for mother. These concepts do describe the earth as having the "implications of the idea of one who creates, makes new, or provides for life," but they do not literally translate to that specific familial relationship.[22] While the relationship to the earth is sometimes translated as Earth Mother, which is accurate in a relational way, this should not be mistaken to be the same as a goddess figure that is worshipped.[23] If one is to understand *Mazikaamikwe* it must be done from the proper Anishinaabeg linguistic-conceptual experience. The relationship to the earth, or *Mazikaamikwe*, will only be misunderstood if it is conceptualized from a hierarchical logic from a eurowestern perspective. *Mazikaamikwe* is not exalted or worshiped as in eurochristian fashion, it is part of this web of relatedness.

Noodin continues on this path of Anishinaabe conceptual integrity with a discussion of a narrative about a storm. She shares a *dibaajimowin* (personal narrative) in its original Anishinaabemowin and then provides a translation to demonstrate the care that must be given to the text and the translational process. In this narrative, a young man describes getting water from a spring towards the end of winter. He arrived to find the spring full of muddy water. He took some of that water back to his camp and asked an old man what it meant. The old man said that within two days there would be a big thunderstorm. After this thunderstorm had come and passed, it melted all of the snow still left on the ground and the spring once again ran clear. While these types of narratives get translated all the time, rarely is it done with precise explanations of the original Anishinaabemowin, which can get at the differences in relationship to the environment. Noodin explains,

> The description in *Anishinaabemowin* of the shift in weather is subtle and precise. The atmosphere not only gets warmer, *gii aabwaa*, there is a warm wind that strengthens when the thunders arrive, leading to a combination that produces lightning. Most interestingly he says, *gii-waabndaaan waasmowaad giw Nimkiig* (I saw the lightning in Thunder), in a way that implies the lightning has a simple relationship with the viewer. This is made clear by his use of *waabndaa*, an inanimate transitive verb. However, the *Nimkiig*, the Thunders, are more complex. The verb he uses to describe hearing them is a transitive animate verb. More important than any implication of 'animacy,' which many speakers say is an inaccurate term, the switch in verb types shows that there is a difference between lightning and thunder. This is a cultural perspective not clear in English, and one that relates to other words and stories.[24]

This example helps to demonstrate some of the fundamental differences in an Anishinaabeg relationship to the environment. Within the Anishinaabeg linguistic-conceptual world we can see here, no noun will directly translate as nature and instead there is a reliance on action (verb) and experience. In this narrative the Thunders are described as a type of person, and a person that is associated with the melting of the snow and the muddying of the spring. While this is not a causal relationship in the eurowestern sense, there is a relationship of power associated with the Thunders that affects the environment that the Anishinaabeg live in. If one attempts to translate the phenomenon in these narratives using the eurowestern natural/supernatural dualism, then the experience of the Thunders as people and the relationship of the storm to the muddying of the spring would be attributed to the supernatural, that which is outside of the laws of nature. This dualism is simply unintelligible to the Anishinaabeg, for whom all experience is part of the same conceptual world. If it is used as a lens to attempt to comprehend a narrative such as this, it will euroform the narrative into something analogous to a eurowestern experience at the expense of the Anishinaabeg reality.

A. I. Hallowell attempted to describe this difference, and it is what led him to coin the phrase "other-than-human person." Again, he should be given some credit in that he was attempting to articulate deep cultural difference; however, he lacked an effective methodology to get at those differences he sensed all around him. For example, he also attempted to describe the Thunders and their other-than-human status. In one description he does help to demonstrate this concept of a single world in which all of their experiences were considered a unified reality. In "Ojibwa Ontology, Behavior, and World View" he discusses a boy who believed that he had seen a Thunder perched on a rock during a thunderstorm. The boy ran back to his lodge and got his parents to show them, but the Thunder was no longer there. In giving his village a description of the Thunder Bird, the elders were skeptical because almost no one had ever seen one in this way. However, their minds were changed "when a man who had dreamed of *pinèsï* verified the boy's description."[25] This is a good example of all experiences being given the same weight. A separate man's dream helped to verify the boy's sighting of a Thunder. This would never be allowed to happen within a eurowestern conceptualization of nature, and would at best be written off as a supernatural phenomenon. More likely, the boy would be told that his experience was just in his imagination and did not "really" happen, as that would allow the eurowestern system of thought to stay intact.

As this linguistic-conceptual methodology is followed through to demonstrate the depth of cultural differences between the Anishinaabeg and the eurowest, we can point to particular concepts and ways in which those concepts help to identify how these two groups relate to their environments. If we add to this discussion the dialogical relationships between these words and ideas as they relate to their respective cultures, then the difficulty of translating these concepts becomes even clearer. In the eurowest, when we think about nature through the lens of cognitive linguistics as a radial category, then we can see how nature is not a universal concept applicable to all people and places, but is a culturally particular concept that comes intimately related to the material/nonmaterial, the natural/non-natural, and the natural/supernatural dualisms. Nature as a concept is also shot through in meaning with the last several hundred years of actions that demonstrate dominion of humans as superior to and disconnected from that nature. When the word nature is uttered, it comes preloaded with all of this eurowestern conceptual baggage dialogically related to its particular cultural uses. We cannot assume that the meanings associated with the concept of nature are universally applicable in all places. At a deep level, from a eurowestern worldview, which negotiates relationships with its surrounding environments through the lens of these dualisms, we can see how those lenses significantly affect the meanings associated with those words. If only a surface translation takes place between nouns, then the relationships and actions associated with those nouns do not get called into question. For example, there are forms of life that make up the woods called trees in the English language. In Anishinaabemowin they are called *mitigoog*.[26] On the surface this would seem like an easy, noncomplicated translation. However, the simple utterance of a noun does not get at the underlying relationships, actions, and concepts embedded in those nouns. Following the *mitig*/tree example, a deeper translation of cultures can demonstrate that a *mitig* is a noun in the *maaba* class and in Anishinaabe culture is often considered a coequal form of life. In numerous narratives, *mitigoog* can become teachers and helpers, for example when a young woman lost her husband and spent over a year in the forest with a tree, who then taught her valuable knowledge that she was able to take back to her village to help them.[27] Also, when the actions associated with *mitigoog* are considered, this web of relatedness again comes to the fore. *Mitigoog*, like other forms of life, are not elevated to the status of heroes or worshiped beings, but all life is recognized as valuable. *Mitigoog* are sometimes cut down for their use as building materials for lodges, drums, and canoes. However, when these actions of taking the life of a *mitig* is negotiated, the tree is talked to as a person, the actions are explained to it, and an offering is made to help recognize its life and sacrifice.

However, if we look closer at the actions associated with trees in the eurowest, then a very different relationship can be recognized. Trees are recognized as living, and except for extremely rare circumstances, they are considered lower forms of life. While there may be stories that discuss trees as important or even someone to talk to (think Shel Silverstein here), they are considered metaphorical and not an action that could happen to people "in reality." Furthermore, the actions that are allowed in the cutting down of trees, both for individual firewood and the clearcutting of forests for the purpose of making money, then the place of trees in relationship to eurowestern humans becomes clearer. In the eurowest, hierarchy is used as a logic to order life from the most important (most complex) to the least important (least complex), with humans on top and trees falling far below other living creatures. In the actions of cutting trees, no recognition is given that a life is being taken and there are no offerings to attempt to bring balance back to the whole of life. Trees can be used and abused as a material for human consumption with little to no recognition that they, both individually and together in large groups, provide a significant function in the larger realm of life. While scientific inquiries have recently begun to recognize the function of trees in the production of oxygen and point to the problems associated with deforestation, the logic of the hierarchy of life is still intact in that the largescale consumption of trees is still a significant problem throughout the world. With a deeper recognition of the relationships to *mitigoog* as forms of life and how that functions within Anishinaabeg thought, the futility of a surface translation can be easily seen. While someone from each culture can point to a *mitig* and say what it is called, the deeper relationship to that *mitig*, other *mitigoog*, and the rest of life demands a much longer discussion to understand the cultural differences involved.

The previous discussion helps to bring to the surface the underlying power that a worldview offers in providing a logic to organize and conceptualize the necessary relationships to the rest of life. The above examples of Thunders as people embedded in Anishinaabemowin helps to demonstrate the fundamental difference in the logic of relatedness between Anishinaabeg culture and the eurowest. For the Anishinaabeg, the world is conceptualized as a large interrelated family to which all life belongs in a web of relatedness. In the eurowest, the relationships to the rest of life are organized in a hierarchy of relatedness with humans on top of a racialized, gendered, sexualized, anthropocentric hierarchy. These two vastly different logics for organizing relationships to the rest of life result in very different cultural manifestations in the everyday. The logic of hierarchy as manifest in environmental destruction by a culture of racialized, gendered, sexed, and anthropocentric hierarchies has been self-evident at this point. However, the logic of the web of relatedness as manifest in Anishinaabeg culture and language is not so obvious. So the question remains, what does this web of relatedness look like and how does it manifest in Anishinaabemowin and culture?

Chidibenjiged: That Which Makes All Things Belong

As the preceding discussion has demonstrated, we cannot perpetuate a naive reliance upon eurowestern terms like nature to communicate something complex like our relationships to the rest of life. When we think in depth about the dialogical relationship that nature has to other interrelated eurowestern concepts like the natural/supernatural dualisms that are unintelligible within an Anishinaabeg concept of relatedness, the process of translating this Anishinaabeg worldview must use a starting place from well within that culture. Thankfully, we have other concepts central to our understanding of the web of relatedness that have not been confused or distorted by the euroforming power of imposed colonial translations. To effectively follow this new path of conceptual decolonization, we must carefully translate from these new starting points and explain as best we can what that means or looks like in English, while at the same time being clear about what it is not. In this way, we as Anishinaabeg can take a greater control of the translation process.

To understand an Anishinaabeg logic of the web of relatedness, it is helpful to discuss the concept of *chidibenjiged*, or "that which makes all things belong."[28] I begin with this concept because it functions as an important principle or ideology for Anishinaabeg culture, and because it very rarely shows up in the eurowestern written record.[29] This last point will help to make the translation process potentially less problematic as it is not currently confused with any eurowestern conceptualizations. First of all, to suggest the translation of "that which makes all things belong" is rather unsatisfying. Clearly, *chidibenjiged* is a type of power, since it can "*make* all things belong." In a verb-based language this is important to emphasize. Secondly, Anishinaabeg negotiate the world as entirely spatially located, so like *manidoo*, *chidibenjiged* as a power must also be quasi-material. However, as we will see, this concept is thought of much more as a guiding principle or knowledge than as an entity, even though it must be a quasi-material energy if it has the power to make. As a concept it is seldom mentioned, which accounts for it being missed by almost all of the anthropologists and travelers who have written about the Anishinaabeg. It is commonly understood in communities with first-language speakers. There is also no particular iconography associated with it. There are no statues, pictures, charms, or other items in the material culture that would suggest that this is an important concept. Of course, with no iconography, there is no anthropomorphization of *chidibenjiged*. It has no body, no visible form, and it is certainly not gendered. Finally, *chidibenjiged* is a helpful place to begin the translation of the web of relatedness because it is free of association with any sort of hierarchical relationship in Anishinaabeg communities. It is not exalted, placed on high, or fetishized in any way. Built within the knowledge of *chidibenjiged* is the simple truth that there is a power or energy that "makes all things belong." This is an unconditional mandate that all life associated with Anishinaabe Akiing belongs to that place.[30] This foundational principle in Anishinaabeg thought on the topic of relatedness places all of life on the same democratic plane of existence. No one form of life is greater than another, so there is a necessity to make sure that our interactions with other forms of life do not kill them off as a group.

This brings me to two important points about *chidibenjiged* and relatedness. First, the group, or community, is the primary social unit in Indigenous thought, not the individual. So when we think about "all belonging," we are speaking about communities of life. Therefore, *wawageshkag* (whitetail deer) or *makwag* (bears) belong as a species or community of life, the individual is secondary in importance. If the individuals all belong singularly then it would be impossible to hunt, fish, and harvest other food because we would be going against this principle of belonging. Secondly, when we think about the verb-based action orientation of the language, it should come as no surprise that the emphasis of a concept like *chidibenjiged* would be focused almost entirely on putting its meaning into action. We can push this emphasis on verbs in relationship to *chidibenjiged* by demonstrating its etymological association with the verb *dibendaagozi*, translated as the act of belonging.[31] In this form it is an intransitive animate (*maaba*) verb, meaning that someone does something. For instance, *n'dibendaagoz* (I belong). If we make a more complex utterance that may be used in conversation, one may say *makwa nindibendaagoz* (bear clan is where I belong) to announce their *doodem* relationship.[32] As a concept, *chidibenjiged* demonstrates a large sense of belonging, as all of life belonging in the complex system of life. *Chidibenjiged* is only realized as we help to promote belonging in our web of relatedness. It is not so important what it is—power, energy or principle—only that we live in a way with the rest of life that promotes belonging.[33]

As I have already stated, there is almost no mention of the concept of *chidibenjiged* in the written record. Unsurprisingly, where it does come up is in the writings of A. I. Hallowell. This is simultaneously a testament to the care with which he negotiated his time among the Anishinaabeg in Berens River, and an acknowledgment of the incredibly difficult task of translating what he learned into meaningful knowledge about this group of people. He was giving greater attention to the Indigenous voice associated with his interpreter William Berens, and Hallowell's work demonstrates some of that voice with his comprehension of knowledge, such as the inclusivity of the concept of person in Anishinaabe thought. However, his work simultaneously demonstrates some of the pitfalls and blind spots that are still a problem for us today in our own processes of translation. Hallowell's treatment of *chidibenjiged* is worth spending the necessary time critiquing because it helps to show the gravitational force of worldview as an almost inescapable framework of knowledge in the process of cultural translation.

In his article "Some Empirical Aspects of Northern Saulteaux Religion," Hallowell suggests that the concept of *chidibenjiged* is on the top rung of a hierarchy of power and is the "'owner' of the world [and] is both the most remote (highest?) and powerful of all beings."[34] If it were just the imposition of a hierarchy of power in which Hallowell places this concept, it would still be problematic as it undermines the knowledge of *chidibenjiged* as "that which makes all things belong," but his attempt at bringing understanding to this important term goes far beyond that. He continues,

There is one spiritual entity, however, which neither manifests itself in the conjuring tent, appears to man in dreams, nor has even been seen by the waking eyes of any human being. This is Kadabendjiget or K'tchi-ma'ni-tu, the supreme power in the universe. Perhaps the best English equivalent to the native term is Lord. Even from the standpoint of Saulteaux religious philosophy this spiritual entity is purely conceptual. Kadabendjiget is not specifically anthropomorphized in respect to bodily form or sex, nor is there any trace of iconographic representation. Yet by implication this power possesses the faculties of sentience, omnipotence and presumably omniscience. Kadabendjiget is the Creator and Ruler of all things, if I have fathomed the native mind sufficiently. In terms of the religious system itself, in short, he is the Boss of Bosses, the Owner of the Owners. And since the notion that everything has its boss is so fundamental to their beliefs, Kadabendjiget is a logical necessity, if not logically prior in their whole scheme. Yet because the name of this supreme power is so seldom mentioned—I mean because of a positive tabu, which implies respect and veneration—the casual inquirer might mistakenly characterize this religious system as polytheistic. In my opinion this notion of a High God is indubitably aboriginal.[35]

I will begin a brief analysis of this passage on *chidibenjiged* with the positive aspects of Hallowell's description. First, he is correct in asserting that *chidibenjiged* does not manifest itself in any ceremonies or dreams. There are no narratives of *chidibenjiged* as an entity coming to speak to any Anishinaabeg, nor is there any mention of it intervening in any community. Second, there is no specific iconography of *chidibenjiged*. No paintings, statues, or painted cliffs that resemble it. Third, with no tangible manifestations, the concept is almost entirely conceptual. It is a concept that one can think about, but in this sense it functions similarly to an important principle or saying.[36] Finally, it is not anthropomorphized. Since there are no known manifestations of this concept, no type of body is possible to describe, let alone be gendered as male or female. These four points are important to keep in mind as they help to provide the initial moves from an Anishinaabeg starting point of translation. These modest beginnings could have provided Hallowell with some radically different thinking about the concept of relatedness in his descriptions of Anishinaabeg culture. However, as we will see, he is simultaneously making other moves with these accurate descriptions that euroform the concept of *chidibenjiged* into an analogy of a eurowestern concept of a High God.

There are five significant problems with Hallowell's discussion of *chidibenjiged* that need to be addressed. First, his suggestion that *chidibenjiged* is the "Creator" is problematic, both because of the spatiality of all existence in its intimacy with Anishinaabe Akiing, and by association, the unification of all life within the same universe of existence (i.e., no supernatural). This is a common mistake because of the assumed universality of the concept of a Creator, and creation from nothingness. However, as I have demonstrated, this eurowestern concept of Creator is unintelligible within Anishinaabeg thought. Secondly, *chidibenjiged* as Lord and Ruler is highly problematic. Lord and Ruler brings with it a number of dialogically related words and concepts from feudal Europe that have no Anishinaabeg equivalent. These European concepts are shot through with the concepts of being on the top of a hierarchy of relationships, which again is significantly opposed to the web of relatedness that *chidibenjiged* represents. Furthermore, "Lord" euroforms the concept of *chidibenjiged* into a palatable analogy of religious hierarchy, which is closely associated with the male gendering of European society. Thirdly, the translation of "Boss of Bosses and the Owner of the Owners" also has the same problem as "Lord" in its imposition of the relationship of hierarchy onto Anishinaabeg thought. While Hallowell is correct that there is a concept of a *manidoo* leader of animal and plant groups, a more accurate way to translate this idea would be *ogimaa*, or leader. To be a "Boss" or "Owner" implies not only a hierarchy, but a relationship of power and ownership that also has no equivalent in Anishinaabeg thought.[37] An *ogimaa* of an animal like a *makwa* (bear) makes much more sense. Within it, *ogimaa* suggests not only leadership, but also responsibility to take care of that animal group. Understood within an Anishinaabeg sociopolitical context, *ogimaag* are primarily speakers for the group they represent. There is no authority to impose ideas or decisions on those whom you represent, only to speak for them. Also, if done poorly, an *ogimaa* can be replaced by the group who is represented rather easily. These more democratic associations embedded in the concept of *ogimaa* cannot be presumed within the eurowestern sociopolitical-economic context of "Boss" and "Owner." Fourthly, the suggestion of "High God" as an equivalent has many of the same problems as "Lord." There is no hierarchy and no concepts that can effectively translate the outside-of-creation problem associated with a Creator God.

Furthermore, if Hallowell is going to stay logically consistent in his correct assertion that *chidibenjiged* is "not specifically anthropomorphized in respect to bodily form or sex," then High God cannot be used as a translation because any association to God as a concept is both anthropomorphized, sexed, and in the colonial project raced as a white male body.[38] Here Hallowell struggles to come up with an effective way of communicating something that is drastically different than anything in eurowestern culture. He even slips in his ability to communicate a non-sexed body in his use of the pronoun "he" three sentences after he declares *chidibenjiged* nongendered.[39] In this instance we can simultaneously understand the difficulty of finding a nongendered eurowestern equivalent to *chidibenjiged*, and hold a standard of translation that is at least logically consistent. Finally, one of the primary reasons that Hallowell has these difficulties in translating *chidibenjiged* is that as a concept it is automatically conflated with *kitchi manidoo*. While *chidibenjiged* is rarely spoken of, *kitchi manidoo* is more often mentioned in Anishinaabeg life. The meaning of *kitchi manidoo* and the extent to which it is mentioned in contemporary Anishinaabeg life is a subject that will get a more thorough treatment further on. However, these two words represent different concepts within Anishinaabeg thought. *Chidibenjiged* is largely conceptual and focused on generating lifegiving actions and culture; it is "that which makes all things belong." While important as a basis of understanding the relatedness to life, it is not at all a theistic concept. *Kitchi manidoo* literally translates as "big, or important *manidoo* (quasi-material life energy)."[40] However, in the colonial project this concept is often taken out of Anishinaabe context and placed into a eurowestern religious hierarchy similar to the treatment that Hallowell has given it above. This euroforming of *kitchi manidoo* has created considerable confusion in trying to comprehend Anishinaabeg culture and thought, and is perpetrated by both Anishinaabeg and non-Anishinaabeg alike. While this concept is important in Anishinaabeg thought, it has taken on a multitude of meanings in our contemporary colonial setting, so a more thorough defining of the term will wait until that process of colonization and decolonization can be elaborated.[41]

In the above examples, it becomes clearer how the process of translation and understanding those translations is affected by worldview. From the Anishinaabeg starting place, *chidibenjiged* is associated with a web of relatedness, literally as "that which makes all things belong," and has no direct eurowestern cultural equivalent. As an almost entirely conceptual phenomenon, the primary focus of *chidibenjiged* is the action (verb-based language) that is associated with belonging.

The Anishinaabeg actions dialogically associated with *chidibenjiged* are offerings for taking a life for food, making sure one uses all that one takes from other life, and the ceremonies around making sure that life taken is done in a thankful manner. The closest manifestations of *chidibenjiged* would be the *ogimaag* of the animals, which Hallowell euroforms as "Bosses," which help take care of that respective animal species. The translations that Hallowell offers above euroform *chidibenjiged* into an Anishinaabeg analogy of God. Whether "High God," "Lord," "Ruler," or "Creator," Hallowell's descriptions have none of the comprehension of an Anishinaabeg web of relatedness, and instead impose a framework of eurowestern religious hierarchy onto Anishinaabeg culture. An Anishinaabeg comprehension of *chidibenjiged* is then completely lost within a eurowestern worldview of hierarchy, dialogically related to religious and spiritual concepts that are unintelligible within Anishinaabeg thought. In this sense these translations fail Wiredu's test of translational symmetry since the religious concepts that Hallowell offers for *chidibenjiged* fail to carry its meaning into English, and certainly, concepts like "High God" are similarly unintelligible or misunderstood within Anishinaabemowin.

These problems of translation are not as new as one may think. Throughout the primary documents recording European initial contact with Indigenous North America, there are numerous examples that demonstrate a recognition that the two cultures are different to the point of unintelligibility. Margaret Noodin demonstrates this longstanding problem of translation in her book *Bawaajimo: A Dialect of Dreams in Anishinaabe Language and Literature*. She gives the example of Gabriel Sagard, who visited Anishinaabe Akiing and noted that

> Les mots de Gloire, Trinité, sainct Esprit, Anges, Resurrection, Paradis, Enfer, Eglise, Foy, Esperance & Charité, & autres infinis, ne sont pas en usage chez-eux (The words Glory, Trinity, Holy Spirit, Angels, Resurrection, Paradise, Hell, Church, Faith, Hope, and Charity and a multitude of others are not used by them).[42]

Here we can see in the era of early colonial encounter that this problem of translation was fully recognized. However, throughout the process of colonization, these eurochristian words and worldview get imposed on the Anishinaabeg, and the lines of difference between the two cultures is blurred. Noodin continues in her analysis, suggesting these problems that Sagard has identified are common in Anishinaabemowin. She gives the example that "'hell' is simply *maji-ishkodeng*, a bad fire without the implications of religion and darkness carried by the English word."[43] This is a good example as it helps to demonstrate that within an Anishinaabeg worldview, *maji-ishkodeng*, if ever used, would be representative of a fire that just smolders and does not warm or cook sufficiently, or something that consumes too much and takes more life than it gives. However, if one is "thinking with a colonized mind" and using Anishinaabemowin to describe a eurowestern religious term, it can carry with it all of the fire and damnation that the church authority intends for it.[44] In this way we can get a firsthand glimpse into the flexibility of language as a platform of communication. Theoretically, it could be entirely possible to live within a eurowestern worldview and culture and speak entirely Anishinaabemowin if the Indigenous language would only be used to describe a eurowestern life. *Maji-ishkodeng* can then be euroformed and filled with the Christian concepts of fire and damnation. Thankfully, this type of complete colonization has not happened. However, we do live with a significant amount of colonial confusion within Anishinaabemowin as much of the eurowestern religious, political, and economic world has been incorporated into our language and lifeways. As Noodin demonstrates, the danger here is that "Words can represent worldview and identity. Language can shape narrative and leave traces of that shape long after it has been translated."[45] Since much of our lived experience, our actions is governed by a colonial economic and political experience, even those of us who work diligently to decolonize our thoughts and actions live a significant part of our lives with the actions of colonization.

Even though there has been a significant problem of the colonization of Anishinaabemowin, there has also been a lot of work towards the process of decolonization in the past few decades. This work has helped us to begin to regenerate our languages and lifeways towards a more meaningful and healthy Anishinaabe existence. As these examples demonstrate, much more time and care must be given to the translations that we use to communicate across this cultural gap. This is made all the more essential when one considers the cultural differences at the depth of worldview. The logic of the web of relatedness has no cultural equivalent in eurowestern thought. Therefore, we must start the process of translation well within Anishinaabemowin. In that line of thinking, *chidibenjiged* is best thought of as an ideological representation of the logic of a web of relatedness. As a word it represents a worldview, and when that worldview is followed with action it represents part of an Anishinaabeg identity. For this identity to be lived out, it is best done in close relationship with the rest of life with reciprocal giving. But when conflated with *kitchi manidoo* and overrun with eurowestern hierarchical meaning, as is done in Hallowell's translation, it represents an entirely different worldview. *Chidibenjiged* is "that which makes all things belong" and does not have a eurowestern cultural equivalent. Any mention or discussion of translating it as "God" or "Creator" must be resisted as that mistranslation functions as an ongoing form of colonization of our minds.

Lost in Translation: *Kitchi Manidoo* and the Process of Decolonization

In the middle of the twentieth century, American colonization was nearing its completion. The centuries of war, disease, and displacement were followed up with the theft of children into the genocidal process of the boarding schools, and very little was thought to be left of once very strong Indigenous nations. In the face of this ongoing oppression, Indigenous peoples began a process of regenerating their lifeways and asserting both treaty and human rights in the public sphere.[46] These movements took shape throughout the 1960s and 1970s in multiple forms. Often called the Red Power movement, these decolonizing energies gained strength as elders and young people in our communities began the process of regenerating the languages and actions that are associated with an Anishinaabe way of life. The languages and ceremonies that had gone underground and out of sight of the colonial authorities began to blossom again. Looking back now from the vantage point of forty years of action and scholarship, what has become readily apparent is the depths to which colonization has entrenched itself in our own thinking. As the above example with *chidibenjiged* has shown, it is not enough to just speak Anishinaabemowin, but we must continually root out the colonizing frameworks of thought that have embedded themselves within our own minds and actions. In short, for those of us interested in decolonization, we must be in it for the long haul. When we consider the web of relatedness as part of the Anishinaabeg worldview that provides a guiding logic for developing proper relationships to the rest of life, then it is necessary in this process of decolonization to make sure that our language is associated with concepts that are consistent with that logic. As we will see, there is reason to call into question any presumption of consistency, even among first-language speakers.

When we think of the use of the concept of *kitchi manidoo* in the process of colonization, a number of issues quickly arise. For example, in the missionary work of Peter Jones, his usage is problematic in its conflation with the eurowestern concept of God. Clearly, Jones's intention was the process of missionizing other

Anishinaabeg, so the intended translation of God as *kitchi manidoo* is relatively simple in that he was part of a colonial machine attempting to communicate a biblical concept of the Christian God in Anishinaabemowin.[47] However, it becomes very complicated when we think about the message received by the potential converts. Just what did the Anishinaabeg who heard Jones speak think about this concept of *kitchi manidoo*, and how did they conceptualize it? How did a people who conceptualize the world as spatially oriented and intimately related to their particular places receive a message of "good news" about someone from a distant place that is part of a foreign culture that is effectively destroying their homelands? These moments of colonial missionization are also points that demonstrate the extraordinary difficulty of communicating across worldviews.

When we move to the period of decolonization in the late twentieth century, sorting out the differences in worldviews and the problems associated with translation are no less complicated. The work of Basil Johnston and his use of *kitchi manidoo* helps to demonstrate the process of decolonization as his use of the concept has shifted over time and because it is embedded in a much larger body of Anishinaabeg knowledge. In his book *Ojibway Heritage*, Johnston begins with a description of "*Kitche Manitou* (The Great Spirit)" fulfilling a vision:

> In this dream he saw a vast sky filled with stars, sun, moon, and earth. He saw an earth made of mountains and valleys, islands and lakes, plains and forests. He saw trees and flowers, grasses and vegetables. He saw walking, flying, swimming, and crawling beings. He witnessed the birth, growth and the end of things. At the same time he saw other things live on. Amidst change there was constancy. Kitche Manitou heard songs, wailings, stories. He touched wind and rain. He felt love and hate, fear and courage, joy and sadness. Kitche Manitou meditated to understand his vision. In his wisdom Kitche Manitou understood that his vision had to be fulfilled.[48]

In this fulfillment, "Out of nothing he made rock, water, fire and wind. Into each one he breathed the breath of life."[49] After that he made the contours of the land, plants, animals, humans, and then "The Great Laws of Nature."[50] According to Johnston this world was destroyed and remained a water world for many generations before *Giizhigokwe* came to this earth. When these passages are read in English, there are five problems that jump off the page to suggest a colonization of Anishinaabeg thought. First, in this passage *kitchi manidoo* is sexed as male with the pronoun "he." This is problematic as the Anishinaabeg culture is considered to be centered on the balance of energy, so a male creator could be thought of as out of balance. Secondly, the translation of *kitchi manidoo* as "The Great Spirit" also raises a problem in the area of spatial existence. If being or existence is intimately tied to space in the form of *ayaa* (to be, there), then any translation suggesting spirit falls flat in its inability to carry the necessary relationship to space. Thirdly, while origins can be important, that Johnston begins this book with a narrative that closely resembles the Bible offers some difficulty. This move places Anishinaabeg culture in relational mimicry to eurowestern culture. Its placement at the beginning of the book suggests a linear movement of time, again similar to that of the Christian Bible. Fourthly, this "Great Spirit" created "out of nothing" the entire universe. Again, this also runs into problems with its inability to be spatially configured. This would cause us to follow the same theological problem that Christianity has had, which is if God is outside of the universe (since it was created out of nothing), then can God participate in the world and intervene? Since there are no known narratives dealing with this problem, even if by a childlike suggestion that *kitchi manidoo* can do anything, then this is probably a poor translation. Finally, a male "great spirit" that "created" the universe so closely resembles the male Christian God that the conceptualization associated with this passage is that this is just the Anishinaabeg notion of God, so it is analogous to the Christian God, which comes with its associated logics of linear time and hierarchy in tow.

However, Johnston is not a theologian and he cannot necessarily be held accountable to a standard of technical theological language, discourse, and doctrinal history. Hence, this critique deserves a further unpacking to set it into a larger conversation about worldview, translation, and the decolonization of Anishinaabeg thought. When we negotiate this critique in the context of a larger discourse of decolonization, we come to a better understanding of the depths of the colonization of our own minds and the need to further this type of work. When we look at the larger body of Johnston's work, we can see some movement in his thought over time. In this larger context these passages, while still problematic, can be seen along with the other positive decolonizing moves that he does make.

First, while Johnston does allow for the gendering of *kitchi manidoo* as "he" in his early writings, in later texts he does offer a corrective. In *The Manitous: The Spiritual World of the Ojibway*, he offers an etymology of *Kitchi Manitou*, suggesting that "when the Anishinaubae people predicated the term Manitou of God, they added the prefix 'Kitchi,' meaning great. By this term they meant 'The Great Mystery' of the supernatural order, one beyond human grasp, beyond words, neither male nor female, not of the flesh."[51] This passage has other problems associated with terms like "supernatural" and the notion of "mystery" associated with *kitchi manidoo*; however, naming the concept as "neither male nor female" is a positive step in the process of decolonization. By claiming a nongendered status for *kitchi manidoo*, it moves to differentiate the culture away from the colonial patriarchy associated with Christianity and the rest of eurowestern culture. Again, the narratives are powerful in that they set primary examples for the Anishinaabeg to follow in their own societal structures. In this case, with no divine patriarchy to follow as a standard, it can allow for the promotion of more gender-balanced political and economic systems since no one gender is responsible for the creation of the entire universe.

Johnston's discussions of *kitchi manidoo* also have a more subtle decolonizing movement throughout his work. Even in *Ojibway Heritage*, he spends very little time in the discussions of *kitchi manidoo* itself. He uses these brief stories as primers to describe how the Anishinaabeg came into being. In both *Ojibway Heritage* and *The Manitous*, these brief descriptions of *kitchi manidoo* are quickly followed with the entrance into the other important *manidoog* and characters in the Anishinaabeg cultural narratives. More importantly, unlike the Christian narratives, *kitchi manidoo* does not require adoration, or threaten and destroy other peoples, or intervene on behalf of the Anishinaabeg. When reading the larger body of Johnston's work, it is clear that the emphasis in the culture is not on an ultimate creator (whether gendered or not) but on the relationships forged with the *manidoog* in the land in which they reside. Most of his writing paints a much larger picture of the many *manidoog* that the Anishinaabeg are in relationship with like *Mazikaamikwe*, the four sons of *Winona* (particularly *Nana'b'oozoo*), *manidoog* of the forests and water, sprites, the winds, other plants and animals, and the *wendigo*.[52] By emphasizing the larger relationships of the Anishinaabeg, the narratives that Johnston give help to deemphasize the distant relationship to *"Kitchi Manitou"* and point the process of decolonization towards the land and the *manidoog* that reside there with us. It is these relationships to the land that help to sustain us in the everyday. There are no Anishinaabeg power moves that call upon *kitchi manidoo* to take care of us or to vanquish enemies as in the Christian narratives. The Anishinaabeg, according to Johnston and his body of work, are responsible for forging reciprocal relationships with the surrounding environments of humans and other-than-humans.

In the process of rekindling these relationships with the rest of life, it is necessary for the Anishinaabeg to experience these *manidoog* in their lands. This is where the problem with a Great Spirit of *kitchi manidoo* comes into play. By relying on a framework of Christian thought and a translation of spirit, *manidoo* and its spatial location are lost in that translation. While people can and do experience other-than-human persons in their lives, the conceptualizations of those experiences can be minimized or lost completely in relying on a foreign framework of thought that can euroform those experiences in a Christian framework of a nonspatial reality.[53] Johnston's work does buy into that Christian framework, but he does make attempts to differentiate *kitchi manidoo* from that foreign system of thought. In *The Manitous*, he attempts to further a definition of *manidoo*, suggesting that "Manitou refers . . . to the unseen realities of individual beings and places and events that are beyond human understanding but are still clearly real."[54] He also makes a further move to differentiate an authentic Anishinaabeg understanding of *manidoo* when he describes the multiple uses of this term in Anishinaabemowin, correctly naming that we use "manitouwun to refer to some curative or healing property in a tree or plant" and "manitouwut to refer to the sacrosanct mood or atmosphere of a place" or "manitouwih to allude to a medicine person with miraculous healing powers."[55] These linguistic-conceptual moves help to give a deeper understanding of both the language and the multiplicity of concepts that are associated with *manidoog*. If someone is paying attention to Johnston's critique, they will be able to ask important questions about the problems of spirit as a translation for *manidoo*. While his printed work is still grounded in the nonspatial and nonmaterial Christian framework in his association with spirit, Johnston does begin the process of problematizing those translations so that other scholars can continue this work.

The concept of time is essential in the process of decolonization. The Christian framework of a linear progression of time is the overarching temporal relationship that the globalized world uses. While cyclical concepts of time are understood, they do not function as the underlying logic of the worldview in relation to time. Hence, it is necessary to be critical when conceptualizing our work in temporal relationships. While Johnston does often begin his books with a discussion of *kitchi manidoo* as creator of the universe, this relationship to linear time is deemphasized in the rest of his narratives. While it is necessary to start with *Winona* and the West Wind's sexual encounter to get to the birth of the four brothers, these narratives are set after *Giizhigokwe* but not in direct relationship. This temporal disjunction to different sets of narratives in *The Manitous* helps to decenter a linear thought and allows Johnston to introduce the reader to a larger set of Anishinaabeg narratives that do not necessarily have a particular order. This narrative style mimics a traditional storyteller who would tell narratives that are meaningful to the community at that particular place and time, with no need to give a linear sequence of events. The events in the land are the power behind the narratives, not the linear progression of the narratives. This narrative style is best seen in his book *Ojibway Ceremonies*, where he weaves a complex narrative of the life of *Mishi-Waub-Kaikak* (the great white falcon), a fictive person he uses to introduce the reader to a community of ceremonies used by the Anishinaabeg. The narrative is told following the life of *Mishi-Waub-Kaikak*, but within each ceremony that he goes through, multiple layers of narratives are told that demonstrate the cyclical nature of time in Anishinaabeg culture as they tell and retell the narratives and ceremonies that are used to sustain the people in the northern Great Lakes. While both a linear and cyclical conceptualization of time are communicated, linear time fades to the background in the narratives as the cycles of ceremonies are told and retold in traditional fashion. In this complex pedagogical fashion, Johnston is able to decenter linear time and reintroduce cyclical conceptualizations of time in the narratives.

Finally, the problems associated with *kitchi manidoo* creating the universe out of nothing should be kept in perspective. This mimicking of a Christian creation narrative is problematic as it does emphasize linear time. However, the Christian problems associated with a God who is relied upon to intervene in the lives of the community do not come into Anishinaabeg narratives because there is a much different relationship with *kitchi manidoo*. In following Johnston's retelling of Anishinaabeg narratives, it is not *kitchi manidoo* who comes to aid the Anishinaabeg, but a significant number of other *manidoog* who take turns teaching the Anishinaabeg important lessons. *Nanapush* (*Nana'boo'zoo* in Johnston's work) becomes the Anishinaabeg trickster who often teaches important lessons and gives gifts of medicine. While Johnston's work does deemphasize the Christian notion of a God that is both distant and reachable via prayer for help with his introduction of a much larger group of Anishinaabeg narratives, this association of *kitchi manidoo* as a creator is problematic in ways that are difficult to be undone.

Returning to the process of decolonization, it is important to place Johnston's work in a larger context from which we can make useful critiques. While it does suffer from its relationship to a Christian framework of hierarchical relationships, his work has been helpful in other capacities. His in-depth introduction of the reader to a larger world of Anishinaabeg narratives helps to give a much better understanding of the wealth of relationships that are associated with the people. His emphasis on introducing Anishinaabemowin into his texts also has helped to provide a proper Anishinaabeg methodology for decolonization. Johnston's writings, in combination with numerous others who have taken up this difficult work, have helped to create the cognitive space for successive generations of Anishinaabeg to be reintroduced to their own culture, lifeways, language, and worldview. In this cognitive space the process of decolonization can take root in the ground in which the language is being spoken and the stories are once again being told. In this intergenerational project, Johnston's work has helped untold numbers of people to feel a pride in themselves for being Anishinaabeg, and allowed for greater access to narratives and language that has helped people to also take up the work of rebuilding their communities.

Decolonizing Colonial Cyphers

Following this trajectory of Anishinaabeg decolonization, we can identify the shifting uses of a concept like *kitchi manidoo*. Considering a longer trajectory of Anishinaabeg thought from Peter Jones to Basil Johnston, we can see that while the use of the term has had some decolonizing effect in its ability to conceptualize a relationship to life differently, it would be difficult to fully transform the concept since it has been mired in God talk for so long. In this sense, *kitchi manidoo* is a confused category, having multiple meanings at the same time ranging from another way to say God, to Godlike, but different from the Christian God. Stated in another way, *kitchi manidoo* functions as a colonial cypher. Here there are two meanings of cypher that are useful. First it means zero, or having no capacity. Considering the unintelligibility of nonspatial concepts within Anishinaabemowin, *kitchi manidoo* as related to God and spirit is a cypher because it has zero capacity to carry those meanings, unless one is willing to think with a colonized mind. In the same fashion, religious concepts in the English language also have zero capacity to comprehend an ontology grounded in spatial existence. Second, cypher can mean a secret or hidden meaning. When we think of the multiple meanings that have been and are attached to *kitchi manidoo*, it can have hidden meanings when it is being uttered in a room or written down as text. With *kitchi manidoo* being attached to many different concepts, it can be difficult to know what is being communicated. This is where it is useful to think about *kitchi manidoo* as having hidden or encrypted meanings. It is possible for someone to say *kitchi manidoo* and think they are communicating an Anishinaabeg concept, and for someone who is listening to come away with the idea of God, or vice versa. Furthermore, since the concept has been so closely associated with a Christian framework of a nonspatial deity, it is possible to speak this Anishinaabeg word and still have its meaning be well within a eurowestern framework of dominion, linear time, and hierarchy. The dialogically related doctrinal history of God, church, spirit, and the logics of dominion, linear time, and hierarchy can come along as encrypted messages within Anishinaabemowin. This is another example of thinking with a colonized mind. It is essential to disconnect Anishinaabemowin from these foreign meanings and frameworks of thought. For the process of decolonization, it is most important that the worldview is embodied more and more. While *kitchi manidoo* as a concept has helped to shift the discourse towards a cognitive space for decolonization to happen, since it is still so tangled within a eurowestern framework, it may have outlived its ability to provide more space to think and live a life more Anishinaabeg.[56]

In a more recent linguistic turn, the term *gizhe manidoo* has gained a certain currency among a number of Anishinaabeg communities. This concept also follows a similar trajectory as *kitchi manidoo*, so a deeper look at the development of its usage can be useful for a discussion of decolonization. According to Bob Williams, an Anishinaabeg elder from Northern Michigan, *Gizhe Manidoo* is synonymous with the "Creator."[57] Williams continues to give a deeper explanation: "The first part of that word means the kind, uncreated spirit. When you talk about something that's gizhe, you're talking about something that hassles the mind."[58] Here Williams makes a clear translation of *Gizhe Manidoo* as Creator. However, there is no in-depth follow-up to demonstrate what that Creator is or does. His discussion of *gizhe* as "something that hassles the mind" is also curious in that he is suggesting that this *manidoo* is active in the lives of humans. But again, very little else is given as a deeper elucidation of this concept.[59] In a poem about water by Winona LaDuke, *Gizhe Manidoo* is translated as "creation."[60] Basil Johnston provides two separate entries in his *Anishinaubae Thesaurus*, one for *Kitchi-Manitou* (God, The Creator, The Great Mystery) and one for *Kizhae-Manitou* (The Respected, Revered Mystery, another term for the Creator).[61] Nichols and Nyholm give the definition of *gizhe manidoo* as "God (especially in Christian usage)."[62] This range of definitions suggests that *gizhe manidoo* is no less problematic a category than *kitchi manidoo*, with a range of meaning that suggests both an Anishinaabe and a eurowestern worldview depending upon how, by whom, and in what context it is being used. However, when we look deeper at its structure, *gizhe manidoo* does offer some different ways of thinking about relationships.

While it is useful to think about words and concepts in their common usage, as that can help to associate those words in particular relationships and contexts, it is also important to go into the etymology of the words, as that helps us to get deeper into the linguistic-conceptual analysis. We already analyzed *manidoo* and attempted a definition that takes into consideration the spatiality of an Anishinaabeg worldview, naming *manidoo* as a quasi-material life energy. *Gizhe* is a morpheme of *giizis*, the sun. Here, the concept of *gizhe* is grounded in its origin as a quantum source of heat energy. So an utterance of *gizhe manidoo* is a naming of the quasi-material life energy and heat that originates from the sun. This definition can be seen in the imagery of both *kitchi manidoo* and *gizhe manidoo* as the sun, often depicted with arrows pointing away in four directions. While theoretically, both *kitchi manidoo* and *gizhe manidoo* could be words associated with this concept of quantum heat energy, only *gizhe* is etymologically associated with that source of heat. *Kitchi*, as a prefix, is rather vague and usually means very big or very important. This etymological discussion does help to give a deeper elucidation of the words and associated concepts, but in and of itself that does not necessarily demonstrate what is correct or the best option. That question can only be decided by communities of people. However, this discussion does offer a warning for anyone interested in the process of decolonization.

When the underlying frameworks of knowledge that worldviews represent are taken into consideration, special attention needs to be paid to not just the language being used in the process of decolonization, but the relationship to the worldview as well. Even though there has been a shift in some Anishinaabeg communities to *gizhe manidoo* from *kitchi (gitchi) manidoo*, a brief survey of the literature raises a number of red flags about whether or not an Anishinaabeg worldview is being represented. Within these few examples we can easily see some divergent paths. For Nichols and Nyholm, and Johnston, there is clearly only a slight shift in meaning between the two concepts. Both of these dictionaries still presume a universality between Anishinaabeg culture and that of the eurowest at the level of worldview since the definitions for both *kitchi* and *gizhe manidoo* make reference to a Christian God or Creator. However, as we have seen, the presumption or imposition of a universal understanding represents the colonization of the Anishinaabeg mind. If the translation of *gizhe manidoo* as God were to be accepted, then that would simultaneously accept the eurowestern worldview of dominion over land, linear time, and hierarchy associated with this concept. This doctrinal heritage comes in tow with any utterance of God, whether the speaker wants to or not. As we know, those worldview logics are foreign to Anishinaabemowin and Anishinaabe thought.[63]

When we look at the translations given for *gizhe manidoo* by Williams and LaDuke, we no longer have a direct correlation to the eurowestern worldview associated with God. Here the shift to creation or Creator is useful to help us think about relationships and the process of decolonization. Notwithstanding the problems associated with creator and creation language that has already been stated, there is a move here by these authors to demonstrate a different conceptualization and relationship to life. If either of these authors had wanted to communicate the concept of "God," that would have been easy enough to use as a translation. However, these two passages represent a shift in thinking about the concept of *gizhe manidoo* away from the hierarchy and dominion associated with God to the life that the people are surrounded by and interact with. Particularly in LaDuke's poem, she says "Gi-bizhigwaadenimoa Gizhe Manidoo maji-mashkii . . . To poison the waters is to show disrespect to Creation."[64] Here *gizhe manidoo* is used to represent the whole of life that is affected by polluting rivers. Williams does not associate *gizhe manidoo* with a larger narrative but gives a simple definition as "Creator," representing that which causes that creation to come into being. While his definition does not range as far from God as LaDuke's, it does demonstrate a shift in thinking from God to creator that has been popular in Anishinaabeg and other Indigenous communities in the last few decades.

When we think about this range of usage for the concept of *gizhe manidoo*, we clearly see a dissonance happening within the culture. This should come as no surprise considering the significant amount of cultural upheaval that the Anishinaabeg have experienced. With the large and growing population of Anishinaabeg over a vast territory along with the local autonomy that is inherent in the culture, this sort of diversity in language and thought makes perfect sense. However, as the desire and actions of decolonization continue to move the people, there are a number of decisions that must be made along the way. This decision-making process can be better developed if there is a grounding methodology that helps to give linguistic-conceptual parameters that further push Anishinaabeg closer into a web of relatedness with their surrounding environment. Here I am suggesting that a more clearly articulated and critically defined Anishinaabeg worldview can help to provide a mooring for the cycles of decolonization. That cycle was regenerated in the late 1960s as many people stood up for themselves as Indian and then Anishinaabeg people. This standing up helped to stir a greater pride in the Indigenous communities that in turn helped to bring more people together to participate in actions like powwows, ceremony, drumming, singing, and street actions. At these actions many people were (re)introduced to their respective languages as songs were sung and ceremonies were conducted in Indigenous languages. These actions taking place with Anishinaabemowin in turn helped to reify that sense of pride and became a (mostly) positive cycle for decolonization that has continually reproduced itself over the last four decades. This positive cycle of decolonization has held Anishinaabeg actions (ceremony, drumming, singing, and many other everyday actions) in dialogical tension with the learning of Anishinaabemowin. While this process has been a positive development in Anishinaabeg communities, we have to remember that this process is simultaneously held in tension with lived eurowestern daily actions of late capitalism. Furthermore, the starting place for most of the Anishinaabeg who are participating in this complex, tensioned-filled environment is the English language and its associated eurowestern logics of dominion, linear time, and hierarchy. Again, when we honestly think about this complex dialogical and tension-filled cultural space that most of us live in, then having differing opinions as to what *gizhe manidoo* means is completely under-standable. While a certain amount of diversity in thought is healthy and a simple reality for a large culture group like the Anishinaabeg, the continual straddling of two very different worldviews and associated actions is extraordinarily difficult to sustain. A critical definition of worldview, if it is accepted and brought into the cycle of decolonization, may help to further the cause by assisting people to select trajectories of thought and action that are more congruent with the relationships associated with their own worldview. However, since the starting place for the larger movement of decolonization for most of us takes place well within the lived actions of late capitalism and the eurowestern worldview, and there is currently no consistent, logical mooring to guide the process of decolonization away from the foreign logics of the eurowest, we cannot presume that there will be ongoing decolonizing movement into the Anishinaabeg logics of an intimate relationship to localized space, cyclical time, and living in a web of relatedness. A reliance upon the myth of linear progress would be an enacting of a eurowestern logic itself. This potentially improved dialogical relationship of Anishinaabeg actions and language held in tension by this Anishinaabeg worldview can help ground this process in a common set of logics. While this introduction of a set of logics can improve the process of decolonization, there will also have to be a greater discussion as to just what Anishinaabeg actions and relationships look like in this place of late capitalistic decay in Anishinaabe Akiing. What are Anishinaabeg best relationships and practices? What part will language play in the process? How are *kitchi manidoo* and *gizhe manidoo* to be understood? The idea here is not to impose regulations or a strict system to adhere to, but to work towards bringing the dissonance in Anishinaabeg thought back into a healthy diversity of a single worldview.

For the process of decolonization to continue in a positive manner, it will be necessary to work towards living in closer relationship with the rest of life in this web of relatedness. *Kitchi manidoo* as a concept is supposed to help us conceptualize the world in a way that is conducive to that way of living. However, since it is so confused with foreign logics of eurowestern religious language and its nonmaterial and nonspatial existence, as a cypher for eurowestern relationships to life it may cause more problems than it solves. Words as symbols are not only related to their respective referents (objects), they are also related to the multiple meanings that they have. Following a dialogical trajectory, these words are related to other similar words that together inform each other's meanings. For this reason, in the process of decolonization it is essential to think deeply about our language and the necessary translations that we use. To return to and enrich our relationships with the rest of life as embodied in concepts like *nametoo* and *chidibenjiged*, Anishinaabemowin will provide an essential component of those relationships as it has for our ancestors. These relationships as mediated through Anishinaabemowin can be strengthened and help return us to healthier communities as they are practiced. In this way a positive cycle of decolonization can be sustained through the cycle of language revitalization, positive interactions with the rest of life, and reciprocal gifting in those relationships. Then the logic of the web of relatedness will again be manifest in the actions of the Anishinaabeg consistent with the concept of *chidibenjiged.*

Inawendiwag: They Are Related to Each Other

When we methodologically use Anishinaabemowin to demonstrate cultural difference, it can be useful to describe social situations and relationships that are most closely associated with the development of that language. Hence, I will begin with relationships in an Anishinaabeg village. Again, the village is the center of Anishinaabeg life. It is where people live most of their lives and negotiate most of their relationships. The importance of relationships are so prevalent that it is most common for people to call each other by their relationship to each other, so a baby boy does not just say *n'inga* (my mother), *n'oos* (my father), *n'okomis* (my grandmother), and *n'mishomis* (my grandfather), which is common in many cultures, but also *niijikiwenh* (my brother) and *n'indawema* (my sister).[65] These same relational names (*niijikiwenh* and *n'indawema*) are also used when addressing what are considered cousins in eurowestern culture, and *n'ninoshenh* or *n'nimishoome* are used when addressing their aunt and uncle, respectively.[66]

While so far the emphasis on relationship in Anishinaabemowin is different than what is commonly used in eurowestern culture, when we move outside of what is considered the nuclear and extended family the differences compound. For a young man negotiating his way through the world, *n'niijikiwenh* is also used to address a male friend.[67] A more accurate translation for *n'niijikiwenh* would be my brother, cousin, friend. This common language to describe brother, cousin, and friend demonstrates some significant differences as to the social relationships at play in Anishinaabeg communities. In this sense, the distinctions between sibling, cousin, and friend do not exist as they do in eurowestern culture. In Anishinaabe-mowin and thought, there is an equality in relationship that functions to keep social relationships on an equal plane. There is no hierarchy of relatedness or importance as one moves further away from the self, to brother, cousin, second cousin, friend, acquaintance, and stranger as there is in the eurowest. Furthermore, the social relationships encompassed in the concept of *n'niijikiwenh* extend beyond the village to other villages near and far. It is common protocol when traveling to other places that one should seek out and find food and shelter with someone of the same *doodem*, or clan. While there is a closer relationship within a given *doodem* that is understood, the language used to describe someone who is of a different *doodem* is the same as someone within. Also while traveling, protocol would suggest a formal greeting for the *ogimaag* (leaders) of the other village as *n'okomis* and *n'mishomis* (my grandmother and my grandfather). Within Anishinaabemowin we see a world in which the people live closely related to one another, even if they live at a distance and only meet them once. The protocols for engaging with other people and the language that is used suggests a familiarity that does not exist in the eurowest.

It is important to push the importance of this difference between these two cultures and aver that social relationships are organized around fundamentally different logics. The language of this large Anishinaabeg family is an institutional manifestation of the ideology of *chidibenjiged*. Here we can see the logic of a web of relatedness underlying an ideological principle of "that which makes all things belong," and the Anishinaabeg institution of the village being organized around this concept of belonging conceptualized as a family. This logic of relatedness is practiced in the everyday as the people talk to each other, call each other by their respective relationship, and participate with all of life as a large family. When "all things belong," then there is a built-in logic for the people both to include all of life into their world, and to develop social and political means to be able to act in ways consistent with that logic. With this in mind, it should come as no surprise that Anishinaabeg and other Indigenous peoples are practiced in the art of democracy, consensus building, and the ability not only to treat with other groups of people, but to have ceremonies dedicated to maintaining those agreements over time. These methods of treaty engagement are the consequence of groups of people who are guided by a logic of a web of relatedness and have organized their culture consistent with that logic.

It should also be noted that there are formal ceremonies for naming people that the Anishinaabeg engage in. However, these names are rarely used in a public setting. A person's first name is usually given soon after birth and is given in a *waawiindasowin* (naming ceremony). This name is given by elders in the community who can communicate with *manidoog* about the child, and the name reflects qualities or attributes of the person.[68] This name is designed to help the child to develop into the person they are supposed to be in relation to the community. Again, this name is known by the people closest to them and may or may not be known by a larger group of people. This use of naming is important as in the everyday, a person exists primarily as part of a web of relatedness in the community as *n'niijikiwenh* (my brother, cousin, friend), *n'nimisenh* (my sister, cousin), *n'kawiss* (my son), *n'daanis* (my daughter), *noozhishenh* (grandchild), *indoozhim* (nephew), or *indoozhimis* (niece).[69] In this large family of the Anishinaabeg there is a lack of emphasis on the individual as represented above. A person exists primarily as a relation to the rest of the community. In an Anishinaabeg village the primary social unit is the large family that is the community. Persons are as important as they help the village to function well.

This is very different in the eurowest as a person's name sets them apart as an individual and is used as an identifier in public. While the eurowestern person does understand themself as related to their immediate family, there is a hierarchy of relatedness within the nuclear family of mom, dad, brother, sister as most important, then moving to an extended family of grandparents, aunts and uncles, and cousins as not as central to the family. Outside of the family the language is very different in English, moving from forms of blood relations to neighbors, friends, work or classmates, acquaintances, or strangers. Again, this hierarchy does not occur in Anishinaabeg thought. This emphasis on the relationship to community is what Tink Tinker is referencing when he suggests that involvement in "ceremonial life of a community is typically engaged in 'for the sake of the people' and not for the sake of individual salvation or personal spiritual self-empowerment."[70] In an Anishinaabeg community one is first a part of a community, and one's individuality is understood within that communitarian context.

This human Anishinaabeg community is also intimately related to their local environment. This shift to the larger other-than-human community is still in many ways conceptualized as a large family. When *Giizhigokwe* fell from the sky, she was welcomed and given a place to land even during a time of great difficulty. The other animals, who were already present on the earth, are clearly the elder relatives here in this place. For their generosity in providing food, shelter, clothing, and medicine they are considered *gichi-aya'aa* (elder). This position of *gichi-aya'aa* is held in high esteem in communities and helps to guide the type of relationship that Anishinaabeg communities hold with the rest of life that surrounds them. The maintenance of these relationships are essential to the Anishinaabeg as it is these animals and plants that provide daily sustenance for the entire community. Providing sustenance for the younger humans is also set forth in the *Giizhigokwe* narratives as *makwa*, the bear, gave of himself so that *Giizhigokwe's* children could eat.[71] This narrative functions as a guiding principle that helps the Anishinaabeg to conceptualize this large web of relatedness to the rest of life. Here we can see the logic of *chidibenjiged* play out in narrative form. The elder animals were clearly guided by a notion that all things belong, even those things that are not from this world like *Giizhigokwe*. All things belong, yet all of those things need to eat to continually belong. Here it is important to name that the belonging here is afforded to communities, not the individual. When *Giizhigokwe* is welcomed to the earth, it is for all humans. The same logic of communities is followed for all of life. *Makwag* (bears) belong as a community, so it is okay to kill a few for the sustenance they can provide. This goes for all of life. This concept of belonging as a community helps to keep in perspective the reality of life needing to feed on life. It is not each individual who belongs but the species as a whole. In this way this large web of relatedness can continue as life can feed on life, thereby sustaining each species.

This form of relationship and belonging can also be seen in the relationships between villages, both within Indigenous nations and between different nations.

Villages that sat near to each other would often practice reciprocal relationships in a multitude of ways. If they shared a boundary for hunting and fishing territory, then any disputes that would arise would be handled by the village leadership councils. These disputes were part of the intervillage dynamic, but certainly not the only factor. Villages were also held in reciprocal balance by a gifting economy. In this sense, if one village was overflowing in a certain resource like fish because they were near a large body of water, they could gift a village further inland that did not have as many fish. The village inland could also gift the village near the water with something that they too were overflowing in. These two villages then each received the best from each other and held one another in a positive mutual-interdependent status. Furthermore, villages near each other would also have a number of intermarriages between them, further strengthening the bonds between the communities.

These mutually beneficial trade and decision-making strategies were present in communities that did not share the same language or were not in the same confederacy, yet were spatially located near enough to each other where it was still beneficial to enter into agreements. Here it is important to remember that while there were loose national affiliations like Anishinaabeg, the primary identity and sociopolitical location was the *doodem* and the village. Therefore it should be of no surprise that villages near borders with other linguistic and culturally different people would necessitate some sort of relationship.[72] This type of village-to-village relationship would be very similar to the one described above, with each village gifting the other their best, communicating to resolve disputes, and sometimes intermarrying.[73]

The above descriptions of Anishinaabeg community life give a brief overview of the language of family as it plays out in village life and in the relationships with the surrounding environments. There is another layer of relationships that also must be discussed. In addition to what is commonly seen and understood in Anishinaabeg life, there are also the powerful relationships with the *aanikoobijigan* (ancestors) and the *manidoog* that must be acknowledged. First, the wisdom attributed to the ancestors is accessible in both the many *aadizookaanag* and *dibaajimowin*, and continually in ceremony. Ancestors are a vital part of the Anishinaabeg community as they provide the narrative mooring for the continual practice of proper relationships. They speak through the narratives, continually telling and retelling the lessons necessary to keep the people acting in ways that help to provide the flourishing of all life, for all the relatives. The ancestors also speak in ceremonies like *maadootsiwan* (purification lodge) and others to help guide the people towards lifegiving actions and relationships. This access to ancestors also goes for the *manidoog*. Many *manidoog* are around in the land to be in relationship with the people. These quasi-material life energies are also available via narratives and in ceremony. They continually bring knowledge and help to the people as long as the people are actively listening. The *manidoog* are of a different type of person, so they may take many different forms as they have the power of metamorphosis, yet they are often tied to particular places. This is often how villages and particular places get their names. The people will encounter a *manidoog* in a particular place, interact with that *manidoog*, and those encounters will help give shape to the names of those *manidoog* and places. These powerful experiences are then told and retold across generations and may eventually make it into the realm of *aadizookaanag*, where they will be brought out in the winter months for the people to remember those lessons.[74]

In this description of Anishinaabeg village life, we can better see the manifestation of the worldview of a web of relatedness in the everyday. The people are intimately connected to each other in a web of familial relatedness, which extends to other communities, the surrounding fauna and flora, and to the ancestors and *manidoog* as manifest in the narratives and the land. Each member of this large community of life is a coequal partner in, and responsible for, the flourishing of all life. Here the ideology of *chidibenjiged* is useful as it represents a focal point or principle that helps to guide actions consistent with this web of relatedness since all things belong. The language of family in the institution of the village provides an inclusive framework for interacting with each other as the people negotiate their lives in the everyday to provide sustenance for each other while simultaneously promoting the flourishing of all life.

When the gaze of this theory of worldview is directed towards eurowestern culture, a very different picture comes to light. Starting with the individual in a family, the person is related to their immediate family as brother, sister, mom, and dad. Moving to an extended family we see grandparents, aunts, uncles, and cousins as still family, but related to a lesser degree according to fractions of blood quantum. As one is distanced from blood relatives, the language of family is no longer used and is replaced with variations depending on the social situation as friend or acquaintance in social settings, and colleague or coworker at work. Again one can see the logic of hierarchy at work as one is distanced from their nuclear family relationships.

When this eurowestern person is engaged in the everyday, their relationships are primarily guided by a hierarchical logic. In church, Christian ideology provides a framework of hierarchy as the Aristotelian Chain of Being is mimicked in Christian theology with God as the apex of existence, followed by Jesus, then the church hierarchy of priests, and lay people.[75] The epitome of this language of hierarchy can be seen in the Anabaptist tradition and the sometimes stated belief that humans are not even worms in the eyes of God.[76] While the language of family is sometimes used for a larger church family, those relationships are very different from those of the Anishinaabeg. In eurowestern culture there are multiple words that people can use to describe one another in a church setting, including friend, acquaintance, brother/sister, enemy, and deacon. In Anishinaabemowin if someone goes to another village, the proper language is that of family as stated above. There simply are not other options to call each other by.

The logic of hierarchy is also prevalent in the ideology of capitalism. Here the best example would be the prominent corporate structure of CEO on top, followed by a group of vice presidents, upper management, middle management, and workers. Here the up-down image schema that cognitive linguists speak of is useful in thinking about the hierarchy of capitalism.[77] If one is to improve their standing in capitalism, they are "climbing the ladder" of success. If someone gets a promotion they are "moving up." In the capitalist ideology, money provides a method and outward manifestation for placement in the social capitalist hierarchy. The more money one makes at work, the more it provides the outward manifestations of that success in the form of houses, cars, and clothes, all clearly identifiable markers of a capitalist hierarchy.[78] The logic of hierarchy is given a pure expression in the ideology of capitalism and the institution of corporate American business as the acquisition of the necessities of food, shelter, clothing, and medicine are directly tied to the achievement of that person on the economic hierarchy in the everyday. This logic of hierarchy is replicated throughout American society, from the nuclear family, to church, and even in the university classroom.

Science as an ideology provides an interesting point of departure for this chapter, as within its trajectory of development in the eurowestern canon we can see a growing dualism in thought. First, in its origin and development into the early twentieth century, there is a clear hierarchical logic involved in thought. This can be seen in scientific taxonomies that use complexity as an organizing mechanism with humans as an organism on top of a hierarchy of biological complexity with amoebas and other single-cell organisms at the bottom. Furthermore there is a significant relationship between the development of science as an ideology and capitalism. The resources necessary to conduct more and more complicated experiments have been funded via the growing capitalist elite. This relationship has kept science in a form of bondage with capitalism, where the development of scientific knowledge has been at the beck and call of capitalism's desire for the creation of more wealth.[79] Scientific experimentation has required more and larger inputs of money to purchase equipment and build facilities for the acquisition of more knowledge. While this sounds benign thus far, it is important to point out that this relationship has favored the capitalist desire for the accumulation of wealth, as it is far more likely to fund experimentation that will result in the improved technologies that will benefit the acquisition of more money. Capitalism has been the driving force behind this trajectory since both science and capitalism have been in the eurowestern conscious.[80] Finally, the anthropocentrism evident in Christian thought also has functioned to influence scientific knowledge. Within the eurowestern canon, humans have been presumed to be superior to and separate from the natural world. This anthropocentric hubris has allowed for the violence and destruction of entire species and ecosystems in the name of development and progress. Not only has this violence manifested over and against the rest of life, but the conceptualizations and theories of human development have consistently used hierarchy as an organizing method in the theories of racialization and sexism that have littered countless scientific books throughout the nineteenth and into the mid-twentieth centuries. In this sense it is clear that the development of scientific knowledge has been guided by the eurowestern logics of hierarchy and the manifestation of colonial power.

However, throughout this same period, even while the bulk of scientific inquiry was directed consciously and unconsciously towards the acquisition of wealth, there has been another trajectory of thought that runs counter to this narrative of the scientific justification for racialized and gendered hierarchies of power. From early in the Enlightenment period there have also been inquiries that demonstrate a common relatedness among different species. While this knowledge of relatedness also spawned the theories of the hierarchies of race, there is also a development of different thought over time.[81] As the eurowestern scientific gaze was fixed upon the local environments both large and small, there has been the recognition of intricate and complex systems of interrelatedness. Within the human body there has been a recognition of not only the complex chemical systems that make up the human body at the cellular and subcellular level, but also the genetic similarity among all humans. Furthermore, scientific inquiry has been able to recognize the complexity and interrelatedness not only of other forms of life with each other, but between humans and those systems. Here the unconscious belief in the separation of humanity from nature has been challenged as the obvious influences of human progress and development have created untold destructions and extinctions for much of the rest of life with which humans share their environments. This trajectory of scientific thought has demonstrated a growing dissonance within eurowestern culture between the longstanding anthropocentric hubris evident in Christianity, capitalism, and much of scientific thought, and the growing theories of interrelatedness in biological and astronomical systems that surround all of us. This dissonance is a welcome issue for many Indigenous peoples as it allows for a new discourse of translation with which to communicate to non-Indigenous peoples about what is happening to our environments and the necessity to reverse those trends. As many of us like to use jokes to discuss this trend of scientific recognitions of the relationships of life, we jest that now, after several hundred years of the development of scientific thought, they are finally catching up to Indigenous knowledge that has been here since time immemorial.

Conclusion

This dualism in eurowestern scientific thought is exemplified in an experience I had at Rocky Mountain National Park. I was part of a class studying environmental conflict resolution and we went on a field trip to Rocky Mountain National Park to discuss some of their work. Particularly, we discussed the controversy surrounding the reestablishment of a wolf population in the park for the purpose of helping to control the elk herds that had become so numerous that they had begun to damage other groups of fauna and flora. Ultimately, we were told, they chose not to bring the wolves back to the park because the land area that the park controls is not big enough to support a healthy wolf population. Furthermore, there was a lot of opposition from local ranchers who feared that the wolves would prey on their livestock. However, this still left the problem of the too-numerous elk herd. Several possibilities were on the table to help control the elk, which included limited public hunts, and even a plan to shoot female elk with a hormonal contraceptive. We were told that the problem in regard to the elk numbers is that they do not have any natural predators in the area.[82] Upon hearing this, without thinking, I blurted out

"WAIT! Are you saying that the Arapahoe, Cheyenne, and Ute peoples had not been hunting elk in these valleys for thousands of years?" I could not believe what I was hearing. No natural predators? While it is understandable that the wolves were not there to do their part, for a national park employee to suggest that humans were not part of this natural environment demonstrates a significant dissonance in the scientific ideology.

This example helps to demonstrate how two competing ideologies can function within a single person and in society as a whole. Clearly, this park employee is a trained scientist and holds the title of research administrator and ecologist. The science behind the intimate relationships between predator and prey regarding the wolves and elk is known in intricate detail, including the positive benefits of such a relationship. However, when the relationship of the local humans to the elk is conceptualized, the deep-seated worldview of dominion over nature and an anthropocentric separation from that natural world took over. Even though this park employee and others who were a part of the elk and wolf discussions had training that must have covered evolutionary biology and the acknowledgment of humans as a developing part of the natural world, according to the language that described the primary problem for the elk, humans were not considered a part of the natural world. This example helps to demonstrate the extraordinary power of a worldview to sustain itself even in the face of contradictory evidence.[83] So strong is the eurowestern belief in the superiority and separation of humans from the natural world as embedded in the logic of dominion that it is evident even in people trained otherwise, who interact with interrelated environments on a daily basis. I should also note that thankfully, the plan for elk contraception was dropped and a supervised hunt for cow elk was conducted for the first time just a few weeks before we went to the park for the visit. Once again, natural predators of the elk were allowed to participate in natural actions to keep the elk herd in check.[84]

This dualism evident in the scientific ideology in the above example is not just a problem for eurowestern peoples. For the Anishinaabeg as well, there is a dissonance between the web of relatedness that is embedded in Anishinaabeg culture and the hierarchy of contemporary eurowestern religious, political, and economic life that we all must negotiate at some level. Even with the considerable decolonization that has happened in the last four decades, this imposed dualism of thought and lived experience represents a constant threat of extinction, which the Anishinaabeg and other Indigenous peoples must contend with. While there have been improvements in the pedagogy and implementation for the survival of

Anishinaabemowin, the time of the lived experience that is consistent with the logic of a web of relatedness still pales in comparison to that spent involved in the day-to-day struggles within eurowestern religious, political, and economic language and thought. This dualism of lived experience creates an ongoing struggle. When we think of the emphasis on action within Anishinaabemowin as a language anchored in the verbs as the center of thought, this problem of dualism comes to the surface. It is not enough to think about being Anishinaabeg. A discursive ontology is a contradiction for a people who are anchored in verbs and action. A full expression of being Anishinaabeg is extraordinarily difficult in contemporary America as the lived expressions and actions associated with that culture are difficult to participate in. The next step in decolonization is to bolster the lifegiving aspects of Anishinaabeg culture and work to regenerate the lifeways that are consistent with the logic of a web of relatedness.

The central place that living out this web of relatedness has in Anishinaabeg culture helps to shed some light on Article 13 of the 1836 Treaty of Washington. Even under the duress of being far from Anishinaabe Akiing to sign away even more land, the *ogimaag* who signed the treaty were still able to press for the stipulations of hunting and fishing on the ceded land until the land was required for settlement. When we take into consideration the power of the worldview of a culture like the web of relatedness for the Anishinaabeg, then we can understand Article 13 from the experience of people who still hunt and fish on the ceded lands today. Not only are we still in Anishinaabe Akiing, hunting, fishing, sugarbushing, collecting firewood, cedar, food, and medicine, we have a lot to show non-Anishinaabeg peoples how one can live in the upper Great Lakes in a lifegiving way. While we still can participate in some of the same activities, many of those activities have been significantly altered. For example, one cannot safely eat fish from the *k'chi gumiing* (the Great Lakes) more than once per week because of the significant levels of toxins in the water. In this sense, when we think about what entails the right to hunt and fish on ceded lands, those rights are directly impacted by the economic and political activities of "settlement." From an Anishinaabeg perspective, the right to fish in the Great Lakes is being violated by the massive amounts of industrial pollutants that have accumulated in the Great Lakes and their associated rivers and streams. These pollutants have infected the food chain and have rendered the fish too toxic to live on, too scarce to catch, or completely annihilated altogether.[85] Clearly, when the right to hunt and fish on ceded lands was written into the Treaty of Washington, it was there to make sure that the surviving Anishinaabeg would have access to a necessary food source. In this way, this food source has been taken away from the Anishinaabeg, and we can think of the polluting of the Great Lakes as a violation of the Treaty of Washington.

The imposition of a hierarchical relationship to "nature" has proven to be more than just discursively problematic for the Anishinaabeg and other peoples who live in the Great Lakes, but the pollution, deforestation, and intentional destruction of Anishinaabeg language and lifeways have manifested in the destruction of important food sources as well. This destruction of food sources has forced people to partake in the hierarchical practices of obtaining primary foodstuffs from capitalist sources where a proper relationship to a piece of meat under cellophane is an impossibility. While one may think that all of these genocidal actions have been effective, we are still here in our homeland. Some of our actions may look different, such as our methods of hunting, our dress, and our modes of transportation, but we are still Anishinaabeg, living in Anishinaabeg Akiing. This survival is a testament to the tenacity of both a people and a worldview. Many of the relationships that were written into the Treaty of Washington in Article 13 are still practiced today. They have been altered, some have changed, but the relationships to the ancestors, our *doodemag*, the *manidoog*, each other, and the rest of life are still available to us. The next step in decolonization is to find ways to strengthen those lifegiving relationships for ourselves and other peoples who are willing to live in a functional relationship.

CHAPTER 5

A Logic of Balance

C losely associated with a web of relatedness is the fourth component of worldview that gives further direction to the actions necessary for living. There is a guiding logic to the action and maintenance of these relationships to the rest of life that help people to conceptualize how to negotiate their daily lives in the acquisition of food, shelter, clothing, and medicine. For the Anishinaabeg, the worldview component that conceptualizes these relationships is a logic of balance that grounds our cultural thought and action. The web of relatedness builds a foundation with the concept of *chidibenjiged*, which recognizes that for us, all things belong. The logical trajectory of thought from the worldview of balance extends this belonging and prescribes the interactions between and within species to make sure that no one species overcomes or devours another to the point of extinction. The logic of balance helps to assure that all of life can flourish as interrelated communities. The richness of life to its fullest extent is highly valued in Anishinaabeg culture, and is given ideological expression as *mino bimaadiziwin*, or the good life.[1] This concept demonstrates an ideological understanding of an overall purpose of Anishinaabeg culture, to promote and diligently work for the flourishing of all life in our lands.

When we reflect on the Treaty of Washington and Article 13 with "the rights of hunting on the land ceded with the other usual privileges of occupancy, until the land is required for settlement," from the Anishinaabeg perspective we know that these conceptualizations are driven by the complementary logics of belonging and balance.[2] The actions of hunting associated with the logic of a web of relatedness as witnessed in the concept of *chidibenjiged* are given shape with the logic of balance. For example, we know that *wawageshkag* (whitetail deer) belong as a community in Anishinaabe Akiing, and that we hunt them for food, clothing, medicine, and tools we can make from their bodies. However, hunting also constitutes an act of violence against these relatives. Here we can think about balance in two meaningful ways. First there is a responsibility for hunters to prepare for the hunt, to purify themselves, and to communicate to the *wawageshkag* that they are coming to hunt in a good way, with a good mind and a good heart. If one is able to kill a deer, then an offering will be given to the deer and it will often be told that it will provide food for the hunter's family and that the family is very thankful that the deer gave its life for that purpose. So in this preparation, kill, and offering for the individual animal, a sense of balance for the act of violence is being sought after. Balance can also be thought of in a second meaningful way. Many communities of animals live in the same land and must negotiate their communal lives with each other. In short, life feeds on other life to survive. If one species were allowed to devour all of its food sources, then it would soon suffer since it would have little to no food left. Hence, the logic of balance has been a guiding force behind the flourishing of all life that even precedes *Giizhigokwe* and the entrance of humans to Turtle Island. Balance is not just an anthropocentric conceptualization of life, it is something that is understood by all of life. Here we can see the second conceptualization of balance as the ebb and flow of an equilibrium between species that depend on each other for life. So from an Anishinaabeg perspective, written into Article 13 of the Treaty of Washington is a cultural knowledge that understands that the right to hunt and gather the necessities for life is guided by a logic that all of life belongs and that we are responsible for participating in actions that help the flourishing of all life. This is an important part of the experience of the Anishinaabeg understanding of this treaty that can be easily missed without a further elaboration of our worldview.

Since the signing of the Treaty of Washington in 1836, Anishinaabe Akiing has been radically altered. While there were once ebbs and flows of complex ecosystems in a positive tension always seeking balance, this was destroyed with clearcutting forests, industrial farming, industrial manufacturing, and energy production, all of which spewed huge amounts of pollutants into the land, water, and air. This "settlement" of Anishinaabe Akiing has meant an ongoing cycle of violence against ecosystems and the flourishing of life that has never recognized these complex interactions between species. Now that we live together in this place, it is possible to reexamine the logics complicit in this destruction and to think through what systems of thought may help to reestablish flourishing for life. The logics of balance as seen through the lens of an Indigenous worldview has a lot to offer in addressing these problems that confront us all.

Mino Bimaadiziwin: The Good Life

Much has been written about *mino bimaadiziwin* in recent scholarship, so much so that one could argue that it has reached a certain fad status in academic writing.[3] However, this attention demonstrates that many people are searching for a better way of life that they are not achieving in contemporary capitalist culture. For that reason, *mino bimaadiziwin* is a concept that is worthwhile spending some time with. In this section I will look at a small number of examples to get at a usable definition and then use that definition to demonstrate a connection to the logic of balance as a component of an Anishinaabe worldview.

A good starting place is an etymological discussion of *mino bimaadiziwin*. *Bimaadizi* is a root verb that means "to live, be alive," and the addition of the suffix *win* changes the verb to a noun.[4] *Mino* is a prefix that simply means "good, nice or well."[5] So from a literal perspective, *mino bimaadiziwin* does translate as "the good life" or "living the good life." However, as a definition, that leaves a lot to be desired. When *mino bimaadiziwin* is uttered in our communities, the culture recognizes a rich set of relationships that demand our attention. It is the attention to those relationships that we now turn to.[6]

One of the more cited references to *mino bimaadiziwin* comes from Winona LaDuke. This should come as no surprise as she is both a well-known Anishinaabekwe and respected leader and activist for Anishinaabe Akiing. In her book *All Our Relations*, she gives a short yet potent discussion of *mino bimaadiziwin* that has struck a chord with many people. She uses this three-page discussion as a conclusion for the chapter titled "White Earth: A Lifeway in the Forest." This discussion makes two important points about *mino bimaadiziwin*. First, she begins the section by stating, "There is no way to quantify a way of life, only a way to live it. *Minobimaatisiiwin* means 'the good life.' Used in blessings, thanksgivings, and ceremonies, it refers to the lifeway."[7] She elaborates on what this Anishinaabe lifeway is by giving examples from people in the White Earth community and the surrounding region. Ronnie Chilton demonstrates that an important time of renewal is in the spring sugarbush, annually making maple syrup and sugar. The activities of the White Earth Land Recovery Project (WELRP) further demonstrate the importance of a relationship to the land, where their actions have helped to reclaim stolen reservation lands and helped to return the sturgeon to the rivers and lakes of the area.[8] Furthermore, these lifeways of intimate relationship with the land and life of Anishinaabe Akiing are demonstrated in the 65 percent of the people on White Earth who hunt for both deer and small game, and almost half of the population who participate in gathering wild rice.[9] Lennie Butcher furthers this discussion with his own hunting activities, stating that "I wasn't born to be rich, I was born to live a good life."[10] These brief examples all push the point of *mino bimaadiziwin* as a lifeway, a praxis, in close relationship with Anishinaabe Akiing and the surrounding life in that land. Secondly, she adds an important element to the definition when she writes, "Like the eternal Spring, after the freezing Winter, there is always a rebirth. *Minobimaatisiiwin. Mi'iw*."[11] Here she makes an important connection of *mino bimaadiziwin* as a constant renewal of life and the lifeway, not only of the fish and the rice, but also of Anishinaabe lifeways themselves. Jim Dumont extends this discussion of the regeneration of Anishinaabe lifeways, stating that "How it will manifest itself and find expression in this new time comes as a part of the responsibility of how we go about the revival and renewal."[12] I would suggest that the attention that *mino bimaadiziwin* has received as a concept is largely predicated on this strong desire to regenerate these Anishinaabe lifeways.

Anishinaabe scholar and activist Leanne Simpson has also worked towards a useful definition of *mino bimaadiziwin* in her book *Dancing on Our Turtle's Back*. In this book she works towards a cogent meaning of this phrase, adding to LaDuke's concept of continuous rebirth that *mino bimaadiziwin* "means living life in a way that promotes rebirth, renewal, reciprocity, and respect."[13] These additions are useful as they help to give a deeper understanding of *mino bimaadiziwin* in an Anishinaabeg context. Here Simpson connects this important concept of a good life not only to the concept of rebirth, but also to the reciprocity that is grounded in the logic of balance. Reciprocity, the act of giving back, is what the hunter is doing when they offer tobacco for the life of the deer. Furthermore, she adds, "although there are many ways to live the good life and that within Nishnaabeg contexts, there is no dichotomy between the 'good life' and the 'bad life,' rather living in a good way is an ongoing process."[14] Here she makes a helpful distinction that the good life associated with *mino bimaadiziwin* should not be conflated with a Manichean framework of good and bad. The good life is sought after by the community; it is the goal that the people work towards. This is important as there is not a heaven-and-hell analogy or a fear tactic used to guide the people toward the good life. *Mino bimaadiziwin* is reason enough to act in ways that help to promote the flourishing of life.

Another useful take on *mino bimaadiziwin* can be seen in the work of language instructor Amy McCoy. Her master's thesis, titled "Minobimaadiziwin: Perceiving the Good Life through Anishinaabe Language," also helps to develop a deeper understanding of the good life in an Anishinaabe context. She emphasizes action and *mino bimaadiziwin* as a "dynamic process, not an 'it' to be understood mechanistically and practiced through routine."[15] Here her discussion mirrors LaDuke and Simpson, naming *mino bimaadiziwin* in a process of cultural rebirth and renewal. Her distinction that *mino bimaadiziwin* cannot be attained through "routine" also helps to comprehend the complex cycle of thought and action that "requires spiritual practice, thought, reflection, interpretation, and reinterpretation."[16] Furthermore she specifically states that "the centrality of minobimaadiziwin is manifest by its intergenerational continuity."[17] While one can say that the concept of intergenerationality is embedded in LaDuke's and Simpson's suggestion of rebirth and renewal, McCoy clearly articulates the long-term process that *mino bimaadiziwin* represents in Anishinaabeg communities. Her qualitative study of Anishinaabeg thought about *mino bimaadiziwin* helps to demonstrate the intergenerational cycle of thought and action that is happening in many Anishinaabeg communities to push beyond survival into flourishing.

Both LaDuke and Simpson make important connections in their brief analyses of *mino bimaadiziwin*. By naming the "good life" as a lifeway, they suggest a grounding in action that is congruent with a verb-based Indigenous language. It is in the participation with the rest of life that *mino bimaadiziwin* is achieved. All three authors emphasize the concepts of rebirth, renewal, and the intergenerational necessity embedded in the actions of the good life. This grounds the definition of *mino bimaadiziwin* in an Anishinaabeg concept of cyclical time. *Mino bimaadiziwin* is not a linear achievement; it is manifest in the ongoing changes in life from birth, growth, maturity, senescence, and rebirth. This helps to demonstrate the interconnected nature of worldview. The logic of balance intersects here with the logic of cyclical time as life in Anishinaabe Akiing continually renews itself.

This intersectionality of Anishinaabeg logic as manifest in *mino bimaadiziwin* is one of the reasons that the concept has taken on a growing importance in many Anishinaabeg communities. It represents a deep ancestral truth about how to regenerate lifegiving actions and communities.

Balancing Narratives

The above discussion of *mino bimaadiziwin* demonstrates a contemporary understanding of "the good life"; but if the logic of balance is a deeper cultural construct, then we must also look to the Anishinaabeg narratives for evidence of its usage. Thankfully, this is a relatively easy task, as balance as a logic is embedded as an object lesson in a significant number of Anishinaabeg narratives. Also, for better or worse, quite a few of these examples are already in print.[18] This section will give evidence of balance as a worldview in Anishinaabeg narratives.

Considering Basil Johnston's prolific publishing career, it should come as no surprise that some of these narratives have been published in his books. More importantly for this topic of balance, two of his more recent endeavors have focused on this subject. Both *Walking in Balance: Meeyau-ossaewin*, and *Living in Harmony: Mino-nawae-indawaewin* present narratives centered on these concepts of balance and harmony.[19] These two books are important because they make these narratives accessible and offer them in English and in Anishinaabemowin. This inclusion of both languages is a bold step in centering Anishinaabemowin where it can be recognized and used as first-language instruction and competency. It is interesting to note that in these narratives, Johnston chooses the terms balance and harmony as the titles as opposed to a description of *mino bimaadiziwin*. Here we can see a slightly different take on the concept of achieving a balanced life.

One of the representative narratives from *Walking in Balance* that demonstrates the central place of balance in Anishinaabeg culture is titled "Never Take More Than . . ." Johnston begins this narrative with the statement that "Our ancestors were fond of saying: 'Don't take more than you need. There is more than enough for everybody, more than enough.'"[20] The narrative then goes on to discuss *Nana'b'oozoo* and his difficulty obtaining enough food for his family. For this failure he was ridiculed by his wife, and his children would ask why the other hunters were better than their father. In his travels, he asked some heron (a large water bird) for help. The heron first discussed amongst themselves whether or not they should help him. They agreed that "If it was only *Nana'b'oozoo* I [they] wouldn't help him one bit. Let him help himself. But let us help the children. Are we not supposed to be 'Good People' caring for others?"[21] So the heron tell him how to successfully get fish, with the warning that "If you need three trout take them but not more. They'll be there tomorrow."[22] Then, like clockwork, *Nana'b'oozoo* proceeds to follow the directions to catch the fish, but caught up in his success, fails to stop at three trout and catches more than he and his son can carry home. When he returns to the site of the fish with his wife to help carry them home, they have turned into ice. Once again, *Nana'b'oozoo* failed to become a successful fisherman.

The object lesson of the narrative is obvious: *Nana'b'oozoo* was unable to feed himself and his family because he failed to follow the basic directions of all animals, never take more than what you need. This is a consistent theme of narratives too numerous to mention. However, there are other points to make about this narrative that may not be so obvious to all of the readers. First, the concept of the "Good People" is invoked by the heron, clearly aligning them with the Anishinaabeg in the narrative. This suggests that it is not only we as humans who understand this concept of balance as taking only what you need, but the other animals comprehend this teaching as well. We also see the power of community in this telling. As the heron describe, if it were only *Nana'b'oozoo* they might let him suffer because he has shown that he often does not follow directions. However, since he is responsible for feeding his family, he is given advice on how to catch the fish. The importance of community for the Anishinaabeg associated with *Nana'b'oozoo* are invoked simultaneously with the trout. The Anishinaabeg can be sustained by the trout if they only take what they need. If they take too many trout then they will be at risk of depleting the population. This lesson is told and retold in many narratives.[23]

In his book *Living in Harmony*, Johnston continues the retelling of narratives in English and Anishinaabemowin as well as the concepts involved in living in harmony with the rest of life. In the narrative titled "The Last Shall Have Leftovers," he elaborates the desire for harmony between species. This narrative describes how the birds got their colors. Johnston begins, "A long time ago all birds were white. Crows, ducks, pigeons, hawks, eagles, turkeys, ravens, owls were white in color."[24] They needed no color to distinguish themselves because they knew each other by their voices and their songs. However, upon coming to a powwow held in the spring by *Pukawiss* to celebrate the renewal of life, they were questioned as to why they were not painted.[25] It was explained that the other species could not tell them apart, so they decided to let *Pukawiss* paint them at his lodge the next day. All of the birds showed up to get painted and *Pukawiss* sat at his work all day, painting one after the other using their favorite colors and patterns. In an attempt to be the prettiest bird, Raven, Jay, Seagull, and Eagle ran to the back of the line. Johnston explains, "While the other birds were being painted, these four were jostling and doing what they could do to outwit the other so that one of them would be last and gain the advantage of outdoing his rivals in the beauty of his dress."[26] Raven and Eagle fought the most, ultimately leading Raven to pummel Eagle's head with his beak and knock all of the feathers out of it. However, Jay was fourth from last and got the blue he was looking for, and Seagull was satisfied with a little bit of gray for his wings and back, with a touch of gold for his eyes. Next was Eagle; still steaming from the beating he received, he demanded, "I want all the colours!"[27] However, *Pukawiss* replied that he no longer had all the colors to choose from, just brown, white, and gold. Sore from his beating, Eagle flew away and watched as Raven took his place as last to be painted. He too exclaimed, "I want all the colours!" but now all that was left was black.[28]

Once again, the object lesson is obvious: that fighting amongst each other to be the best looking will turn against you. However, relating this narrative to the specifics of Anishinaabeg culture will take some more coaxing for many readers. First, *Pukawiss* takes on the task of helping to form life into the colors that we recognize today. His is an important role as one of *Winona*'s sons who help to teach the Anishinaabeg how to live in the world appropriately. This helps to demonstrate the multiple actors involved in shaping the world into what it is that we know today. Hence, discussions of a single "creator" do not fit with the larger corpus of Anishinaabeg narratives. Secondly, when we go to dances, we have traditionally painted ourselves in a vast array of colors and ways that represent our *doodemag*, or clans.[29] This phenomenon of painting is not practiced as often today, but can be important as an expression of *doodem* relationship in a community setting. There is a built-in irony to the story that it is *Pukawiss* who teaches about the problems of vanity since he struggles with that himself. This leads to the more obvious object lesson that while painting is beneficial for the community, the relationship to this painting must be kept in balance as vanity can lead to social disharmony. The harmony of the community comes first.[30]

The narratives that Johnston shares help to further the discussion of the embedded logic of balance as a worldview in Anishinaabeg culture. They ground these concepts within the structure of Anishinaabeg narrative culture, which demonstrates them as deeply held and old beliefs.[31] This aspect of worldview is reproduced each time the narratives are told and retold to successive generations of people. When the narrative of the heron is uttered in a room of people, they are reminded of the necessity of taking only what you need, as taking more throws communities of other life out of balance. It may be more accurate to say, never take anything without thinking of the economic and ethical consequences of your actions. In times of drought it would be necessary to take very little of some things since they are struggling during that time. In the years of an exceptionally good fish run, it would be okay to take more and store it for the coming months since there is an ample supply. It is important to push this analysis to a greater complexity since the on-the-ground situations necessitate complex thought. When this narrative was told, it would call all of this experiential complexity into the room with it. When the narrative of *Pukawiss* painting the birds is spoken, it reinforces the need for social harmony both within and between species. For these harmonies to be maintained, we must be thankful for what we get and not aspire to better than our own community, or any other community of life. These narratives and others like them demonstrate the underlying logic of harmony between species. This logic of balance is represented in the ideology of *mino bimaadiziwin*, structured in ceremonial places like *madootsiwan* (purification or sweat lodge), and performed in the everyday as tobacco and food offerings as we always work towards that balance.

Homeostasis, Equilibrium, and the Logic of Balance

While balance is a concept that can be considered common knowledge, we cannot assume that balance is understood as a dynamic system of interrelated ecosystems in constant complex tension with each other. It is just that type of complex thinking that is represented in the Anishinaabeg logic of balance. Here it is helpful to think about Kwasi Wiredu's conception of parallel translations as a means of testing the validity of this discussion. As we will see, it is necessary to connect the concept of balance to a larger discussion of medical and ecological knowledge where the dynamic interplay of complex systems is more clearly articulated. The eurowestern terms homeostasis, equilibrium, and harmony together provide a deeper understanding of complex systems in collaborative tension with one another. While none of these concepts individually carry the entire meaning of Anishinaabeg logic, together they can provide a cogent translation that can allow a non-Anishinaabeg person to comprehend what is being communicated in this worldview.

Basil Johnston helps to push us towards a complex understanding of balance with his shift to harmony. The narratives that he uses make clear that "When our people speak of 'living in harmony' they mean that people should live in good will and peace as men and women of the same blood ought to work and live together in friendship. They used 'mino-inawau-daumoowin' or 'mino-nawaemaugaewin' to express this special kinship with other beings."[32] Here the association of good relationships is close to the notion of harmony as "order or congruity of parts to their whole or to one another."[33] It is no surprise that Johnston would use this as a translation as singing, music, and dancing are so important in Anishinaabe culture. His use of harmony in association with narratives (especially with *Pukawiss*, the dancer and singer) gives an artistic feel to the notion of Anishinaabe culture as the building of rich complementary relationships. Here Johnston pushes towards a deeper understanding of an Anishinaabe logic of balance.

We can also move further towards a meaningful definition of the logic of balance as we once again turn to the scientific knowledge of medicine and ecology. The concepts of equilibrium and homeostasis offer possibilities of coming to deeper understandings of the Anishinaabe worldview. When we think about the concept of equilibrium as "a condition in which all influences acting upon it are cancelled by others, resulting in a stable, balanced or unchanging system," we can see some possibilities for comprehending the dynamics of a complex system.[34] In the English language we see the use of equilibrium to denote the result of a complex system working effectively to balance itself out. Equilibrium is thought of as a system achieving its optimal status. From the Anishinaabe side, it is useful to think of equilibrium as a goal that is sought after as communities of life relate to one another. The goal of *mino bimaadiziwin* is the continual rebirth or annual reproduction of that complex system of life. Here it is important to make two points. First, balance is achieved through having life and death alternating. Life and death balance each other out in the yearly cycle of birth, growth, senescence, purity, and rebirth. The cycle is balanced by having both life and death built into it. Secondly, within Anishinaabe thought, balance is a goal we work to attain, but do not always achieve individually. Hence, we have narratives of people falling short of their responsibilities and needing ceremony to restore them and their relationships with appropriate offerings and behavior.[35] This suggests a recognition of our own failures, and this fallibility extends to other animals as well. *Mino bimaadiziwin* is not a perfect norm from which we deviate, but a dynamic system in which we participate, each form of life working to sustain itself and others in the process.

Equilibrium as a "stable, balanced and unchanging system" works well as the stated goal of the Anishinaabeg worldview of balance, not as the day-to-day reality.

From the eurowestern medical terminology, homeostasis also pushes us down the road of a meaningful discussion of the Anishinaabe logic of balance. Homeostasis can be defined as "the tendency of an organism or cell to regulate its internal conditions, such as the chemical composition of its body fluids, so as to maintain health and functioning, regardless of outside conditions. The organism or cell maintains homeostasis by monitoring its internal conditions and responding appropriately when these conditions deviate from their optimal state."[36] The regulation of body temperature is an example of homeostasis where humans can sweat to release too much heat when the internal temperature gets too high, or shiver to create more heat when the temperature is too low. We can extend this recognition of a dynamic thermoregulatory system to other processes in life as in cellular respiration or the maintenance of ecosystems. In homeostasis we can see the regulatory processes at work to demonstrate the possibility of agency in the actions of regulation. The human body receives feedback from temperature receptors and then acts to correct if the temperature deviates from its optimal state. This happens both at the unconscious level of shivering to generate heat, and at the conscious level of adding clothing or moving to a warmer area. This recognition that there will be moments that deviate from the desired norm (equilibrium) built within the meaning of homeostasis is helpful in describing the logic of balance. In Anishinaabe conceptualizations of interacting with the rest of life, there are methods of reading the signs that our relatives offer us. A hard winter that is cold with a lot of snowfall will be difficult on the local deer, who will struggle to find enough to eat, but this would offer hibernating animals like bears relatively easy access to protein when they come out of their dens from the deer who have died.[37] In this case, the deer may be down in numbers over a period of a few years while the bear may have an initial boost of numbers the next year as those cubs born will have good access to food.[38] Here we can see an ecological example of the complex interactions between species, which can recognize imbalance in a larger system (deer dying off) and a reaction to that imbalance (bears eating well.) Homeostasis offers a useful conceptualization of the logic of balance as it can encapsulate a significant amount of complex interactions in its meaning.

Balance as a concept is a useful translation for an Anishinaabe worldview, but to fully grasp the complexity of an Anishinaabeg conceptualization of the world, this meaning must be given an added depth. This is where the concepts of equilibrium and homeostasis help to highlight the dynamic complexities of the interactions of life. Following Wiredu's method of testing translations, balance in and of itself would not pass the test as it does not necessarily communicate a dynamic interplay of multiple entities working together as a much larger system. Here equilibrium helps to comprehend the optimal state of *mino bimaadiziwin*, and homeostasis offers a useful understanding of a complex system regulating itself towards the goal (or goals) of equilibrium. Balance, expanded in meaning by equilibrium and homeostasis, offers a much more accurate translation of this Anishinaabe logic. It is also important to think about this logic of balance as a system of thought that is much more than an anthropocentric musing about nature. It is a logic that is understood by all of life from the micro (cellular and subcellular) to the macro (ecosystems and biospheres). It is not a human invention, but an intelligent recognition of the methodical functioning of life learned by paying attention to our elder relatives and the lessons that they offer us. It is this intelligent learning that is represented in the Anishinaabe narratives that remind us of these lessons about how to properly interact with our relatives. The Anishinaabe worldview of balance is the logical incorporation of those teachings over time.

A Logic of Balance in Cultural Theory

Now that we have a better understanding of an Anishinaabeg logic of balance, we can further demonstrate this worldview as it plays out in the culture. As I have already discussed, *mino bimaadiziwin* is an ideological manifestation of that logic of balance which helps to give conscious direction for the development of institutions and experiences that promote the flourishing of life. Again, if we think about the institution of the *doodem* we can begin to see how this worldview is acted out in the village. The *doodem* is the instrument of acquisition and distribution of the necessities of life, including food, shelter, clothing, and medicine. It is within the *doodem* structure that these goods are sought after, acquired, and distributed. The *doodem* family structure teaches these ethical standards associated with the logic of balance and provides the accountability to maintain these standards.

Each *doodem* provides leadership for their specific relationship to life for the larger Anishinaabe community, so the *makwa doodem* (bear clan) has certain responsibilities for making sure that ceremonies involving bears are actualized.

More often than not, one cannot kill or eat their own *doodem*, so a member of the bear clan cannot kill bears, but can use bear medicines taken from the animal with proper ceremony. These practices help to maintain balance not only within the *doodem*, as it would be cannibalistic to eat of your own kind (bear clan eating a bear), but also for the larger relationships of all the people of the village to the bears in that area. Problems could occur if the rituals associated with bear hunting or use of bear medicines were allowed to deviate from their prescribed norms. In this way, the *doodemag* together provide the maintenance of a complex set of relationships with the local flora and fauna as they perform ceremonies that help to maintain the health and wellbeing of these relationships. As many of our narratives remind us, when we fail to perform these ceremonies, these relationships can be altered. The love and power associated with these relationships is not unconditional; they come with significant responsibility. Again we can go to the concept of *doodem* as translated as a noun, but that belies the power of responsibility that comes with a *doodem*. It is important to remember that within Anishinaabe thought the focus is on verbs and actions, so a *doodem* is primarily understood in the actions that are associated with that clan. These actions not only keep the larger community in balance with the local environment, but they also keep the ceremonies going, the people fed, clothed, in good health, and if done well, they will also be laughing along the way.

I have already described some of these rituals and ceremonies that are necessary to maintain proper relationships as people are going about their daily business of acquiring food, shelter, clothing, and medicine, so I can be brief here. Often, when one is harvesting food either from plant or animal life, it is thanked for what it is providing and a small offering of tobacco is given for the life that is being taken. This type of offering is about demonstrating the recognition of that life as valuable. It is the mindfulness of those relationships that should be emphasized in this interaction. Furthermore, as the narrative of *Nana'b'oozoo* and the heron demonstrates, it is essential that we only take what we need for the basics of life. Greed is destructive to multiple forms of life since it is not just humans who count on those plants and animals for sustenance. For the optimal state of relationships to be realized, we must participate in ways that promote the flourishing of all life. When we are mindful of our actions and take only what we need, then we are working to promote *mino bimaadiziwin* as we go about getting our own sustenance. In this way our actions help to reinforce the narratives of the heron, *mino bimaadiziwin*, and the logic of balance.

I have already begun to discuss the eurowestern conceptualizations of the interrelatedness of life in the medical and ecological fields. The concepts of equilibrium and homeostasis are indications that eurowestern scientific knowledge is capable of understanding the complex interrelatedness of life. However, within the eurowestern framework of thought, this comprehension of the complexity of life is compartmentalized within particular fields of knowledge, in this instance in medical and ecological knowledge. These subcategories of eurowestern thought lack the ethical connections to more powerful societal agents such as political and economic systems. Hence, the ethical concerns that are brought out by the actions of mining, deforestation, energy production, and corporate farming can fall on deaf ears as those industries do not have to be held accountable to ecological standards unless relevant laws are passed in the political process. While there have been and certainly still are attempts by environmental groups to rein in mining, energy, and lumber companies' actions within the political process of the United States Government, these are extraordinarily difficult to negotiate considering the significant budgets that these companies have to fight against environmental legislation. Corporations have the financial power to influence the political process to create legal buffers around their endeavors that function to deny ethical claims that can be made. Furthermore, they not only have the power to decide what ethical standards they can be held accountable to, they also have the power to help influence public opinion with media messaging.[39] These conflicting desires for ethical consideration of ecological systems do not have an Anishinaabeg equivalent. In an Anishinaabe village everybody is held accountable to the same ethical standard, which is in the logical extension of the logic of balance.[40]

Good and Evil as a Relational Method

The logic of the eurowestern worldview that conceptualizes its relationships to the rest of life is a Manichean dualism of good versus evil. This dualism has been crafted and applied to many relationships within the historical development of its thought. This Christian formulation has taken on many other names, but the logic stays consistent. The same logic embedded in the good/evil dualism is also animating the civilized/savage, light/dark, farmer/hunter, and city/wilderness dualisms. Each of these dualisms follows the same logical pattern in the process of colonization where the civilized eurowestern must defeat the savage, light must triumph over dark in all of its racialized meaning, the farmer will win out over the hunter, and the establishment of civilized cities will overpower and tame the wilderness. Here we can see the logic of singular universality where the dualism is a conflict that must be resolved to satisfy the logic. Of course, for this logic to continually function there must be a fresh supply of dualisms to overcome. Hence, when we follow some of the political and economic trajectories of the United States Government and its associated corporatocracy, we can see this Manicheanism continually play out. As Indian people we were the original colonial fodder on which eurowestern powers cut their teeth as they eradicated, killed, and then civilized in the march across this continent. Once that process was considered complete at the turn of the twentieth century, new and improved enemies were found to continue the process. Here politics and economics get conflated in the communist threat and the Cold War, as the godless communists were considered to be always on the point of taking over the country to outlaw our freedoms. This threat followed its course and was eventually eradicated, only to be followed by the threat of radical Islam and their hatred of our freedoms. Free-market democracy is the only singular, universal, legitimate political and economic system that continues its civilizing mission for the whole world.

When applied to the rest of life, this Manichean dualism has laid waste to millions of acres of forests and gouged huge holes in the earth's crust in the name of profit. In this process, the wilderness is "tamed" so that there are materials to build the cities. In this system of thought, the worldview of Manichean dualisms is manifest in the ideology of free-market democracy. The Manicheanism from Christianity has been extended into the political and economic realms in the colonial process and has functioned well to justify the takeover of other people and places in the name of God, democracy, and/or capitalism. These ideologies have spawned institutions, called corporations and the Department of the Interior, that administrate the destruction of lands for the purpose of profit and the manifestation of the "universal" true culture. These institutions then administer the daily actions of mining, lumber, and energy production at the expense of the rest of life. The workers are rewarded for their service with a paycheck, which reinforces the institutions from which it came and the ideology that it serves.

While this sketch is correct in its brief description of the manifestation of Manichean dualism as a eurowestern worldview, there are resistances to this manifestation of colonial destruction. There are attempts to rein in corporate pollution and destruction within eurowestern culture in the environmental movements in the twentieth century, but there has been little movement in that direction.[41] Here we can see the current dissonance in the eurowestern system of thought as many people want to espouse the goals of being kind to nature with actions like recycling and reusing, but the capitalist system of production and consumption allows very little movement in that direction so that it can continue to make profits. The logic of Manichean dualism is still very much intact within political and economic thinking, even though there has been a growing concern about the destruction of the planet. However, we are so dependent upon capitalism to provide the basics of food, shelter, clothing, and medicine in the United States that living outside of that destructive system is considered an impossibility, and even moderately altering the consumption patterns of people is a significant challenge. These larger changes, which some environmentally conscious people are looking for, are nowhere to be found in the same worldview that has created the problems in the first place.

Conclusion

The eurowestern worldview and its Manichean logic based on the presumption of a singular universal offers a particular way of negotiating relationships with the rest of life. However, contrary to what the mantra of eurowestern universalism is as perpetrated through colonialism, it is not the only way of negotiating these relationships. The Anishinaabe worldview provides a very different trajectory of thought that functions to prescribe the interactions between species. This logic of balance promotes the flourishing of all life and is demonstrated in two powerful ways. First, the concept of *mino bimaadiziwin* is an ideological manifestation of this worldview, which prescribes the relationships between life not just as the "good life," but as the rebirth, renewal, and intergenerational lifeways that are congruent with cyclical time. While *mino bimaadiziwin* has received a lot of attention as of late, it is a concept that has been around for a long time in our communities and is indicative of a growing interest in living a life more closely associated with Anishinaabeg logics and teachings. In this way, *mino bimaadiziwin* has been a useful ideological concept in the ways that it has provided a focal point for the dialogical relationship of thought and action around Anishinaabe cultural renewal. Secondly, Anishinaabe narratives offer a powerful pedagogical tool for teaching people about the logic of balance that is embedded in the cultural teachings. As Basil Johnston consistently demonstrates, the lifeways associated with living in harmony and balance with the rest of life are in the narratives for us to think about, hear, speak, and discuss in our communities. Countless narratives demonstrate not only the consequences of failing to live up to our responsibilities to the rest of life but also the benefits when we do. What we see here in regard to the Anishinaabe worldview are the complementary actions of old (narratives) and new (attention to *mino bimaadiziwin*) working together to return the people closer to Anishinaabe lifeways.

It is necessary to return to those lifeways because we were pushed so very far away from them in the process of colonization. The 1836 Treaty of Washington represents an important moment in that push as it ceded much of what is now known as Michigan. The overemphasis on boundaries, the parcels of land for a few individuals, and the fact that the treaty "negotiations" took place in Washington, DC, all represent significant shifts away from the ability to properly participate in relationships grounded in an Anishinaabe worldview. Yet, Article 13 still reminds us of the agency of the treaty signers and their ability to still put in the "right to hunt on ceded lands and the usual privileges of occupancy." Once again, we must think about what this article means in accordance with an Anishinaabe worldview that is necessary to fully comprehend the heteroglossia of Article 13. For hunting and other activities to be able to take place, there must be a certain amount of space available for there to be intact ecosystems. However, as we saw throughout the twentieth century and into the twenty-first, the space available for ecosystems to negotiate their own complex sets of relationships was thrown out of balance. The extent of environmental destruction wrought on Anishinaabe Akiing has only continued and reached an extent where much of the land and waters are unrecognizable from what they were when this treaty was signed. *Mino bimaadiziwin* is now called into question, not just for a few species, but for all of us who still live here.

Conclusion

A n analysis of the 1836 Treaty of Washington offers a range of possibilities for Anishinaabeg. While legal theorists can negotiate the technical language of the treaty and its contemporary meanings, that analysis can miss the deeper cultural meanings represented in Article 13. Now that we have a more thorough understanding of an Anishinaabeg worldview and its associated ideologies, institutions, and everyday experiences, we are in a better position to comprehend just what was being protected in that article from our own perspective. When we think of that treaty negotiation and signing, we can get a picture of not only a world in flux, but also the spatial grounding and the relationships at stake in "the right to hunt and the other usual privileges of occupancy."[1] Even though in the leadup to Michigan statehood there was greater economic and political pressure being placed on the Anishinaabeg, much of the Indigenous lifeway was still intact. While some of the furbearing animals had been depleted, there still was access to fish and other game, not to mention the gardens and other cultivated crops like blueberries in the area. Ceremonies like *madootsiwan* (purification lodge) and *Midewiwin* ceremonies were still taking place (among many others). There were still Indigenous medicines available and people to properly use those treatments.

In the villages, *doodemag* (clans) are still intact for the purpose of identity and leadership. Anishinaabemowin was still the primary language being spoken, though a few people had learned to speak and write in English at this time. In short, the Anishinaabe lifeways associated with the worldview of an intimate relationship to localized space, cyclical time, living in a web of relatedness with life in balance were still largely intact. Some of the specific cultural experiences were altered, such as clothing, utensils, some living quarters, and hunting tools and traps, yet the logics embedded in the worldview were still congruent with the ideologies, institutions, and everyday experiences of Anishinaabeg. At the same time there were eurowestern economic experiences, institutions, and ideologies that had caused a certain dissonance in Anishinaabeg communities. Our communities were also still reeling from the ongoing diseases that had dwindled our population down and shaken the confidence in our methods of handling disease. It is these altered but intact communities that the treaty signers came from.[2] They were shipped off to Washington, DC, and after they were given a tour of the manifestations of American exceptionalism and power, they were ushered into rooms to negotiate away much of their homeland.

Since the socio-ideological horizon of the U.S. Government and their agents is so radically different from the Anishinaabeg, from their perspective, the experience of the Treaty of Washington was quite different. This treaty represents their dominion over the land as part of the linear progress of Manifest Destiny. They assumed the top position in their imposed hierarchy of relationships and were vanquishing the primitive other in their march from sea to shining sea. I believe that it is safe to say that the American treaty negotiators fully believed in their own presumed superiority and knew full well that the primitive races of people before them would either assimilate into God's chosen people or would fade away in the face of such a superior race. Hence this treaty was all but a foregone conclusion, and necessary to make the hostile takeover of Anishinaabe Akiing seem like an honorable and legal change in title. Ultimately, this treaty and many others like it were necessary steps to make the takeover of Indigenous lands seem like it was done with all of the legality and civility associated with American exceptionalism and its latent white supremacy.

Thankfully, these Anishinaabe *ogimaag* (leaders) had the foresight to "stipulate for the rights of hunting and the other privileges of occupancy."[3] However, it is difficult to translate just what is embedded in that utterance of Article 13 from their perspective. Hunting is not to be confused with a leisurely activity for the elite or even an economic subsistence activity. Embedded in the utterance of Article 13 is a snapshot of an entire way of life that is to be preserved if we are to take the treaty seriously. To properly understand what this treaty represents, it is necessary to take a deeper look at the worldview and culture of the Anishinaabeg from within the frameworks of thought and language that we use to negotiate the world. We must engage this retranslation of Anishinaabemowin and Anishinaabe thought to break through the colonial confusion that has come to impose its definitions and meaning onto Anishinaabe and other Indigenous peoples. These carefully crafted myths of the Indian as primitive held in anachronistic time, whose identity is defined by their historical use of material culture, have created false knowledge of an entire continent of peoples. Hence, it is necessary to both critically define worldview and give particular examples from within Anishinaabemowin to accurately articulate the meaning of Article 13.

Using a definition of worldview as an interrelated set of cultural logics that orient a culture to space (land), time, the rest of life, and provides a prescription for how to relate to that life, gives us a starting place to comprehend the cultural depth of Article 13. In this orientation to land for Anishinaabeg we see a logic of an intimate relationship to a localized space. This intimate relationship can be seen in the language in multiple sites like place names, those villages as centers of spatial location, and concepts like *Mazikaamikwe*, or Earth Mother. However, the depth of this intimacy is best seen in Anishinaabe ontology. From the verb *ayaa*, or to be, we can see more than just a surface relationship to land. The use of this verb is only intelligible when it is related to a particular place; hence its definition really is "to be, in a certain place."[4] This ontological position demonstrates the deep connection that we have to our land. Literally, there is no intelligible existence outside of a particular spatial location. This has significant repercussions for the translations of concepts like *manidoog*, or the quasi-material life energies. Spirit, as a nonspatial and nonmaterial entity, cannot communicate the spatial intimacy embedded in the Anishinaabe worldview and the logic of intimate relationships to localized space. In this sense, if this translation of *manidoog* as spirit is allowed to stand, it works to erase this ontological intimacy in space. Even though it is clear in the language of the Treaty of Washington that we were supposed to be removed west of the Mississippi River, the Anishinaabe *ogimaag* still insisted on the inclusion of Article 13.[5] Furthermore, removal from Anishinaabe Akiing was successfully resisted, and many of us still resided in the ceded territory that would become the State of Michigan.

The logic of cyclical time is also part of Article 13. Even though the treaty language uses a terminus of twenty years for annuity payments, Article 13 is free from any such limit of time. While Anishinaabemowin can negotiate both cyclical and linear time, the logic that fundamentally orients the culture in its space is clearly cyclical. As Hallowell was able to correctly identify, *giizhig* (day) and *dibiki giizis* (moon) are not divisions of continuous time, they are recurring events.[6] Anishinaabeg culture follows this cyclical logic throughout the *giizhig*, *dibiki giizis*, the seasons, and the year, celebrating this cycle of rebirth of *Ziigwan* (spring), growth of *Niibin* (summer), senescence of *Dagwaagin* (autumn), and the purity of *Biboon* (winter), all to begin again as signaled by *Makwa Giizis*, bear moon (February). Each season had its own economic activities and sets of narratives that helped to give meaning to village life and activity. It is easy to see that this way of life is free from notions of linear progress and the project of development. The Anishinaabeg world is about the annual rebirth and flourishing of all of life as a primary purpose of us all being in this place.

This concept of flourishing is essential to understand if we are to intelligently interpret Article 13. In the subsequent years since 1836, missionary, traveler, and anthropologist accounts of our culture have imposed a concept of a struggle to survive. While under colonial control this did become true in the loss of economic resources and culture, it was not always the case. The starting place for understanding our worldview and the logic of a web of relatedness is the flourishing of all life. For Anishinaabeg, this flourishing is just what we experienced as part of this large web of related life in Anishinaabe Akiing. From the *aadizookaanag* (origin and ideological narratives) we have learned from our elder relatives who were already here when *Giizhigokwe* came to this place that there are proper ways to relate to each other. The concept of *chidibenjiged* helps to conceptualize these proper interactions since it *makes all things belong*. This belonging provides a grounding ideology for proper relationships as it necessitates careful action in how a group of people negotiate their way through the world to provide themselves with food, shelter, clothing, and medicine using their relatives. This logic of the web of relatedness and the ideology of *chidibenjiged* functions to promote the flourishing of all life because it helps to keep in check the greed or carelessness that could result in the extinction of a relative. Furthermore, that life is linguistically conceptualized as family relationships demonstrates the level of reverence involved in this web. This recognition of relatedness is embedded in Article 13. For Article 13 to make any sense, there must be a continuation of that related life in Anishinaabe Akiing. While it is written in English and does not specify this web, considering that the Anishinaabe *ogimaag* spoke Anishinaabemowin and negotiated this web of relatedness in the everyday, it would be ridiculous to suggest that their negotiation of relationships with the rest of life would not follow this logic taught to us by our elder relatives.

Closely associated with the web of relatedness is the logic of balance. This fourth logic of worldview complements relatedness by providing a prescription of how to negotiate those relationships. This notion of balance, as imbued with a sense of complex dynamic relationships of harmony, homeostasis, and equilibrium, represents a guiding principle that shapes interactions with life to achieve the goal of the flourishing of life. *Mino bimaadiziwin* is an ideological manifestation of this logic of balance that is representative of the rebirth, renewal, and intergenerational lifeways that are congruent with cyclical time. *Mino bimaadiziwin* as the good life is used as a linguistic tool to evoke memory of flourishing and the desire to return to that state of being in Anishinaabe Akiing. When the logic of balance is followed in our relationships with the rest of life through the daily and yearly cycles of time in Anishinaabe Akiing, then life can flourish. While there had been some altering of Anishinaabe Akiing with the fur trade, the flourishing of life was still very much intact in 1836. There would also be a communal memory of life with more beaver and what that meant for the logic of balance. That balance had been shifted, but the availability of food, shelter, clothing, and medicine was still abundant for the Anishinaabeg at this time. From this perspective, Article 13 can be seen as an attempt to secure what flourishing there still was for the benefit of the Anishinaabeg communities and the rest of life for future generations.

When these interrelated logics of an intimate relationship to space, cyclical time, living in a web of relatedness, and a prescription of balance are used as a linguistic-conceptual method for analyzing the Treaty of Washington and Article 13, we can come to a much better understanding of why this article was included and what it actually means. Anishinaabemowin is the only vehicle that can help to elucidate this worldview as it provides the proper articulation of these fundamental orienting logics. As I have demonstrated, Anishinaabemowin, when carefully translated from an authentic starting place within the proper cultural framework, can function as a corrective against the assumed colonial universality in eurowestern culture. Eurowestern religious language embedded within nonspatial and nonmaterial meaning cannot effectively comprehend our intimate relationships to localized space. The colonial logic of dominion over land, given divine sanction by religious language and codified in the United States legal system, is both unwilling and incapable of comprehending Anishinaabeg relationships to land. After 1836, the Anishinaabeg and our relatives with whom we share this land would come to suffer under the control of this foreign set of logics.

After 1836, what was left of flourishing would continually deteriorate in the face of colonial expansion, as lumber, mining, and agricultural interests would pave the way for the "development" of steel, and eventually the automobile industry, all spewing pollution into the land, water, and air. Life in Anishinaabe Akiing, for us and all of our relatives, would quickly move from flourishing to a struggle for survival under the logics of capitalism and the extraction of wealth from the land at the expense of almost all of its inhabitants. This period saw not only the oppression of the land, but also the theft of generations of children into the boarding school death camps, where they had the Indigenous stripped from and beaten out of them. When the children were stolen away, this left a significant void in the communities where they were taken from, trading the children for the trauma of loss. The inherent racism of the twentieth century only compounded these problems. The boarding school survivors who were able to eventually return to their communities came back with little to no knowledge of parenting except for the violence they experienced by boarding school staff. This violence and abuse was then internalized and practiced within our own communities, often by our own people.[7] This social dysfunction was then lifted up as evidence of our inferiority in comparison to the civility of the white, patriarchal nuclear family and community, thereby erasing the previous century of brutal violence that was perpetrated on our families and communities.

But memory can be amazing. People experienced varying degrees of violence, and through it, some still were able to speak Anishinaabemowin, attend ceremony, and live in close relationship with the rest of life. This more traditional way of life was altered, yet still available as many people began returning to the ceremonies, the language, and back towards the relationships that are healing. As this returning shifted into movements, communal actions began taking place all over the country. As the American Indian Movement was gaining momentum with the Trail of Broken Treaties and the Wounded Knee Occupation, in Anishinaabe Akiing, Albert Leblanc set his gill nets in *Kichi Gumeeng* (Lake Superior) in accordance with the 1836 Treaty of Washington and Article 13. This was in defiance of State of Michigan rules prohibiting the use of gill nets. This case would eventually go the Michigan Supreme Court, and was adjudicated in favor of Anishinaabeg and our treaty rights.[8]

This was part of the trajectory of fishing rights controversies that were roiling in Michigan, Wisconsin, and Minnesota throughout the 1980s as Anishinaabeg and other Indigenous peoples were participating in their ancestral traditions, which were protected under this treaty.[9] This would eventually lead to the 2007 Inland Consent Decree, an agreement between the Anishinaabeg Nations who signed the 1836 Treaty of Washington, the State of Michigan, and the U.S. Government. This decree was a legal agreement covering the inland fishing rights, hunting, trapping, and the gathering of traditional foods and medicines on state and federally "owned" lands.[10] Clearly, these lands have yet to be "required for settlement."[11]

These events of *State of Michigan v. Leblanc* and the 2007 Inland Consent Decree are important decolonizing moments. They have helped Anishinaabeg to have better access to traditional lifeways, which are expressions of the worldview and its interrelated logics. I give this brief narrative to discuss the tenacity of worldview and its ability to reproduce itself in the face of incredible difficulty. I begin with flourishing because that is an Anishinaabeg starting place to discuss colonization. If we allow the articulations of survival to explain our culture, then we have bought into a colonial technique of erasure. I push this point because when speaking about court cases in the English language, it could very easily get conceptualized in a logic of linear progress where this narrative of the 2007 Inland Consent Decree becomes a successful inclusion of Anishinaabeg into American democracy, and the past wrongs of a previous generation of Americans were courageously rectified. If this logic of progress is allowed to structure the narrative, then the decolonizing power of these actions would be erased. For the 2007 Inland Consent decree to remain a viable decolonizing energy we must resist the narrative of inclusionary politics and remain independent Indigenous peoples. While the narrative of decolonization is a useful lens to discuss these contemporary events, this discussion has yet to be fully realized.

There are two primary points to make from this study. First, when we take the Anishinaabeg worldview and Article 13 seriously, the subsequent industrial "development" in the treaty lands represents a gross violation of this treaty. Article 13 requires the habitat necessary for the flora and fauna to exist for this treaty provision to remain intact. Furthermore, the pollution in the Great Lakes has significantly undermined our ability to live in ways that are spelled out in this treaty. While it would be nice to make this argument in court, it would be likely to fail. The political and economic power behind the status quo is such that it would take a lot more than a well-crafted legal argument to turn the tide of environmental destruction. This study is not intended to provide another move towards recognition by the colonial government, though other people could use it for that purpose. I am not interested in waiting around for other people to recognize the difficulties in living an Indigenous life in Anishinaabe Akiing. As the *Lyng* decision has demonstrated, "Even assuming that the Government's actions here will virtually destroy the Indians' ability to practice their religion, the Constitution simply does not supply a principle that could justify upholding respondent's legal claims."[12] A belief in overturning the legal status of Indigenous peoples and land in the eyes of the colonial government would have to be taken on faith. By definition, faith is belief in the absence of experience. A reliance upon legal methods to demonstrate a transformation of the legal landscape could be an exercise in thinking with a colonized mind, whereas we are asking permission to be in relationship to our homelands. Many of those relationships are still available, and it is most important that we experience those relationships intergenerationally. This is the power of Albert Leblanc and many others who have taken it upon themselves to participate in cogent relationships, regardless of what others may say.

The second point from this study is to provide a useful methodology to decolonize our thinking within the linguistic-conceptual confusion that presents itself in the everyday. To this end, we can finish with a quote from Vine Deloria Jr.'s final book, *The World We Used to Live In*. He begins this volume with an astute observation of the preceding forty years of renewed ceremonial life of Indigenous peoples in the United States. In this book he states,

> Even on the most traditional reservations, the erosion of the old ways is so profound that many people are willing to cast aside ceremonies that stood them in good stead for thousands of years and live in increasingly meaningless secularity. The consumer society is indeed consuming everything in its path. It is fair to say that the overwhelming majority of Indian people today have little understandings or remembrance of the powers once possessed by the spiritual leaders of their communities. What we do today is often simply a "walkthrough" of a once-potent ceremony that now has little visible effect on the participants. The exercise of spiritual powers still continues in some places but lacks the definitive intensity of the old days. Like the Christian sacraments, the mystery is largely gone and in its place is the perfunctory recitation of good thoughts not unlike the mantras of self-improvement books and videos that remind us we are our own best friends.[13]

There are many questions to ask of this passage, but I think one of the main responses can be, if this is even somewhat accurate, then why was that power diminished? Furthermore, what can be done to turn the tide of colonial thinking and participate in the reproduction of those powers? The development of this theory of worldview and an associated linguistic-conceptual method of retranslating our own cultures offers a methodological response. While there are many reasons why Indigenous peoples have had difficulty regenerating ceremonies and their powers, including the violent removal from our homelands, stealing our children, and reducing many of us to states of poverty with economic and political dependence, we still have before us the problem of regenerating relationships to land and ceremony that are conducive to the flourishing of our ancestors. When we think seriously about the ways in which the English language and concepts of religion have taken a significant role in mediating our daily experiences, we can see just how devastating that mediation can be. When a group of people find themselves up against considerable odds, the language of hope is often uttered. But there is a glaring problem with that thought. Hope is not a method. Rather than focusing on the work of external actors, as Anishinaabekwe Leanne Simpson states,

> our most important work is internal, and the kinds of transformations we are compelled to make, the kinds of alternatives we are compelled to embody are profoundly systemic. I am strongly interested in building an Nishnaabeg presence, and Nishnaabeg present, that embodies and operationalizes the very best of our nation because this is what we have always done.[14]

I believe that the regeneration of a life more Indigenous can be engaged through a complex dialogical relationship of experiencing the land and all of our relatives within the linguistic-conceptual frameworks that our linguistic-conceptual world has to offer. This cycle of action and reflection is exactly what our ancestors did on a daily basis. There is every reason to believe that a reengagement with that Anishinaabe dialogical praxis will provide the next level of experiential engagement that can provide a better life for those that are yet to be born.

NOTES

PREFACE

1. I am using eurowestern here as a term that encapsulates the cultural influences of colonization that have emanated from western Europe during the colonial period of 1492 to the present time. By defining the cultural influences of early colonialism in this way, I can cover the colonization of the French, English, and Spanish empires, as well as the American colonization that then ensued in Anishinaabeg land. All four of these colonizing countries share very similar colonizing discourse and cultural influences when it comes to the domination of the land and the Indigenous peoples who were already here.

2. Treaty of Washington, 1836, online text available at https://turtletalk.files.wordpress.com/2008/05/7-stat-491.pdf. There is no further explanation of what this article means in this treaty. This one sentence stands alone. See Matthew Fletcher's remarks in "Nation to Nation: 15 Great Nations Keep Their Word," at https://www.youtube.com/watch?v=sLfjvxBMvAs.

3. While the court case was decided in 1979, the consent decree outlining the parameters of the treaty rights was not entirely worked out until 1985. This initial decree expired in 2000 and was renegotiated. The inland hunting and fishing rights were added to this renegotiation in 2004, which went into effect in 2007.

4. AIRFA was actually a resolution in Congress and for that reason was not necessarily an enforceable law. However it was supposed to be a guiding principle according to which government and court decisions would be made. There have been revisions to AIRFA, yet they still lack the enforcement structure that would protect our lands and our relationships to them. Even though AIRFA in section 2 "directed the president to require the various federal departments to evaluate their policies and procedures, report back to Congress on the results of their survey, and make recommendation for legislative actions," the directives have yet to be followed up on in a meaningful manner. Vine Deloria Jr., *God Is Red: A Native View of Religion* (Golden, CO: Fulcrum Publishing, 1992), 268. For a brief, yet informative summary of AIRFA and other key American Indian law cases and statutes, see Ward Churchill and Glenn Morris, "Key Indian Laws and Cases," in *The State of Native America*, ed. M. Annette Jaimes (Boston: South End Press, 1992), 13–21.

5. *Lyng v. Northwest Indian Cemetery Protection Association*, 485 U.S. 451. Considering that there continue to be more attempts at protecting our lands from "development" within the U.S. legal system, not all American Indian people agree that the *Lyng* decision is the type of watershed moment that I am suggesting it is.

6. *Anishinaabe* is the traditional name for the original people of the Three Fires Confederacy of Ojibwe, Odawa, and Bodewadmik peoples in what is now the northern and western Great Lakes area of the U.S. and Canada. Terms such as Chippewa, Saulteaux, Ottawa, and Potawatomi have been used, but European and American colonizing forces have imposed those terms upon us, and hence many of us choose to use Anishinaabe when referring to ourselves. The plural of Anishinaabe is *Anishinaabeg*, and *Anishinaabemowin* is our language. *Akiing* is the locative version of *aki*, land.

7. State of Michigan, Department of Environmental Quality, File No. GW1810162, http://turtletalk.files.wordpress.com/2010/01/kennecott-fdo.pdf.

8. Clifford Geertz, *The Interpretation of Cultures* (New York: Basic Books, 1973), 14.

9. In regard to religion, the First Amendment states, "Congress shall make no law respecting the establishment of a religion, or prohibiting the free exercise thereof." These are usually split up into two parts, the first being the "establishment clause" and the second being the "free exercise clause." More often than not, the free exercise clause comes into play for American Indian land cases. From the Bill of Rights, available at http://www.archives.gov/exhibits/charters/bill_of_rights_transcript.html.

10. Deloria, *God Is Red*, 95 n. 1.

11. George (Tink) Tinker, *American Indian Liberation* (Maryknoll, NY: Orbis Books, 2008), 123.

12. Kwasi Wiredu, *Cultural Universals and Particulars: An African Perspective* (Bloomington:

University of Indiana Press, 1996), 96.

13. In this project I will be using the double-vowel spelling system in my regular usage of Anishinaabemowin. However, as I will be quoting a number of other authors, when quoting them directly I will be using their own spellings of Anishinaabe words. While most people using Anishinaabemowin use the double-vowel spelling system, it is not a universally accepted orthography, and there are still variations on spellings of words within the double-vowel system.

14. This description should not be misconstrued as a relativist argument. As I will demonstrate, this worldview and associated concepts within Anishinaabemowin can be translated into English. What I am arguing for here is that the starting place for that translation must begin within our own language and take into consideration the worldview of our culture. This translational method will function as a corrective against the colonization of our language and our culture that has happened throughout the colonial period.

15. Leanne Betasamosake Simpson, *As We Have Always Done: Indigenous Freedom through Radical Resistance* (Minneapolis: University of Minnesota Press, 2017). See chapter 1 for a definition, 34–37.

16. Wiredu, *Cultural Universals and Particulars*, 87.

17. Wiredu, *Cultural Universals and Particulars*, 87.

18. Wiredu, *Cultural Universals and Particulars*, 85.

19. Wiredu, *Cultural Universals and Particulars*, 92–93.

20. The protection of our lands via the Constitution and the First Amendment is a complex undertaking, and it should not be assumed that everyone involved is unthinkingly participating in a colonial mentality. Some of the Indigenous people involved know that what we do as Americans is not religion, but others attempt to equate the two and end up doing violence to their own traditions. It is hoped that this study can help to limit the amount of violence that is currently being done to our cultures.

21. Simpson, *As We Have Always Done*, 175.

22. Simpson, *As We Have Always Done*, 178.

23. Treaty of Washington, 1836, online text available at https://turtletalk.files.wordpress.com/2008/05/7-stat-491.pdf. There is no further explanation of what this article means in this treaty. This one sentence stands alone. See Matthew Fletcher's remarks in "Nation to Nation: 15 Great Nations Keep Their Word," at https://www.youtube.com/watch?v=sLfjvxBMvAs.

24. A. Irving Hallowell, "Ojibwa Ontology, Behavior and World View," in *Culture and History*, ed. Stanley Diamond (New York: Columbia University Press, 1960), 21. While Hallowell's

work is problematic in a number of ways, I think his use of "other-than-human persons" is a much better understanding of *manidoog* than is the religious concept of spirit, which is often used as a translation. *Manidoo* is singular, and *manidoog* is the plural form.

CHAPTER 1. WORLDVIEW

1. Treaty of Washington, 1836, online text available at https://turtletalk.files.wordpress.com/2008/05/7-stat-491.pdf.
2. David Naugle, *Worldview: The History of a Concept* (Grand Rapids, MI: Wm. B. Eerdmanns Publishing Co., 2002), 59. It is significant that Kant, according to David Naugle, only used the term once in his writings.
3. Fichte's usage is from 1792 in *Attempt at a Critique of All Revelation*, and Schelling from 1799, *On the Concept of Speculative Metaphysics*. Quote from Naugle, *Worldview*, 60–61.
4. Vincent A. McCarthy, *The Phenomenology of Moods in Kierkegaard* (Boston: Martinus Nijhoff, 1978), 136, quoted in Naugle, *Worldview*, 71.
5. Naugle, *Worldview*, 97.
6. Naugle, *Worldview*, 101.
7. These authors draw from a longer trajectory of evangelical thought working from authors like James Orr, Abraham Kuyper, and Herman Dooyerweerd. Most of them trace their thought from Abraham Kuyper, who worked in the Netherlands and set up the Free University of Amsterdam, a Calvinist school. Kuyper's project was to demonstrate how Calvinism was an entire worldview. See Naugle, *Worldview*, 5–32.
8. Naugle, *Worldview*, 329.
9. Naugle, *Worldview*, 330.
10. James Sire, *Naming the Elephant: Worldview as a Concept* (Downers Grove, IL: InterVarsity Press, 2004), 13.
11. Sire, *Naming the Elephant*, 108.
12. Sire, *Naming the Elephant*, 133.
13. Paul G. Hiebert, *Transforming Worldviews: An Anthropological Understanding of How People Change* (Grand Rapids, MI: Baker Academic, 2008), 15.
14. Hiebert, *Transforming Worldviews*, 55. This relationship to space and time is an essential component for worldview, and an important distinction between Indigenous cultures and those of the eurowest.
15. Hiebert, *Transforming Worldviews*, 23.
16. See Naugle, *Worldview*, chap. 9.
17. Hiebert, *Transforming Worldviews*, 69.

18. For a further explanation of the ability of missionaries to commit acts of genocide while wholeheartedly believing that they are doing "the Lord's work," see George (Tink) Tinker, *Missionary Conquest: The Gospel and Native American Genocide* (Minneapolis, MN: Fortress Press, 1993).

19. Mike Hawkins, *Social Darwinism in European and American Thought, 1860–1945: Nature as Model and Nature as Threat* (New York: Cambridge University Press, 1997), 21.

20. Hawkins, *Social Darwinism*, 21.

21. Hawkins, *Social Darwinism*, 21.

22. Hawkins, *Social Darwinism*, 21.

23. Hawkins, *Social Darwinism*, 32.

24. Hawkins, *Social Darwinism*, 32.

25. Further along, Hawkins makes a distinction between Darwinism and Lamarckism as different worldviews because of their differing views of the mechanism of natural selection (Lamarck as an organism striving for complexity, and Darwin as the struggle for existence). This is another example of Hawkins's definition in play failing to provide the necessary depth of understanding that we are searching for. Stated in another way, if Darwinism and Lamarckism are different at the level of worldview, then what analytical lens do we use to discuss the fundamental differences between Indigenous and eurowestern cultures? Hawkins, *Social Darwinism*, 43–44.

26. See Vine Deloria Jr., *God Is Red: A Native View of Religion* (Golden, CO: Fulcrum Publishing, 1992). See especially chapter 6, "The Concept of History," 98–113.

27. Hawkins, *Social Darwinism*, 107.

28. Hawkins, *Social Darwinism*, 107.

29. Hawkins, *Social Darwinism*, 108.

30. In addition to Fiske's lack of logical consistency, other thinkers like Karl Marx also show this implicit reliance on the sin-salvation-eschaton linear trajectory. For Marx, the sin of capitalism is saved by the communist revolution so that the eschaton of workers owning the means of production can be realized. This is, of course, wildly ironic considering Marx's open disgust with Christianity and religion in general. These examples are helpful for a more refined definition of worldview because they help to demonstrate the tenacity of largely unconscious systems of thought.

31. This definition is from James W. Underhill, *Humboldt, Worldview and Language* (Edinburg: Edinburgh University Press, 2013), 56.

32. Underhill, *Humboldt, Worldview and Language*, 17. Underhill follows Jürgen Trabant's differentiation of weltansicht and weltanschauung, attributing the latter to "a personal stance, a view of the world which is more deeply intuitive than a philosophy"; ibid., 16.

33. Underhill's project is to elucidate the work of Humboldt and to redefine worldview within these linguistic terms.

34. According to Underhill, Humboldt's contribution of weltansicht has largely been lost in English and French as weltanschauung has been associated with the concept of worldview. While it is possible that Franz Boas and Edward Sapir were exposed to Humboldt since they were both from Germany, there is no direct evidence in their writings.

35. Underhill, *Humboldt, Worldview and Language*, 14.

36. Underhill, *Humboldt, Worldview and Language*, 32.

37. Underhill, *Humboldt, Worldview and Language*, 32.

38. John A. Lucy, *Language Diversity and Thought: A Reformulation of the Linguistic Relativity Hypothesis* (New York: Cambridge University Press, 1992), 67.

39. It should be noted that one critique leveled against Whorf is that his analysis of the Hopi language stems primarily from a single bilingual informant in New York. The use of a single informant would seem to seriously limit the weight that has been given to his analysis. See Underhill, *Humboldt, Worldview and Language*, 44.

40. Pascal Boyer, "Cognitive Limits to Conceptual Relativity: The Limiting-Case of Religious Ontologies," in *Rethinking Linguistic Relativity*, ed. John J. Gumperz and Stephen C. Levinson (New York: Cambridge University Press, 1996), 218.

41. Underhill, *Humboldt, Worldview and Language*, 56.

42. A few examples help to demonstrate this point: see Paul Radin, *Primitive Religion* (New York: Dover Publications, 1957); Robert Redfield, *The Primitive World and Its Transformations* (Ithaca, NY: Cornell University Press, 1953); and Ruth M. Underhill, *Red Man's Religion* (Chicago: University of Chicago Press, 1974).

43. Robert Redfield quoted in A. Irving Hallowell, "Ojibwa Ontology, Behavior and World View," in *Culture and History*, ed. Stanley Diamond (New York: Columbia University Press, 1960), 535.

44. Redfield, *Primitive World*, 86.

45. Redfield, *Primitive World*, 91.

46. Geertz, *Interpretation of Cultures*, 25.

47. Geertz, *Interpretation of Cultures*, 27.

48. Geertz, *Interpretation of Cultures*, 89.

49. Geertz, *Interpretation of Cultures*, 131.

50. Geertz, *Interpretation of Cultures*, 129.

51. Geertz, *Interpretation of Cultures*, 141.

52. Michael Kearney, *World View* (Novato, CA: Chandler and Sharp Publishers, 1984), ix.

53. Kearney, *World View*, 66.
54. Kearney, *World View*, 123.
55. Kearney, *World View*, 5.
56. Kearney, *World View*, 67.
57. While Kearney did help to connect worldview to lived experience, his study languishes as a surface analysis because it does very little to negotiate the differences in worldview at a linguistic level. When he does mention Indigenous words to demonstrate his point, he uses secondary sources and allows for euroforming translations of those words.
58. Hallowell, "Ojibwa Ontology," 537. It should be noted, his own bias still evident in the drive toward "objectivity" and the consistent scientific drive towards some "higher" process of understanding is problematic, even though he is working towards a different method of understanding that is helpful.
59. Hallowell, "Ojibwa Ontology," 539. Hallowell himself recognized that the animate/ inanimate dualism was a eurowestern projection and went deeper into this part of the study to attempt to get an emic perspective.
60. Hallowell, "Ojibwa Ontology," 540.
61. Hallowell, "Ojibwa Ontology," 540.
62. Hallowell shares the narratives of informants who had seen stones move in ceremony, and in one case, a *Midewin* leader had a stone that had shapes on it like eyes and a mouth, and with a new knife could tap it and "It would then open its mouth, Yellow Legs would insert his fingers and take out a small leather sack with medicine in it." Hallowell, "Ojibwa Ontology," 541.
63. Hallowell, "Ojibwa Ontology," 543.
64. Hallowell, "Ojibwa Ontology," 537.
65. Hallowell, "Ojibwa Ontology," 543. This lack of a concept of the natural is also demonstrated among Akan-speaking peoples in Ghana by Kwasi Wiredu. See the following discussion of Wiredu.
66. Kwasi Wiredu, *Cultural Universals and Particulars: An African Perspective* (Bloomington: University of Indiana Press, 1996), 96.
67. Deloria occasionally uses the word worldview to discuss deep cultural differences, but does not specifically define the concept. Wiredu has written a paper titled "The Akan Worldview," in which he does gives numerous examples of deep cultural differences, but he does not specifically define worldview as a concept.
68. It should be noted that the suggestion that Wiredu's work falls under an "Indigenous" connotation is mine. His own titles suggest that he is an African philosopher. However, because of the consistent similarities between what he describes as cultural differences

in his work and Indigenous conceptualizations, I make the move to include him under the umbrella of Indigenous philosophy. He is trained as a logician, so the moniker "philosopher" is correct.

69. Kwasi Wiredu, *The Akan Worldview* (Washington, DC: Smithsonian Libraries, 1985), 2.

70. Wiredu, *Akan Worldview*, 2.

71. Wiredu, *Akan Worldview*, 3.

72. Wiredu, *Akan Worldview*, 4.

73. Wiredu, *Akan Worldview*, 4.

74. Wiredu, *Akan Worldview*, 4. Emphasis in the original.

75. Wiredu, *Cultural Universals and Particulars*, 49.

76. Wiredu and other African philosophers have used the Cartesian cogito, "I think, therefore I am," as a means of demonstrating cultural difference. For Africans, and I would suggest other Indigenous peoples as well, the ontological claim of being as framed in the cogito is a particular eurowestern formulation. John Mbiti has commented that the Cartesian cogito is far too individualistic, and suggests that "I am because we are, and since we are, therefore I am" has a communal integrity that is consistent in Africa. However, even more to the point for this essay, Alexis Kagame points out that the verb "to be" is always followed by an association to place, which makes the cogito unintelligible in the Bantu language. So the "utterance ' . . . therefore, I am' would prompt the question 'You are . . . what . . . where?'" Wiredu, *Cultural Universals*, 140. In particular Kagame's example speaks to the importance of spatiality for Bantu people inherent in their linguistic conceptual structure that is consistent with a worldview that is primarily founded in spatial understandings.

77. Wiredu, *Cultural Universals*, 50.

78. Wiredu, *Cultural Universals*, 53.

79. Wiredu, *Cultural Universals*, 55.

80. Wiredu, *Cultural Universals*, 55.

81. Wiredu, *Cultural Universals*, 52.

82. Wiredu, *Cultural Universals*, 55.

83. Deloria, *God Is Red*, 62.

84. Kearney, *World View*, 66.

85. Deloria, *God Is Red*, 71.

86. Deloria, *God Is Red*, 73.

87. Deloria, *God Is Red*, 202. The emphasis is mine.

88. Kearney, *World View*, 66. Clearly my definition of worldview resembles Kearney's in the "logico-structural" aspect, but it differs in many ways as well. In short, my definition

does more to address the fundamental relationships to space, time, and life, and it is not encumbered by an analysis of historical materialism. Furthermore, by confining worldview to the four components of space, time, life, and prescription for relating to that life, it helps to differentiate worldview from ideological aspects of culture. This differentiation will be demonstrated further.

89. Dictionary.com, http://dictionary.reference.com/browse/ideology.

90. Dictionary.com, http://dictionary.reference.com/browse/institution.

91. The Midewiwin Society is a medicinal society that provides a number of functions in many Anishinaabeg communities. It is primarily understood as a healing society that helps to cure sick people and performs a number of life and community renewal ceremonies. It also has a responsibility to hold a significant amount of cultural memory, including migration narratives. For a brief discussion of the Midewiwin, see Edward Benton-Benai, *The Mishomis Book: The Voice of the Ojibway* (Hayward, WI: Indian Country Communications, Inc., 1988), 67–73.

92. This example of everyday lived experience calls into question the power of Christianity as a lived experience when compared to capitalism. While many people claim Christian identity, most, I suggest, would have difficulty naming as many Christian experiences as they could name capitalistic experiences.

CHAPTER 2. SPACE

1. For example, the Haudenosaunee Great Law of Peace was in existence for approximately 500 years before European contact. It stayed intact for another 200 years during the early colonial period and only struggled to continue after the American Revolution and a significant onslaught of genocidal actions.

2. *Mazikaamikwe* is Earth Mother in Anishinaabemowin. Earth Mother is also known as *Shkaakaamikwe*. This concept will be explained later.

3. This specifically refers to Anishinaabeg treaties with the French. These early treaties allowed for trading posts to be built, but were much more about trade relationships than boundaries of land.

4. There is a certain irony here in that the Royal Proclamation officially gave language to the idea that the lands of the Ohio River Valley and area north and west of there (including Anishinaabe Akiing) would be free from new colonizers. The idea was to stabilize relationships with American Indian peoples, but instead it became a justification for the American Revolution as the land-greedy colonists considered it an affront to their freedoms and a symbol of British tyranny. For a deeper analysis see Anthony J. Hall,

The American Empire and the Fourth World (Montreal: McGill-Queen's University Press, 2003), chap. 4, "Revolution and Empire," 294–370. Indian nations throughout this region were suspect, yet hopeful that their lands would be off limits to speculators and squatters alike. But the previous decades had demonstrated that there was little effectual policing that the British government was willing to do to keep Europeans out of the area.

5. The Treaty of Greenville ceded a portion of land north of the Ohio River after a military campaign by the Seneca leader Blue Jacket was defeated at the Battle of Fallen Timbers. The encroachment upon lands north of the Ohio River continued, just as the Anishinaabeg and other Indian nations had suspected. For a further discussion of the Treaty of Greenville and its implications for subsequent treaties, both with Indigenous peoples in the United States and globally over the next two centuries, see Anthony J. Hall, *Earth into Property: Colonization, Decolonization, and Capitalism* (Montreal: McGill-Queen's University Press, 2010), 269–314. See also Barbara Alice Mann, "The Greenville Treaty of 1795: Pen-and-Ink Witchcraft in the Struggle for the Old Northwest," in *Enduring Legacies: Native American Treaties and Contemporary Controversies*, ed. Bruce E. Johansen (Westport, CT: Praeger Publishers, 2004), 135–201.

6. Michigan became the 26th state on January 26, 1837. Similar to the buildup for other states, there was a flurry of treaty activity to secure the proper boundaries needed to officially become a state.

7. During this period of treaty negotiations there were mixed understandings on the part of the Anishinaabeg. From the text of the treaties that recognized specific parcels of land that were set aside for individuals near towns, we can see a better understanding of property in a eurowestern sense on the part of those particular people. This would be similar to understandings of particular family land set aside as hunting or sugar bush territory. Boundaries and responsibility towards particular places would be easily understood; however, the complex legal codes, rules, and regulations that come with eurowestern property rights would probably be new to some of the Anishinaabeg.

8. Treaty of Washington, 1836, online text available at https://www.cmich.edu/library/clarke/ResearchResources/Native_American_Material/Treaty_Rights/Text_of_Michigan_Related_Treaties. There is no further explanation of what this article means in this treaty. This one sentence stands alone.

9. This language would become important in the latter part of the twentieth century as hunting and fishing rights for these ceded territories would become contested once again. This will be further explained in a later section. A. Irving Hallowell describes "usufruct" concepts as how Anishinaabeg relate to the land, stating, "There is nothing in Saulteaux culture that motivates the possession of land for land's sake. Usufruct, rather

than the land itself, is an economic value and land is never rented or sold." Hallowell, *Contributions to Ojibwe Studies: Essays, 1934–1972* (Lincoln: University of Nebraska Press, 2010), 149.

10. For a good description of the common pot, see Lisa Brooks, *The Common Pot: The Recovery of Native Space in the Northeast* (Minneapolis: University of Minnesota Press, 2008).

11. It is certainly debatable what Anishinaabeg and other Indigenous peoples understood these treaties to be. Again, I am not trying to paint the Anishinaabeg as ignorant or naive. My argument for the intelligibility of these concepts of land and relationship to that land will follow in this chapter. Here I am suggesting that when the worldview of the peoples at hand are taken into consideration in the process of translation, then deep cultural understandings of land and relationships are very difficult to translate. Hence, I do not believe that the Anishinaabeg could have fully comprehended the ramifications of the transfer of lands in the treaties since these concepts are dependent upon a deeper comprehension of a eurowestern conceptualization of and relationship to land. At the same time, it would be nearly impossible for the American treaty negotiators to comprehend Anishinaabeg relationships to land, had they cared to try.

12. For example, for Anishinaabeg living in the western portion of Anishinaabe Akiing (Minnesota, the Dakotas, and Saskatchewan) there is an emphasis on the *Nanapush* narratives of origin. In the east (Michigan and Ontario), the *Giizhigokwe* (Sky Woman) narratives of origin are still told. Even within Anishinaabeg thought we can see that the autonomy inherent in the cultural organization allows for polyglossia within Anishinaabeg culture.

13. In an oral tradition, there are also protocols about the telling of this type of narrative. We are supposed to tell these narratives during the wintertime—literally, after the frogs are hibernating in the mud until they come out again in the spring.

14. Basil H. Johnston, *The Manitous* (St. Paul: Minnesota Historical Society Press, 2001), xv–xvi. While Johnston's work does suffer in places from its reliance upon eurowestern categories of thought, this description of Sky Woman is useful. It should be stated, however, that the preface to this narrative of Sky Woman is an example of colonial categories at play in Anishinaabe thought. He begins this chapter by stating, "Kitchi-Manitou (the Great Mystery) created the world, plants, birds, animals, fish, and the other *manitous* in fulfillment of a vision." The use of *Kitchi-Manitou* as a "creator" is problematic in that it assumes a nothingness into which "creation" is placed by a god-like figure. While this and other similar versions are popular among some Anishinaabeg, I am suggesting that this and other versions like it can be misleading, and in certain places

force-fit Anishinaabeg thought into eurowestern categories. Hence, I carefully choose the narratives that I use and how I use them so that I can limit the colonial influences and work to develop a better understanding of an Anishinaabeg worldview.

Furthermore, Johnston and others share another flood narrative where this process of repopulating the land from the Turtle's back is repeated by *Nanapush*. This repetition of narrative is curious in that it repeats the flood narrative, in some cases almost verbatim, and raises a number of questions about the complex set of colonial influences that we have to be careful of. This difference in narrative could be a form of local variation on the flood narrative, whereas the process of re-forming the land and life fell to a male *manidoo*. It also could be recognition of multiple floods that had affected a particular area or people. However, considering the significant colonial influences that we have had to deal with, in particular the patriarchy that has been imposed on us, the shift from a female to a male *manidoo* as responsible for the forming of the land and animals could be representative of, as Wiredu puts it, "thinking with a colonized mind." The shift from Sky Woman to *Nanapush* raises a number of questions because of the wide use of this narrative among many different peoples from the Great Lakes and St. Lawrence Seaway. It can also be indicative of the local variation that I describe earlier.

15. Basil Johnston, *Anishinaubae Thesaurus* (East Lansing: Michigan State University Press, 2007), 1.

16. The suffixes *-ing, -ang,* or *-ong* when added to a word are used to demonstrate a specific location.

17. *Kamig* is the spelling from Frederic Baraga, *A Dictionary of the Ojibway Language* (St. Paul: Minnesota Historical Society Press, 1992), 180. This word is a suffix, used to allude to the ground in a general sense. In Johnston, *Anishinaubae Thesaurus*, he spells it as *kummik*, p. 51.

18. One of the problems of translating the *maaba/maanda* differences from Anishinaabemowin into English is the presumption of an emphasis on nouns in the English language, which does not exist in Anishinaabemowin. There is an emphasis on verbs and action in Anishinaabemowin, which help to determine whether or not a noun is *maaba* or *manda*. This relationship is complex and does not always follow hard and fast linguistic or conceptual rules. For example, while *maaba* nouns are often things that are living, like animals or food, mittens are also considered *maaba*. While it is important to note the *maaba/manda* distinctions in the language, they just play out as they do, and no consistent formulations can be used to describe these distinctions.

19. A. Irving Hallowell, "Ojibwa Ontology, Behavior and World View," in *Contributions to Ojibwa Studies: Essays, 1934 to 1972*, ed. Jennifer S. H. Brown and Susan Elaine Gray

(Lincoln: University of Nebraska Press, 2010), 540.

20. Hallowell, "Ojibwa Ontology, Behavior and World View." The evidence that Hallowell gives includes informants talking about a stone following a *Midé* leader during a ceremony, and another stone that could be "opened" to retrieve medicine that was inside of it. These examples help to demonstrate that for the Anishinaabeg, rocks belonging to a *maaba* category of thought makes sense when their larger experiential world is understood from their own perspective.

21. As Anishinaabeg scholar and linguist Margaret Noori (Noodin) suggests, this translation of *Mazikaamikwe* as "Earth Mother" is problematic as it is not often used, and nowhere in the etymology of the word is the concept of "mother" noted. *Kaamik* is earth or land, and *kwe* is woman, but the words for mother are something different entirely. However, she states that "Basil Johnston and other Ontario storytellers, including Isaac Pitawankwat, use these terms, but in conversations they have led me to understand these words as implications of the idea of one who creates, makes new, or provides for life." Margaret Noori, "*Beshaabiiag G'gikenmaaigowag*," in *Centering Anishinaabeg Studies*, ed. Jill Doerfler, Niigaanwewidam James Sinclair, and Heidi Kiiwetinepinesiik Stark (East Lansing: Michigan State University Press, 2013), 55–56 n. 1.

22. Johnston, *Anishinaubae Thesaurus*, 17. More needs to be said regarding the phrase "breathe the breath of life" in this narrative. It is possible that here Johnston is euroforming the narrative by using a phrase from Genesis 2:7 where God "breathed into his nostril the breath of life." However, Johnston also comes from a generation of people who worked very hard to help regenerate Anishinaabemowin as a living language. Among this group of linguists from the 1970s, they often spoke of their work as "breathing the breath of life" into the language. Furthermore, there are also common understandings around building a fire where one breathes on a fire to give it life. Therefore, there are multiple uses of this phrase that are important in both cultures that Johnston was surrounded by, so no conclusion can be drawn as to the origin of this phrase for him.

23. Here I am also making an argument for the accurate naming of these narratives as origin narratives and not "creation" stories.

24. From *The First Nine Chapters of the Book of Moses Called Genesis*, trans. James Evans and Peter Jones, available at http://eco.canadiana.ca/view/oocihm.91612/7?r=0&s=1.

25. John D. Nichols and Earl Nyholm, *A Concise Dictionary of Minnesota Ojibwe* (Minneapolis: University of Minnesota Press, 1995), 108.

26. This definition comes from personal conversation with Margaret Noodin, November 12, 2012.

27. The Great Lakes region of North America is home to 20 percent of the world's surface freshwater.

28. Kwasi Wiredu, *Cultural Universals and Particulars: An African Perspective* (Bloomington: Indiana University Press, 1996), 89. Here Wiredu is referring to the particular usage of philosophical terms like "creation out of nothingness," warning that their usage comes with a particular lineage of thought that shapes their meaning.

29. This topic of whether or not the *Giizhigokwe* narrative is the "first" narrative is a complicated and difficult task. As I mention above, Basil Johnston does begin *Ojibway Heritage* (Lincoln: University of Nebraska Press, 1990) with a discussion of *Kitche-Manitou* "creating" the universe. However, I do not discuss this narrative for two reasons. First, it mirrors too closely the Book of Genesis. Secondly, it does not specifically relate the Anishinaabeg to the land base that would become *Makinak*, the Great Turtle's back. My discussion centers on relationships to land, so I begin with an analysis of *Giizhigokwe* narratives.

30. It is this common orientation to the land that helps to provide firm relationships in treaties like that of the Haudenosaunee Confederacy.

31. This description of *doodemag* leadership is a structure that is not necessarily in common usage anymore. However, it does represent the socio-political-economic reality of Eshkwagenabi and other signers of the 1836 Treaty of Washington, so it provides a conceptual grounding to understand worldview.

32. As Hallowell puts it, "But this larger whole [Ojibwa as a national group], although readily identifiable, was never at any time unified in any political sense, so that it cannot properly be called a nation or, except by traditional usage, even a tribe." Hallowell, *Contributions to Ojibwe Studies*, 23.

33. George E. (Tink) Tinker, *American Indian Liberation: A Theology of Sovereignty* (Maryknoll, NY: Orbis Books, 2008), 8. This communitarian emphasis among Indigenous peoples is also taken up by John Mbiti in discussing the Cartesian cogito. According to Mbiti, "Whatever happens to the individual happens to the whole group, and whatever happens to the whole group happens to the individual. The individual can only say: 'I am, because we are; and since we are, therefore I am'. This is a cardinal point in the understanding of the African view of man." John S. Mbiti, *African Religions and Philosophy* (Portsmouth, NH: Heinemann, 1989), 106.

34. This brief discussion of village and *doodem* is not an intact system currently. This section describes a "traditional" negotiation of Anishinaabeg life, which was selectively destroyed in the nineteenth and twentieth centuries. While in many communities, the *doodem* still play an integral role in local life and provide for certain relationships, many

people have been separated from these primary identities via the residential schools and ongoing racism. It is necessary for this particular study to discuss the role of the village in its intact form as it provides for the best means of elucidating these Anishinaabeg concepts.

35. For a more thorough discussion of the Anishinaabeg migration from the east, see Thomas Peacock and Marlene Wisuri, *Waasa Inaabidaa: We Look in All Directions* (Afton, MN: Afton Historical Society Press, 2002), 22–27. This writing, like many others, also suffers from "thinking with a colonized mind," as Wiredu would put it, but it does give a decent understanding of the migration narrative. This narrative, which has been kept by the Midewiwin Society (Medicine Society), is a very elaborate narrative, much of which is not in print.

36. The meaning of the word *Ishpeming* is another site of decolonization. Often the definitions for this place include "heaven," because it literally translates as "up above." It is located on the north side of what is now considered the Upper Peninsula of Michigan, therefore, spatially speaking, it is "up above." While Ishpeming as a locative noun is commonly understood as "heaven," it must be noted that no such place exists within Anishinaabeg thought. Heaven is an entirely imposed eurowestern concept, and its use represents a colonization of the language and the mind of those who identify Ishpeming as heaven.

37. Alexis Kagame, "Empirical Apperception of Time and the Conception of History in Bantu Thought," in *Cultures and Time*, ed. Paul Ricoeur (Paris: UNESCO, 1976), 95. Quoted in Wiredu, *Cultural Universals and Particulars*, 140.

38. Wiredu, *Cultural Universals and Particulars*, 141.

39. Wiredu, *Cultural Universals and Particulars*, 141.

40. Wiredu, *Cultural Universals and Particulars*, 141.

41. Kagame quoted in Wiredu, *Cultural Universals and Particulars*, 140.

42. Nichols and Nyholm, *Concise Dictionary*, 71. In Anishinaabemowin, the prefix *izhi-* is quite common, and Nichols and Nyholm follow the *izhi-* entry with seventy-four examples of *izhi-* in use, including *izhichige* (do things in a certain way), *izhi'o* (dress in a certain way), *izhinaw* (see a certain way), and *izhinaagwaad* (have a certain appearance.)

43. Nichols and Nyholm, *Concise Dictionary*, 15, 143. In the dictionary it is written as *ayaa* vii (intransitive verb) be (in a certain place), 15.

44. Wiredu, *Cultural Universals and Particulars*, 141.

45. While occasionally these councils were held at special times for particular decisions, usually these intervillage and international councils were part of a cycle of ritual ceremony and celebration that helped to keep balance not only between humans, but

between humans and the rest of life with whom they share the land. In this way, political decisions about land use and boundaries were made within the context of a larger set of ceremonies that help to keep balance in the larger web of relatedness.

46. Johnston, *Ojibway Heritage*, 16.

47. Johnston, *Ojibway Heritage*, 16.

48. These ceremonies are far too numerous to mention, and vary from community to community, to elaborate specifically. It is also difficult to pin down too many particulars in these types of ceremonies considering the significant amount of cultural dislocation that has happened in the process of colonization. Many of these ceremonies are in the process of regeneration as they were not practiced very often throughout the twentieth century on account of their being illegal, as well as the stigma and racism attached to outward expressions of Indigenous identity.

49. For example, there is a narrative about the deer being taken away by the crows, which the Anishinaabeg had to go fight to get them back. However, the deer were not there against their will; they were treated better by the crows and were not taken for granted as they were with the Anishinaabeg. Once the Anishinaabeg learned their lesson and agreed to take care of the deer properly, they returned to be their food. Johnston, *Ojibway Heritage*, 55–57.

50. Nichols and Nyholm, *Concise Dictionary*, 91.

51. Nichols and Nyholm, *Concise Dictionary*, 77. They also give "Manitou" as part of the definition. Johnston, *Anishinaubae Thesaurus*, 16. He also lists "spirit(s), sprite(s), incorporeal being(s), deity, deities, supernatural being(s), mysteries, properties, attributes, the unseen, intangible reality." *Manidoo* is the singular form, *manidoog* is the plural.

52. Wiredu, *Cultural Universals and Particulars*, 55.

53. Wiredu, *Cultural Universals and Particulars*, 55. However, from Christian sources the concept of the "Holy Spirit" is more than "unseen" since it is conceptualized in both sight and sound. While this is true, Wiredu's discussion of "spirit" as poorly defined still holds true.

54. Wiredu, *Cultural Universals and Particulars*, 141.

55. While spirit in its Cartesian form is certainly "nonspatial and nonmaterial," when one thinks of Christian theology it becomes more complicated. For example, from the third century on, God as a concept gets defined as substance from Greek influences. Substance clearly is associated with a materiality. However, there is a lack of consistency within this trajectory of Christian thought in the sense that in modernity, there is this greater Cartesian influence of the material/spirit dualism, which competes with the notion of

"substance." Furthermore, even if God is "substance," as a Creator "he" is outside of this creation and hence not spatially located here. Again, my critique is ultimately looking towards this notion of relationship to land and the tenacity of Indigenous connections to land.

56. Wiredu, *Cultural Universals and Particulars*, 137.

57. Johnston, *The Manitous*, 2. He also adds that *manitouwih* is a "medicine person," not a spirit. Johnston does not follow the more common double-vowel orthography that other authors use, so *manidoo* is spelled *manitou* in his work.

58. Johnston, *Anishinaubae Thesaurus*, 16. In other places in his work, Johnston consistently relies upon a Christian framework to euroform Anishinaabeg concepts of *manidoog*, and often imposes Christian notions of creation and God.

59. Wiredu, *Cultural Universals and Particulars*, 53.

60. These people with the proper gifts and training are commonly referred to as "medicine people" in the Americas and "diviners" in the African context.

61. In the 1800s, it was first theorized that light was a wave, and then Heinrich Hertz discovered the photoelectric effect, where light when shone upon a surface can eject electrons, thereby demonstrating qualities of particles. For the purpose of this analysis it is unnecessary to follow the full trajectory of Hertz to quantum mechanics; however it is useful to note that light was theorized throughout the twentieth century as having both wave and particle properties. A photon is a particle of light. For a brief, nontechnical description of these developments, see Ralph Baierlein, *Newton to Einstein: The Trail of Light* (New York: Cambridge University Press, 1992), 161–75.

62. *Manidoog* are experienced in many forms since they have the power of metamorphosis. Also, these sparks and lights are also used to describe other powers, such as ghosts, or *jiibay*. These *jiibay* are similar to *manidoog* in that they are spatially located and sometimes appear as sparks, but there are differences as well. *Jiibay* are usually associated with recently deceased people, and sometimes older ancestors where *manidoog* are more associated with larger cosmological powers.

63. I should note that I am using the wave-particle duality as a definition in the general sense that light has properties of both waves and particles, or one could say is "quasi-material." I am not using this definition with a deep technical understanding of quantum theory. However, I believe that it is a useful definition as it helps to push "quasi-material" into more tangible concepts. Also, *manidoo* differs from light in that it has a consciousness that allows it to appear or to not appear on its own. Even when *manidoog* cannot be seen, they are considered to still be there.

64. For a further discussion of *nametoo* and the communication possible, see Heid E.

Erdrich, "'Name': Literary Ancestry as Presence," in Doerfler, Sinclair, and Stark, *Centering Anishinaabeg Studies*, 13–34. Erdrich here focuses on ancestral writing as presence, not on *manidoo* communication specifically, but it does give another example of communication across generations. See also Roger Roulette, "When the Ancestors Moved Around and Left a Presence on the Land," https://ojibwe.net/stories/spring/when-the-ancestors-moved-around-and-left-a-presence-on-the-land/. While this sound recording does not explain the concept, it does provide a use in context of the ancestors moving around to different camps in a three-to-five-year period of time, while "they were keeping in mind where they deserted." These two descriptions of *nametoo* use "presence" as part of a useful definition. I am suggesting this presence is associated with a two-way form of communication between the land and the people, or in the case of Erdrich's piece, between the ancestors and the people. See also Roger Roulette's narrative on *nametoo* available at http://ojibwe.net/stories/spring/when-the-ancestors-moved-around-and-left-a-presence-on-the-land.

65. NRSV Gen. 1:26.

66. NRSV, Gen. 1:28.

67. NRSV, Gen. 2:22.

68. For a more detailed treatment of European colonialism drawing from biblical narratives, see Steve Newcomb, *Pagans in the Promised Land: Decoding the Doctrine of Christian Discovery* (Golden, CO: Fulcrum, 2008). In this book Newcomb uses cognitive theory to demonstrate how European colonization of North America was justified using the conquest narratives in the Hebrew Bible and the ensuing chosen people–promised land mentality. Not only did colonists use this language, but it was codified into U.S. Supreme Court law in the case *Johnson v. McIntosh*. See especially chapters 3, 4, and 5.

69. See Anthony J. Hall's *The American Empire and the Fourth World*, and *Earth into Property*. In these two volumes he traces the trajectory of eurowestern political and economic colonization from early colonization to the global war on terror, demonstrating a consistent thread of colonizing legal strategies that justify for and promote the development of neoliberal global capitalism.

70. The power of renaming locations as part of a conquest was common in Europe. Elio Antonio de Nebrija, a Castillian jurist working for Isabella in 1492, is said to have compiled the first grammar of a European language. When Isabella was presented with it and asked what it was good for, a royal courtier is said to have replied, "Your Majesty . . . language has always been the companion of empire." Quoted in Kirkpatrick Sale, *The Conquest of Paradise* (New York: Alfred A. Knopf, 1990), 18.

71. Albert Memmi, *The Colonizer and the Colonized* (Boston: Beacon Press, 1991), 149.

72. Companion planting is an agricultural technique where certain groups of plants are grown together that mutually benefit each other. For example, corn, beans, and squash have been grown together for millennia because the corn provides a sturdy stalk for the beans to grow up, the beans provide nitrogen for the soil, and the squash helps to provide shade for the ground, which discourages the growth of other competitive plants. Tobacco is widely understood as a natural insecticide.

73. For a brief discussion of the harmful effects of tobacco planting in the Jamestown colony, see Kirkpatrick Sale, *Conquest of Paradise*, 282–83. According to Sale, the monocropping of tobacco would exhaust the soil in five to six years, and then the plantations would be moved further west and the process was repeated. This eurowestern-promulgated ecological disaster was so great that "Even today the tidewater region shows the disastrous effect of plantation-tobacco culture." Sale, *Conquest of Paradise*, 283.

74. According to Kirkpatrick Sale, as early as 1635 the *Jesuit Relations* were reporting that among the "Huron" and "Irokwa" the beavers were already depleted, as on the Massachusetts and Delaware coasts as well. After moving to Saskatchewan and Manitoba for greater supplies, the end of the eighteenth century "saw the 'exhaustion of the beaver fields' and everywhere the 'disappearance of beaver.'" Sale, *Conquest of Paradise*, 290.

75. This analysis does not necessarily suggest a causal relationship between the passages in Genesis and environmental destruction. However, it does describe how a lack of clear ethical constraints on the destruction of the life with which the planet is shared can allow for violence to coalesce to the point of environmental collapse without a large enough backlash to stop it from the people it is hurting. Since the 1960s there have been a number of ecological movements that have worked to steer this trajectory in a different way. However, as evidenced by the annual species loss; the continued mining and extraction of resources, especially fossil fuels; and the ongoing climate change, these movements have yet to coalesce into enough force to significantly alter the political and economic structures that continually develop defense mechanisms to counter these ecological movements.

76. It should be noted that neither the Anishinaabe nor any other Indigenous North American culture has been a static entity. For my analysis this is important because as a people the Anishinaabeg got to the place of effectively negotiating ecological balance because of problems that they had caused previously. Hence, these narratives can be understood as a cultural memory of times when they did treat other animals poorly. In short, we have developed a balanced conceptualization and negotiation with the world because we have learned from our mistakes.

77. Treaty of Washington, 1836, Article 13.

78. *Lyng v. Northwest Indian Cemetery Protection Association*, 485 U.S. 451.

CHAPTER 3. TIME

1. Clifford Geertz, *The Interpretation of Cultures* (New York: Basic Books, 1973), 14.
2. Michael Kearney, *World View* (Novato, CA: Chandler and Sharp Publishers, 1984), 94.
3. Kearney, *World View*, 94. Here Kearney gives the examples in English of "after an hour, ahead of time" as well as temporal sequencing such as "we *come from* the past and *go ahead* into the future," 94 (italics in the original). While these examples do suggest a connection between time and place, they elucidate little about the complex relationships that cultures have to time.
4. Vine Deloria Jr., *God Is Red: A Native View of Religion* (Golden, CO: Fulcrum Publishing, 1992), 70–71. This notion of time as cyclically understood is challenged by Kearney, who suggests the cyclical understanding has been imposed onto Indigenous peoples, and that time is more accurately understood in Indigenous societies as oscillating between two poles. He gives the example of time oscillating between day and night, and seasons between winter and summer. Furthermore he suggests that "it is often inappropriate to . . . a cyclical sense of time. But in the traditional societies to which a cyclical notion of time is usually attributed, circular motion is virtually absent." Kearney, *World View*, 98. However, Kearney misses the significant use of circles in imagery of the earth, sun, moon, and Indigenous villages, not to mention the consistent use of circular motion for Indigenous peoples navigating their way through ceremonies. Indigenous peoples usually travel "sunwise" (clockwise) on numerous occasions when there is a choice presented. Therefore, I will keep with the use of cyclical as an understanding of time.
5. Deloria, *God Is Red*, 63.
6. Robert A. Williams Jr., *Linking Arms Together: American Indian Treaty Visions of Law and Peace, 1600–1800* (New York: Routledge, 1999), 36. All of these concepts are Indigenous in origin and were consistently used in treaty negotiations and relationship building throughout Native North America.
7. Williams, *Linking Arms Together*, 112. The concept of renewal is essential to understanding the ability to keep treaty relationships strong, as each year when the treaty is renewed, there is an opportunity to address any problems or damaging actions to that treaty relationship, and hence resolve those conflicts. The cycle of renewal then is a method of continuing a treaty relationship over time.
8. The spellings of these nations are kept in the original treaty language. Treaty of Greenville, 1795, online text available at https://www.cmich.edu/library/clarke/

ResearchResources/Native_American_Material/Treaty_Rights/Text_of_Michigan_
Related_Treaties.

9. Treaty of Greenville, Articles 1 and 4.

10. Treaty of Greenville, Article 4.

11. Treaty of Washington, 1836, Article 3, online text available at https://www.cmich.
edu/library/clarke/ResearchResources/Native_American_Material/Treaty_Rights/
Text_of_Michigan_Related_Treaties.

12. Treaty of Washington, Article 4.

13. Treaty of Washington, Article 13.

14. Treaty of Washington, Article 8.

15. This is evident in that this treaty was signed and negotiated in Washington, under the customs of European diplomacy. Treaty customs of smoking the pipe and requickening rights that were used at Greenville in 1795 were no longer used. The ongoing conquest and genocide at the hands of war and disease had taken its toll on American Indian peoples east of the Mississippi, and they no longer had the military power to enforce their own visions and customs of treaties and agreements. After approximately 1800, the United States would hold most of the power in these negotiations, and the treaty language reflects this shift in power.

16. George E. (Tink) Tinker, *American Indian Liberation: A Theology of Sovereignty* (Maryknoll, NY: Orbis Books, 2008), 17.

17. Williams, *Linking Arms Together*, 37.

18. Senescence is a much more useful way of describing the life cycle in the fall in Anishinaabe Akiing. Life is reborn in *Ziigwan* (the spring), flourishes in *Niibin* (summer), and decays/ages in *Dagwaagin* (fall), while simultaneously setting seeds for life to be reborn in *Ziigwan* again, after the purification of *Biboon* (winter). Maturity of life could also be used, but is not necessarily associated with the planned movement towards rebirth and continuity. While much of the knowledge about senescence is about the aging process and its link with death, within those discussions is the understanding that life forms reproduce so that life can continue. For example, even in monocarpic senescence, where a single organism like a grass plant is reborn from seed, grows, and decays, it ages and dies in relation to producing seeds that will grow again in the spring. Senescence as a concept is dialogically related to a cyclical understanding of life. See William K. Purves, Gordon H. Orians, and H. Craig Heller, *Life: The Science of Biology* (Sunderland, MA: Sinauer Associates, Inc., 1992), 710.

19. *Aadizookaanag* refers to both the narratives as well as the characters of the narratives. *Aadizookaanag* is the plural form, *aadizookaan* is the singular. John D. Nichols and Earl

Nyholm, *A Concise Dictionary of Minnesota Ojibwe* (Minneapolis: University of Minnesota Press, 1995), 16.

20. I prefer to use the term narrative to describe the events of *Giizhigokwe* and other stories, to guard against the connotations of something related as myth as "untrue." The historicity of an event, whether or not something "really" happened, is a eurowestern issue, associated with the construction of a scientific positivist outlook where reality is divided between the "real" world of nature and science and the "unreal" world of dreams, stories, "myths," and religion. The Anishinaabeg make no such distinctions in their linguistic-conceptual world. All experiences in the Anishinaabeg world are taken as part of the same inclusive reality. Since there has not been a power struggle between science and religion, the Anishinaabeg culture is not split up into competing dualisms.

    According to Jennifer S. H. Brown and Susan Elaine Gray, Hallowell "was clear about the relationship between myth and truth for Ojibwe people. To most outside observers, dominated by western concepts of science and rational thinking, the myths seem utterly fantastic and unrealistic—pure fiction. The Ojibwe, however, could and did accept events in myths as real happenings because for them reality was a more expansive and fluid concept." William Berens and A. I. Hallowell, *Memories, Myths, and Dreams of an Ojibwe Leader*, ed. Jennifer S. H. Brown and Susan Elaine Gray (Montreal: McGill-Queen's University Press, 2009), 118. While this analysis points in the right direction, it is necessary to go deeper into the concept of reality as "more expansive and fluid." To really get at the complexity, one has to delve deeper into the role of these narratives and the possibilities of metamorphosis. Here "fluidity" can mean that humans and other-than-humans are not necessarily distinct, static boundaries, and some people (in an inclusive sense) can transcend these boundaries. Anishinaabeg can draw from not only narratives of these events, but empirical evidence that sometimes these things happen in ceremony. While Hallowell may have understood the "fluidity" for the Anishinaabeg, this translation still allows for a lot of misconception about their culture and is a poor translation.

21. Nichols and Nyholm, *Concise Dictionary*, 83.

22. The narratives are not arranged in a linear fashion and can each be told separately. Each narrative has its own lessons that are used to teach. So each *aadizookewinini*, or storyteller, can choose a narrative that suits the challenges that face that family.

23. It is also important to note that the *aadizookaanag* are also a form of entertainment. People that show a gift for memory are chosen at young ages, and they are taught both the narratives and the craft of performing them. The *aadizookaanag* are only told in the wintertime, usually to small lodges of people, when there is not much else to do during the long winter evenings. A good *aadizookewinini* is a valuable wealth of knowledge for

the people.

24. According to Hallowell, "The recital of myths outside the proper season, moreover, is believed to provoke an unpleasant penalty. It is said by the Saulteaux that toads or frogs (both called one and the other) will crawl up the clothes of a person who tells the sacred stories in summer." Unpublished draft from Hallowell, quoted in Berens and Hallowell, *Memories, Myths and Dreams*, 113. Hallowell had some difficulty getting his informants to relate the narratives, though with William Berens being Christianized, he did not negotiate his life strictly according to these customs and he did share eighteen of the *aadizookaanag*.

25. Hallowell quoted in Berens and Hallowell, *Memories, Myths and Dreams*. Nichols and Nyholm give the definition of *dibaajiimowin* as "story, narrative"; *Concise Dictionary*, 45.

26. *Wiindigo* are other-than-human persons who are usually associated with starvation in winter. They are large, skinny beings who have the ability to devour humans, yet are never able to satisfy their hunger. They represent what happens when greed goes unchecked. *Waabano* ceremonies are more commonly known as "tent shaking" or conjuring ceremonies. These ceremonies are for healing and communicative purposes where the ceremony leader brings the possibility of communication with other-than-human persons. William Berens quoted in Berens and Hallowell, *Memories, Myths and Dreams*, 87.

27. Each animal group is led by an *ogimaa*, or leader. These *ogimaag* are *manidoo* forms of that animal group and help to watch over them. In the *waabano* ceremony, these *ogimaag* often come to speak to the people who are asking for help. In this case, the *mooz* (moose) and *ma'iingan* (wolf) *ogimaag* came and told the hunter that if he wanted to be successful hunting he had to use the meat of the moose correctly.

28. William Berens quoted in Berens and Hallowell, *Memories, Myths and Dreams*, 87.

29. Berens and Hallowell, *Memories, Myths and Dreams*, 85.

30. This ceremony was witnessed by Berens at Thunder Lake; the year is unknown.

31. A. Irving Hallowell, *Contributions to Ojibwe Studies: Essays, 1934–1972*, ed. Jennifer S. H. Brown and Susan Elaine Gray (Lincoln: University of Nebraska Press, 2010), 115. For example, in this process of memory, a person could recall the year of Kurt Cobain's suicide because it was discussed in a class during their senior year of college.

32. Kwame Gyekye, *An Essay on African Philosophical Thought: The Akan Conceptual Scheme* (Philadelphia: Temple University Press, 1987), 169–70. Mbiti as paraphrased by Gyekye. Mbiti makes this assertion based on two East African languages, Gikuyu and Kikamba. Gyekye refutes Mbiti's claim based on the Akan language and conceptualizations of time. In this short eight-page critique, Gyekye uses several means to demonstrate that Mbiti's

generalization of an African concept of time from two languages does not hold for the Akan. He conclusively shows that the Akan do understand a concept of the infinite future, not only with their words that translate as "future," but also through divining activities (which are common practice) where people inquire about future events. See Gyekye, *Essay on African Philosophical Thought*, 169–77, for the full critique.

33. Gyekye, *Essay on African Philosophical Thought*, 172.
34. Gyekye, *Essay on African Philosophical Thought*, 172.
35. Gyekye, *Essay on African Philosophical Thought*, 171.
36. Hallowell gives a similar analysis, though with a lack of depth and using problematic language. He states: "The conventional pattern of dream revelation and the conjuring lodge are, then, institutional means of keeping mythological beings and spiritual entities of other classes constantly contemporary with each new generation of individuals, despite the passage of 'time.'" Hallowell, *Contributions to Ojibwe Studies*, 133.
37. Nichols and Nyholm, *Concise Dictionary*, 60, 61, 165.
38. According to Hallowell, among the Anishinaabeg around the Berens River, their designation for a 24-hour period was *pezagwátabik*, or night. Interestingly enough, this term for "night" was also used as a designation of distance. So if someone was asked how far away they were traveling, they might describe the distance as "two nights away." Hallowell, *Contributions to Ojibwe Studies*, 120–21. Here we see time and space coming together in a single concept. In contemporary Anishinaabemowin, the word *giizhig* is used to denote both time (24 hours) and movement across space (distance traveled in 24 hours.)
39. Nichols and Nyholm, *Concise Dictionary*, 61, 45. While the more formal *dibiki giizis* is used here to differentiate between sun and moon, under common usage the *dibiki* is dropped and the moon is referred to as *giizis* as well. Here it is important to note the economy of Anishinaabemowin in practical use. The *dibiki* can be dropped in situations where it is understood that the moon and not the sun is being discussed.
40. This reference to quantum energy is similar to a scientific understanding of the sun in the eurowest, though it is unclear if it is commonly understood in eurowestern culture that the sun emits this type of energy. This concept of *giizis* and quantum energy comes from personal communication with Margaret Noodin, an Anishinaabekwe linguist, October 17, 2011.
41. "Older Brother" is one familial relationship used. Some Anishinaabeg will use *miishomis*, or grandfather when referring to *giizis*.
42. Hallowell, *Contributions to Ojibwe Studies*, 122.
43. Hallowell, *Contributions to Ojibwe Studies*, 120–21. Temporal divisions of this sort often

baffle eurowesterners who are used to uniform measurements of time. In regard to these six temporal divisions from dawn to the sun over the trees, Hallowell states, "The intervals between the discrete points recognized vary enormously in temporal length as measured on our absolute time scale. But this is irrelevant to the Saulteaux and, of course, it is possible to employ the intervals between any two of the points recognized as a crude measure of temporal length." Hallowell, *Contributions to Ojibwe Studies*, 120.

44. Hallowell, *Contributions to Ojibwe Studies*, 121. More will be discussed as to the important connections to dawn and dusk and their relationship to economic activities of hunting and fishing in a later section.

45. The names of the rest of the week are as follows: *shkwaname giizhigak* (after prayer day), *niizh giizhigak* (second day), *zozep giizhigak* (Joseph's day), *spinaganon* (consecration), *jiibatago giizhigak* (ghost day), *manii giizhigak* (Mary's day). For a full calendar including the numbered day names, see https://ojibwe.net/projects/months-moons/.

46. Hallowell suggests that "The spread of Christianity, then, has been responsible for creating the basis for a new temporal unit in the minds of the Indians. But even so the concept of the week as such does not seem to function very significantly in their life and thought." Hallowell, *Contributions to Ojibwe Studies*, 125. In his realm of experience, the missionaries first came in 1867 and he was making trips to Berens River in the 1930s, so for the Anishinaabeg at the mouth of the river there were roughly sixty-five years of temporal acculturation, which is reflected in these changes. For their relatives further up the river who had at that point little contact with non-Indians and where there was no mission, both the week as a temporal unit and wristwatches were nonexistent. One family in Pekangikum (upriver) did have an alarm clock, but it was "the deferred ting-a-ling of which seemed to fascinate them, rather than its utility as a time-reckoning mechanism." Hallowell, *Contributions to Ojibwe Studies*, 124.

47. These temporal changes, of course, simultaneously came with the imposed necessity of negotiating their economic subsistence from a capitalist wage economy rather than from hunting, fishing, and agriculture. This new economic institution forced them to live regimented by the seven-day week and hourly wage. In combination, this cultural dislocation has forced new relationships that are altering the temporal relationships of the Anishinaabeg.

48. Also, the planet Venus is associated with the feminine in Anishinaabe thought. It is called *Ikwe Anang* (Women's Star) and is related as feminine because of its nine-month cycle where it can be seen both in the morning (morning star) and in the evening (evening star). This nine-month cycle is the same as the gestation period for birthing. See Annette S. Lee, William Wilson, Jeffrey Tibbetts, and Carl Gawboy, *Ojibwe Sky Star*

Map Constellation Guide: An Introduction to Ojibwe Star Knowledge (North Rocks, CA: Lightning Source–Ingram Spark, 2014), 30–31.

49. Thirteen moons do not exactly correlate to 365 days, so according to Hallowell "a seasonal dislocation arises which the Saulteaux correct by adding an unnamed moon to the series." Hallowell, *Contributions to Ojibwe Studies*, 126. Very little is known about how Anishinaabeg handled this as following a lunar calendar has been a casualty of colonization. While there has been resurgence in knowing some of the names of the moons, the Gregorian calendar has been imposed and structures much of Anishinaabeg action in negotiating contemporary daily lives. The list of moon names that follows has twelve named moons.

50. Hallowell suggested that since the attention given to moons was not a succession but a recurring event, "a beginning or ending to their annual cycle is irrelevant." However, in the same paragraph he agrees with Cope that among northern peoples "winter signalizes the 'beginning of the year.'" Hallowell, *Contributions to Ojibwe Studies*, 130–31. However, Johann Kohl, a German travel writer who wrote about the Lake Superior Ojibway, identified that "the moon in February" was the "beginning" of the year as "Many assured me the commencement of the year was typified by this." Johann Georg Kohl, *Kitchi-Game: Life among the Lake Superior Ojibway*, trans. Lascelles Wraxall (St. Paul: Minnesota Historical Society Press, 1985), 120.

51. I added this particular name in place of the *Pokwaagamii Giizis*, or Broken Snow Shoe Moon. I did this because in contemporary Anishinaabeg society many more people participate in sugarbush than wear snowshoes that might break while they are wearing them in crusted snow. This change goes to the point of the variability of naming the moons. Furthermore, since the onset of global warming there has been a shift in the sugaring season in this part of the Anishinaabe Akiing. Before about 1980 very rarely were communities getting sap to run until April. Now, it is often early March when the taps are being put into the trees to collect and boil the sap. In this move I am suggesting that the flexibility of the naming process allows for such changes. That "tradition" holds March as "Broken Snow Shoe" Moon is irrelevant. The naming of the moons is about the important activities and noticeable changes happening around us.

52. *Manidoo* is often translated as "spirit," but because of unintelligibility of a "non-material, non-spatial" entity like spirit, I refuse to use that as a translation. Instead, I keep *Manidoo* as part of the translation, which helps to keep an authentic understanding of the concept, and places responsibility on non-Anishinaabeg to learn about the concept in our own terms. Again, I give a definition of *Manidoo* as a quasi-material life energy.

53. This list of *dibiki giizis* comes from https://ojibwe.net/projects/months-moons/. This list

is from the "Eastern Dialect," except for the addition of *Ziisbakadake Giizis* as explained above. Each moon begins on the full moon and ends the day before the next full moon.

54. Considering this term is used for both the waning and waxing period, it can be assumed that it could be confusing. However, this point in time is used in short-enough duration that it is understood which one is referenced in the economy of the language. Furthermore, if they need to be differentiated, then they could be *nitam* (first) or *ekiniizhing* (second) half-moon, or *jibwaa* (before) or *ishkwaa* (after) the new moon.

55. This point will be further elaborated on in the next section regarding the linguistic formulations of future and past time.

56. Hallowell, *Contributions to Ojibwe Studies*, 126.

57. While there is a recognition of *Makwa Giizis* as a time of regeneration, this should not be misinterpreted as a "new" year as in the eurowestern calendar. There is no conceptualization of linear movement implied in *Makwa Giizis* representing regeneration; it is simply part of a repeating cycle.

58. Hallowell, *Contributions to Ojibwe Studies*, 130.

59. For example, if picking blueberries is being discussed, it is understood that this activity happens during *Miin Giizis*. Yet, more specifically, picking blueberries happens when the blueberries are ready to be picked; hence a description of a specific week or day would be ridiculous from year to year as the berries ripen depending on the seasonal variations, not time.

60. This is somewhat different in eurowestern seasons. With a desire for predictability, control, and accuracy, spring officially starts on March 21, whether or not the weather cooperates.

61. For these narratives see Berens and Hallowell, *Memories, Myths and Dreams*, 132–35. In the latter narrative the winter and summer animals hold a council to compromise on the amount of time each group of animals get to have summer and winter.

62. Carl Gawboy and Ron Morton, *Talking Sky: Ojibwe Constellations as a Reflection of Life on the Land* (Duluth, MN: Rock Flower Press, 2014), 9.

63. Nichols and Nyholm, *Concise Dictionary*, 87. As in many Anishinaabe words, there are many spellings of *Mishibizhii*, and also other closely associated names. The constellation is also known as *gaadidnaway*, which translates as "curly tail" as there is a long tail associated with the constellation. However, *Mmizhibizhii* is also known as the Great Lynx in many narratives. This is due to the use of *bizhiw* used to describe all the big cats of the area, including the bobcat. For a discussion of these differences and their connections to narratives, see Gawboy and Morton, *Talking Sky*, 34–46. See also Lee et al., *Ojibwe Sky Star Map*, 10.

64. For this narrative see Gawboy and Morton, *Talking Sky*, 47–54. For a different version of the *Nanapush* narrative, see Basil Johnston, *Honour Earth Mother* (Lincoln: University of Nebraska Press, 2003), 2–9. In Johnston's narrative *Nanapush* kills a wolf, which is what creates the flood. This diversity of narrative is indicative of the large autonomous population of the Anishinaabeg spread out over a large geographic area.

65. Gawboy and Morton, *Talking Sky*, 12.

66. For a discussion of the narratives of *Biboon*, and versions of narratives of chasing away the Wintermaker, see Gawboy and Morton, *Talking Sky*, 25–33. It is interesting to note that Wintermaker is the only named constellation that is not given in its Anishinaabemowin form. The authors give no explanation for this.

67. There is very little information in the written record about these constellations. While there is more available in Anishinaabeg communities, even there we can see a significant loss of knowledge in the colonial process. Elders are keepers of information and did not always teach all that they could until late in their life. This made the diseases that swept through deadly to both bodies and culture as the elders died at higher rates. Much was lost as whole villages were decimated through wave after wave of disease. Gawboy suggests that "in many places a whole generation was lost, and with them went their knowledge and the stories that went with that knowledge." Gawboy and Morton, *Talking Sky*, 5.

68. This concept of continual rebirth is important in Anishinaabeg culture and is conceptualized in *mino bimaadiziwin*, or the good life.

69. Hallowell, *Contributions to Ojibwe Studies*, 131.

70. *Gikinoonoowin* is also used as a marker of a year. It is used similarly to *Biboon*. Nichols and Nyholm, *Concise Dictionary*, 288.

71. Hallowell notes, "Although winter is the formalized reference for computing yearly intervals in the aboriginal conceptual scheme, the recurrence of the other seasons provides unformalized points of reference that punctuate equivalent intervals." Hallowell, *Contributions to Ojibwe Studies*, 131. In *Chippewa Customs*, Frances Densmore records a narrative of an informant whose father recorded the passing of the year with notches on a stick, and he "had a stick long enough to last a year and he always started a new stick in the fall." Frances Densmore, *Chippewa Customs* (St. Paul: Minnesota Historical Society Press, 1979), 119, 173. This method of recording time must have been a personal use for this man as this type of recording method is not mentioned anywhere else in the record for Anishinaabeg.

72. Cope quoted in Hallowell, *Contributions to Ojibwe Studies*, 131.

73. The ceremonies for reaching puberty for girls were indicated by their receiving their first

menstrual cycle, so for girls this functioned differently. However, while there was not a strict use of age in determining the appropriate time to perform these ceremonies, a general trend was to do this around age thirteen. The physical and emotional attributes of the child would be the primary guide to the decision of when to take the child into the woods.

74. Hallowell, *Contributions to Ojibwe Studies*, 132. The Anishinaabemowin words are from Nichols and Nyholm, *Concise Dictionary*. I chose to stay with the double-vowel spelling orthography of these words to keep consistent with the rest of the words used.

75. In Anishinaabeg culture, there are not particular legal codes that necessitate the year-to-year description of the individual, such as when they can start school, hunt, drive, vote, buy alcohol, or become an elected official.

76. For a description of the use of these verb tenses, see the online resource https://ojibwe. net/lessons/beginner/introduction-to-tenses/.

77. The literal translations are actually, "Yesterday two deer I saw" and "Sturgeon I will cook tomorrow." For purposes of being able to read it more easily, the more user-friendly translation is provided.

78. Days beyond three can be stated as *ingodwaasogonigag noongwa-enji*, or six days from today. However, once someone gets to this many days, often the phases of *giizis* can be utilized at this point to plan ahead seven or more days in the future.

79. Hallowell, *Contributions to Ojibwe Studies*, 126.

80. Kwame Gyekye, *Essay on African Philosophical Thought*, 170.

81. Kwame Gyekye also uses "divining" among the Akan, an activity similar to *waabano* as a demonstration of the infinite future in Akan language and thought. *Essay on African Philosophical Thought*, 175–76.

82. This concept of regeneration is a consistent theme in the *aadizookaanag*, where the characters often go through processes of growth, change, senescence, and rebirth. This cycle of regeneration is part of the same ideological complex of time as a cyclical process.

83. Hallowell quoting unknown informant in an unpublished manuscript, quoted in Berens and Hallowell, *Memories, Myths and Dreams*, 117. Among the Anishinaabeg in Berens River, *Nanapush* is known as *Wisakedjak*, as a result of cultural mixing with Cree relatives.

84. The timing of this particular ceremony makes sense because it would be in the spring when the village would again congregate at their summer fishing camps. This was a perfect way to regenerate the community and to take care of any physical or emotional needs of the community after they have been apart since the fall. There are conflicting reports of the timing of *Midewiwin* ceremonies. They have been linked to spring ceremonies of renewal as suggested above, healing ceremonies during many times of

the year, and also to a cycle around fall annuity payments in the treaty period. This multiplicity in ceremonial suggests that the *Midewiwin* as a society performed numerous ceremonies at different times of the year. See Michael Angel, *Preserving the Sacred: Historical Perspectives on the Ojibwa Midewiwin* (Winnipeg: University of Manitoba Press, 2002).

85. Hallowell, *Contributions to Ojibwe Studies*, 126.

86. This process of shifting economic activities happened throughout the year, going from the spring fish runs to planting crops, setting up summer camps, berry picking, wild ricing, harvesting gardens, and hunting in the fall and winter.

87. Deloria, *God Is Red*, 71.

88. There are actually two creation narratives in the first two chapters of Genesis. In Gen. 1, humans are created together, and in Gen. 2, woman is made from the rib of man.

89. This is Gen. 3: 1–7.

90. Deloria, *God Is Red*, 79.

91. This is Gen. 3: 14–19, where God gives the punishment to Adam and Eve for their transgressions of eating from the Tree of Life.

92. Deloria, *God Is Red*, 80.

93. The actual season is dependent on each denomination. At least among mainline denominations, it would be more accurate to say that the liturgical calendar is Advent to Easter, as Pentecost significantly diminished in importance in the American context throughout the nineteenth and twentieth centuries. For a discussion of Pentecost as historically an important part of the Christian liturgical calendar, see Albert Hernández, *Subversive Fire: The Untold Story of Pentecost* (Lexington, KY: Emeth Press, 2010).

94. This linear trajectory is the same for recent events, relying upon the numbering of years since the birth of Jesus. However, when the geological record is concerned, BP (before present) is used instead of BC (before Christ), since the two-thousand-year difference is numerically insignificant when discussing millions of years.

95. Another example of linear thinking would be when someone is dissatisfied with something like a racist act, one may say, "I can't believe in this day and age . . . ," which presumes a linear progression of cultural morality should be happening. Furthermore, the comedic notion that "we should have flying cars by now" also represents a belief in the linear progress of technology. These examples could go on and on, and they all demonstrate a deeply held belief in the linear progression of time and its effects on developing eurowestern culture consistently over time.

96. Deloria, *God Is Red*, 63. This text was originally written in 1970, so an addendum could be added to this part of the text that includes the recent "war on terror" and its crusade

against radical Islam.

97. Deloria, *God Is Red*, 71. The next line, "but time has little relationship to space," I would suggest is an overstatement. Both in the eurowestern and Anishinaabeg contexts there is a relationship of time to space, however different they might be.

98. Winona LaDuke, *All Our Relations: Native Struggles for Land and Life* (Cambridge, MA: South End Press, 1999), 127.

CHAPTER 4. RELATIONSHIPS TO LIFE

1. Robert Williams Jr., *Linking Arms Together: American Indian Visions of Law and Peace, 1600–1800* (New York: Routledge, 1999), 62. I intentionally omitted the final line of this quote, which states "and protection from feared enemies," because I disagree with Williams on how often this came up before eurowestern contact, or in the "Encounter era." I believe this line of thinking overemphasizes the "harsh realities of survival" as the underlying necessity for treaty making between American Indian groups. I believe that Indiegnous cultures have peaceable relationships as a normative standard, and while there were moments of warfare between groups, most groups succeeded in having effective treaty relationships between neighboring groups most of the time.

2. For a description of Indiegnous protocols used in the 1795 Treaty of Greenville, see Williams, *Linking Arms Together*, especially 71 (seating arrangements), 76 (requickening ceremony), 86 (use of narrative), 95 (mourning ritual).

3. While there were Indigenous protocols used in the 1795 Treaty of Greenville, that does not automatically necessitate negotiating power. While the Ohio Alliance of Natives worked to limit their losses, the United States Government used this treaty to solidify the boundaries that had been fraudulently imposed via the Treaties of Fort Stanwix (1784), Fort MacIntosh (1785), Mouth of the Great Miami (1786), and Fort Harmar (1789), all of which were geared towards stealing the Ohio Valley. One of the tactics used was to pretend after the fact that certain Native Nations were represented when they were not.

4. While there were Indian agents of the Bureau of Indian Affairs who were assigned to serve the local area and were supposed to act in ways to allow for the redress of grievances, rarely did these arrangements meet the needs of the local Indiegnous population.

5. Treaty of Washington, 1836, online text available at https://www.cmich.edu/library/clarke/ResearchResources/Native_American_Material/Treaty_Rights/Text_of_Michigan_Related_Treaties.

6. Treaty of Washington, 1836.

7. Vine Deloria Jr., *God Is Red: A Native View of Religion* (Golden, CO: Fulcrum Publishing, 1992), 88. I also disagree with his use of "man" here to denote humans.

8. For a discussion of linguistic relativity relating to the Sapir-Whorf hypothesis, see John A. Lucy, *Grammatical Categories and Cognition* (New York: Cambridge University Press, 1992); John A. Lucy, *Language Diversity and Thought: A Reformulation of the Linguistic Relativity Hypothesis* (New York: Cambridge University Press, 1992); and John J. Gumperz and Stephen C. Levinson, eds., *Rethinking Linguistic Relativity* (New York: Cambridge University Press, 1996).

9. Ngũgĩ wa Thiong'o, *Decolonising the Mind: The Politics of Language in African Literature* (Portsmouth, NH: Heinemann Educational Books, 1989), 4.

10. Kwasi Wiredu, "The Akan World-View," colloquium paper, Program on History, Culture and Society, Woodrow Wilson International Center for Scholars, May 19, 1985, 1.

11. Wiredu uses the term "Western," not eurowestern to designate the European philosophical tradition. I use eurowestern to stay consistent in language, and I do believe that we are using these two concepts very similarly.

12. Wiredu, "The Akan World-View," 2.

13. Wiredu, "The Akan World-View," 2.

14. Wiredu, "The Akan World-View," 2–3.

15. Wiredu, "The Akan World-View," 3.

16. For a full discussion of the points on Creation, God, transcendence, and spatiality, see Wiredu, "The Akan World-View," 3–20.

17. Wiredu, "The Akan World-View," 2.

18. A. I. Hallowell, "The Role of Dreams in Ojibwa Culture," in *Contributions to Ojibwe Studies: Essays, 1934–1972*, ed. Jennifer S. H. Brown and Susan Elaine Gray (Lincoln: University of Nebraska Press, 2010), 444.

19. I should note that Hallowell's line of thinking here is curious in that while he seems to want to accord Anishinaabeg thought a higher status than primitive, he relies heavily upon others who do not. He notes his description of the inapplicability of the natural/ supernatural dichotomy with Ackerknecht, who states "'Supernaturalistic,' though often used by the best authorities, is quite obviously a misnomer for these primitive representations, as it presupposes the notion of the predictable natural which primitives characteristically do not have." Ackerknecht quoted in "The Role of Dreams in Ojibwa Culture," 455–60 n. 17. Hallowell continues with his disallowance of advanced scientific thinking, this time quoting Bidney in his text, who suggests "the dichotomy of the natural and supernatural implies a scientific epistemology and critical metaphysical sophistication which must not be assumed without reliable evidence." Bidney quoted

in "The Role of Dreams in Ojibwa Culture," 445. Hallowell does not challenge their conceptualizations of Indigenous peoples, and his stated desire to afford Anishinaabeg a higher status comes off as ambiguous at best.

20. Margaret Noori, *"Beshaabiiag G'gikenmaaigowag*: Comets of Knowledge," in *Centering Anishinaabeg Studies: Understanding the World through Stories*, ed. Jill Doerfler, Niigaanwewidam James Sinclair, and Heidi Kiiwetinepinesiik Stark (East Lansing: Michigan State University Press, 2013), 35–36. In the time subsequent to the writing of this book, Margaret's last name changed from Noori to Noodin. In the text I will stick with her present name, Noodin.

21. Noori, *"Beshaabiiag G'gikenmaaigowag*," 36.

22. Noori, *"Beshaabiiag G'gikenmaaigowag*," 55–56 n. 1. These suggestions of *Shkaakaamikwe* as life giving are from Basil Johnston, Isaac Pitawankwat, and "other Ontario storytellers." It is interesting to note some of the regional differences regarding these terms and even the *Giizhigokwe* narratives. Generally speaking, these female narratives are much more prominent in the eastern territory of Anishinaabe Akiing, including eastern Michigan and Ontario. Further to the west, these narratives and usages of relating to the earth as mother are used less often, if at all.

23. Here I am making this comparison to goddess and worship as a method of clearly distinguishing *Mazikaamikwe* and the logics of the web of relatedness as fundamentally different from the eurowestern logic of hierarchy embedded in the Christian-based goddess and worship talk. Too often newcomers to this information will too quickly jump to analogy as a method of understanding, and euroform Indigenous concepts out of their intended logics and into those of the eurowest.

24. Noori, *"Beshaabiiag G'gikenmaaigowag*," 40.

25. A. I. Hallowell, "Ojibwa Ontology, Behavior, and World View," in *Contributions to Ojibwa Studies*, 546–47. This description, while useful, raises some questions about the accuracy of his retelling. Being that all sensory experience is considered part of the same reality, there must have been a reason that the elders were skeptical, or at least really interested in this experience of the young boy. Otherwise, there would be no reason to doubt his experience in the first place.

26. *Mitig* is tree, *mitigoog* is the plural form.

27. For a reading of this narrative, see Eva Marie Garroutte and Kathleen Delores Westcott, "The Story Is a Living Being: Companionship with Stories in Anishinaabeg Studies," in Doerfler, Sinclair, and Stark, *Centering Anishinaabeg Studies*, 61–66. In this narrative the young woman grieves for her husband, who died by going into the forest and sitting at the base of a tree. Over time, the tree helps her to regain her will to live and offers its

own skin (birch bark) and shows the young woman how to make beautiful baskets. She returns to the community with this gift and shows others how to make the baskets as well.

28. This translation is from a personal conversation with Margaret Noodin, October 2010.

29. Even within the growing written Anishinaabe corpus of literature, *chidibenjiged* does not show up in the translational dictionaries most commonly referred to. The Nichols and Nyholm, Baraga, and Basil Johnston references all skip this concept. This may be because these references are reserved for commonly used words and concepts, or that the communities that these speakers come from do not consider it a pertinent concept. Again, there is a lot of diversity among Anishinaabe communities, so *chidibenjiged* may not be known or understood by all communities. It could also be the case that the principles understood in *chidibenjiged* have been transferred to other concepts like *kitchi manidoo*. The process of the shifting meanings of *kitchi manidoo* will be discussed in the next section.

30. While it is helpful to think of *chidibenjiged* as giving an unconditional mandate, as is often the case when this phrase is invoked, there are limits as to what can and cannot be considered as belonging. It is not necessary to say this in many Indigenous communities, but the conditions of belonging in a community are that "all things belong" that are life giving in some way. Clearly, deforestation and killing off of entire species as experienced in the eurowestern colonial project are things that do not belong within this system of thought.

31. John D. Nichols and Earl Nyholm spell this *dibendaagozi* and define it as "be controlled, be owned, belong, be a member"; *A Concise Dictionary of Minnesota Ojibwe* (Minneapolis: University of Minnesota Press, 1995), 45. I got the "act of belonging" definition from personal communication with Margaret Noodin, April 17, 2015. The notions of *chidibenjiged* as associated with control and ownership will be discussed later.

32. There are multiple ways to say what *doodem* one belongs to, and more often than not, a simpler form of *makwa nindoodem* (bear is my clan.)

33. This is a very different method of conceptualization from eurowestern languages based in nouns as they tend to overemphasize the knowing of what a thing is to the exclusion of what it does or teaches us.

34. A. I. Hallowell, "Some Empirical Aspects of Northern Saulteaux Religion," in *Contributions to Ojibwe Studies*, 367. The punctuation around (highest?) is in the original.

35. Hallowell, "Some Empirical Aspects of Northern Saulteaux Religion," 379.

36. I use the caveat of "almost" here to identify the necessity of *chidibenjiged* as an energy that is recognized by Anishinaabeg and other forms of life. If it were purely conceptual,

then it could only exist within Anishinaabeg thought and not be a guiding logic for the rest of life to follow as well.

37. While the verb *zhitoon* could be said to designate an Anishinaabeg equivalent of power and ownership, it does not have the same cultural association as owner or boss. Furthermore, to suggest that the *manidoo* leader of, say, the *makwag*, or bears, "owns" the rest of the bears would take the notion of leadership and responsibility for that species out of an Anishinaabeg context. The larger cultural context that boss and owner have within eurowestern culture does not exist within Anishinaabeg culture.

38. This question of whether or not there is a High God concept among Indigenous peoples is not new. There was an ongoing debate in the early twentieth century as to whether or not Indigenous peoples had this concept before European contact. Alanson Skinner, writing in 1909, suggests that "Certain it is that they were, as is so universal in North America, polytheistic, and that the idea of a single 'great spirit,' (Kitche-manitou) is entirely a European importation; and none are more positive of this than the Cree themselves." Alanson Skinner, "Notes on the Eastern Cree and Northern Saulteaux," in *Anthropological Papers of the American Museum of Natural History*, vol. 9, pt. 1 (New York: American Museum of Natural History, 1911), 59. John Cooper, working with the Cree around James Bay in the early 1930s, comes to a different conclusion, stating that "the concept of the Supreme Being and the practices associated therewith distinctly conform to Indian and non-Christian patterns rather than to Christian ones." John M. Cooper, *The Northern Algonquian Supreme Being* (New York: AMS Press, 1978), 72. Both of these ethnographers use flawed techniques and wildly misinterpret much of their data. Neither one is a reliable source on the matter, but it is important to note the ongoing dialogue and discrepancies that are in the written record on the subject of *kitchi manidoo*. See also George (Tink) Tinker, "Why I Do Not Believe in a Creator," in *Buffalo Shout, Salmon Cry: Conversations on Creation, Land Justice and Life Together*, ed. Steve Heinrechs (Waterloo, ON: Herald Press, 2013), 167–79.

39. In Anishinaabemowin gendered pronouns do not exist; therefore we do not run into this problem of hypersexing concepts when it is unnecessary. This is a consistent phenomenon for languages indigenous to North America.

40. As a reminder, when we think of *manidoo* that quasi-material life energy is spatially located, like light in its dual wave-particle properties.

41. I take up that further elaboration of *kitchi manidoo* in the next section.

42. Margaret Noodin, *Bawaajimo: A Dialect of Dreams in Anishinaabe Language and Literature* (East Lansing: Michigan State University Press, 2014), xvi–xvii.

43. Noodin, *Bawaajimo*, xvii.

44. Here think of the work of Peter Jones and other missionaries who worked diligently to attach Anishinaabemowin to eurochristian concepts as cultural equivalents. In the case of Jones, we get *kitchi manidoo* as an equivalent of God in the Christian sense. Within his particular Anishinaabeg Christian community he worked to bend Anishinaabeg words to eurochristian meaning. Subsequent generations of people were then raised in a community where the meaning of *kitchi manidoo* was filled with concepts and imagery of the Christian Bible. This is a good example of what Wiredu considers "thinking with a colonized mind."

45. Noodin, *Bawaajimo*, xvii.

46. This resurgence of Indiegnous resistance should not be read as a wholly different method of engaging in resistance. There were many forms of resistance throughout the late nineteenth century and early twentieth century that can be seen as a continuum of resistance from the open warfare that was seen in the eighteenth and nineteenth centuries.

47. This is an oversimplification of Jones's work in a larger sphere of colonization. In the midst of the active genocide that was being perpetrated against Anishinaabeg and other Indigenous peoples of the region, his actions of organizing into a Christian community can also be seen as a necessary move for survival. This colonial history is fraught with a number of complex moves and motives that need further attention to successfully negotiate effective meaning making.

48. Basil Johnston, *Ojibway Heritage* (Lincoln: University of Nebraska Press, 1990), 12. Johnston does not follow the double-vowel orthography. When in quotes I will keep his original spelling, but in my own texts I will stay consistent with the double-vowel orthography. He also uses Manitou instead of *manidoo*, so I will use his spelling in quotations and the double-vowel version of *manidoo* in my own text.

49. Johnston, *Ojibway Heritage*, 12.

50. Johnston, *Ojibway Heritage*, 12–13.

51. Basil Johnston, *The Manitous: The Spiritual World of the Ojibway* (St. Paul: Minnesota Historical Society Press, 2001), 2.

52. For discussions of these particular *manidoog*, see Basil Johnston, *Ojibway Heritage*; *The Manitous*; and *Honour Earth Mother* (Lincoln: University of Nebraska Press, 2003).

53. In an earlier chapter, I extended the discussion of spirit as both nonspatial and nonmaterial because I am discussing the mistranslation of *manidoo* as spirit. However, here the mistranslation of *kitchi manidoo* is that of a Christian God. Since God has been defined as "substance" from early in the third century, it can be associated with materiality. However, I would suggest that there is considerable confusion about

this aspect of God within Christian theology; while the "substance" is understood theoretically, because of God's distance from humans and "creation" it also functions as a nonmaterial entity as well. For this purpose of this chapter I will keep the discussions around spatiality and not materiality when I discuss *kitchi manidoo*, and add materiality when discussing *manidoo* and spirit.

54. Johnston, *The Manitous*, xxi–xxii.

55. Johnston, *The Manitous*, 2.

56. Admittedly, this seems like an almost insurmountable task. *Kitchi Manidoo* has been used for many generations and it may have a reference and meaning that continues to be useful to the Anishinaabeg. However, it is important to push the envelope of decolonization and make bold moves for the purpose of providing life-giving culture and relationships.

57. Bob Williams quoted in Amy McCoy, "Minobimaadiziwin: Perceiving the Good Life through Anishinaabe Language" (master's thesis, Michigan State University, 2007), 77.

58. McCoy, "Minobimaadiziwin," 77.

59. It should be stated that McCoy's interview of Williams is not about *Gizhe Manidoo* directly, but the living out of *mino bimaadiziwin*, so it is no fault of the author or of the speaker that there is not a deeper discussion of that topic.

60. Winona LaDuke, "Like Tributaries to a River," in *The Winona LaDuke Reader: A Collection of Essential Writings*, ed. Margret Aldrich (Stillwater, MN: Voyageur Press, 2002), 55. Poem translated by Marlene Stately.

61. Basil H. Johnston, *Anishinaubae Thesaurus* (East Lansing: Michigan State University Press, 2007), 17.

62. Nichols and Nyholm, *Concise Dictionary of Minnesota Ojibwe*, 57.

63. While one could certainly argue for the transformation of the concept of God in its association with *kitchi* or *gizhe manidoo*, considering the gross power imbalance associated with Anishinaabeg communities as compared to their eurowestern neighbors, these desires can be seen as rather naive. In the process of decolonization it is necessary to be very honest with ourselves so that we do not continue to reproduce problems for future generations of Anishinaabeg.

64. LaDuke, "Like Tributaries," 55.

65. The names for brother and sister change depending upon the gender and age of the child in relationship to the sibling. If the individual here is female then the correct relationship would be *nimisenh* (older sister), *nishiime* (younger sister), *indawema* (brother) and *nisayenh* (older brother). Here both *indawema*, *nishiime*, and *nisayenh* are used regardless of gender, so a better translation would be sibling of the opposite sex and younger sibling

respectively. See Nichols and Nyholm, *Concise Dictionary*, entries for brother and sister, 150, 248. The prefix *niin* (I or mine) is shortened to an *n'* as a possessive.

66. These names are for parallel aunts (mother's sister) and uncles (father's brother). For cross aunt (mother's brother) it would be *ninoshenh* and cross uncle (father's sister) it would be *inzhishenh*. For cross cousins the relationship would be named as *niitawis* (male cross cousin who is male) or *niinimoshenh* (cross cousin of the opposite sex). For a female *niinimoshenh* would also still be used, but a male cross cousin would be called *indaangoshenh*. There are differences in language between parallel and cross cousins because cross cousins were considered possible mates in adult life, whereas parallel cousins were not. See Nichols and Nyholm, *Concise Dictionary*, entry for cousin, 161.

67. This is slightly different for a female, who would call a friend *n'niijikwe*. See Nichols and Nyholm, *Concise Dictionary*, entry for friend, 184.

68. It is also possible that someone may receive several names during a lifetime, each given at a different point in their life or for a position of leadership they may have taken on.

69. It should be pointed out that *nozhishenh* is gender-neutral and *indoozhim* and *indoozhimis* are the names for parallel nephew and niece. Cross nephew would be *niningwanis* and cross niece is *nishimis*. See Nichols and Nyholm, *Concise Dictionary*, entries for son, 253; daughter, 164; grandchild, 189; nephew, 218; and niece, 218.

70. George (Tink) Tinker, *American Indian Liberation: A Theology of Sovereignty* (Maryknoll, NY: Orbis Books, 2008), 8.

71. Johnston, *Ojibway Heritage*, 16.

72. Here it is useful to think of the spatial world of the Anishinaabeg. While Bahweting (Sault Ste. Marie, Michigan, or Ontario) would be surrounded by other Anishinaabeg communities, the same was not true of the western boundaries shared with Dakota peoples in what is now called Minnesota, or in the east around the areas of what is now called southern Ontario with the Haudenosaunee peoples. In Anishinaabeg communities that were close to these boundaries there were treaties in place that held the closer communities in positive relationship with one another, most of the time.

73. This village-to-village relationship across international boundaries should not be confused with a larger nation-to-nation relationship where the whole of the Dakota Nation or Haudenosaunee Confederacy would be a part of this local relationship. These larger national meetings would take place from time to time, but were of a different type of relationship than the local village.

74. For an example of this type of community relationship to a place and experience of *manidoog*, see Noodin, *"Beshaabiiag G'gikenmaaigowag,"* 37–38. In this chapter she discusses a narrative from Gregor McGregor from Whitefish River First Nation, who

describes a community interacting with *manidoog* on a rock in a river. After the event they drew pictures of the *manidoog* on that rock. In describing the narrative she states, "The land then becomes a map of understanding, and the task of the *Anishinaabeg* is to record what is seen through narrative and image."

75. The particulars of this church hierarchy would play out differently in different denominations. For Catholics the pope, followed by cardinals to priests could be articulated. For Methodists it would be the Council of Bishops and one could argue the General Conference as part of the hierarchy. That the particulars differ makes no difference as what I am arguing for is the manifestation of a hierarchical logic. That logic holds for any Christian relationship.

76. One could retort here that this is disrespectful to worms as this places them very low in the eurowestern hierarchy.

77. For a deeper discussion of an up-down image schema, see Steven T. Newcomb, *Pagans in the Promised Land: Decoding the Doctrine of Christian Discovery* (Golden, CO: Fulcrum Publishing, 2008), 66–72.

78. While this is clearly an oversimplification, the logic of hierarchy is manifest in the places people live and the cars that they drive. Hence there is an American obsession particularly with homes and vehicles as identity markers of success for middle-class peoples.

79. Here just think of the development of mining technologies and geological knowledge as a necessary means for the greater profit in extracting resources. Technologies such as cyanide leach mining for gold are a good example of this dysfunctional relationship of science and capitalism.

80. For a discussion of this dysfunctional relationship between science and capitalism, see Jean-François Lyotard, *The Postmodern Condition: A Report on Knowledge*, trans. Geoff Bennington and Brian Massumi (Minneapolis: University of Minnesota Press, 1984), 41–47. Lyotard describes this unbalanced relationship between science and capitalism as rooted in the need for the validation of proof, which becomes tied to the ability of the human body to optimize its senses to prove hypotheses. Lyotard states, "No money [to purchase laboratory equipment] no proof—and that means no verification of statements and no proof. The games of scientific language become the games of the rich, in which whoever is wealthiest has the best chance of being right. An equation between wealth, efficiency, and truth is thus established" (45).

81. See Mike Hawkins's book *Social Darwinism in European and American Thought, 1860–1945: Nature as Model and Nature as Threat* (New York: Cambridge University Press, 1997).

82. For a brief discussion of the National Park Service's decision on controlling the elk population, see the Rocky Mountain National Park Elk and Vegetation Management Plan, available at http://www.nps.gov/romo/parkmgmt/upload/elk_veg_newsletter_dec_07_small.pdf. This discussion covers the early stages of implementing the plan. For the full Environmental Impact Statement, go to https://www.nps.gov/romo/learn/management/upload/elk_veg_newsletter_dec_07_small.pdf. For a more detailed fact sheet on the Park's plan and decision-making process, go to the Elk and Vegetation Management Plan Fact Sheet, available at http://www.nps.gov/romo/parkmgmt/elkveg_fact_sheet.htm. As often happens in controversial action, the National Park Service is being sued over the decision not to reintroduce wolves into the park as part of the solution. For a discussion of this suit see Amy Bounds, "Rocky Mountain National Park Wolf Reintroduction Case to Be Heard at CU-Boulder," https://www.dailycamera.com/2012/09/17/rocky-mountain-national-park-wolf-reintroduction-case-to-be-heard-at-cu-boulder.

83. Here I emphasize the contradictory logic that is missed in the discussions of cultural evolution and the linear logic of eurowestern thought. See Hawkins, *Social Darwinism in European and American Thought*, 108.

84. The park employee did make some positive comments on the allowance of hunters into the park. Being that Rocky Mountain National Park (along with many other park systems) needs the entrance fees from the visitors to keep itself afloat, a certain amount of care around the matter is understandable. There was fear among the park employees that if the public consumers of the park were to see the hunting in the form of dead elk, that it would negatively affect the public. However, according to this employee, the hunters were few and discreet in their movements, and there were no negative encounters or feedback that she was aware of.

85. For a brief overview of the effects of colonization on Great Lakes ecology, destruction, and water quality, see EPA, *The Great Lakes: An Environmental Atlas and Resource Book*, especially chap. 4 titled "The Great Lakes Today: Concerns," available at http://www.epa.gov/greatlakes/atlas/glat-ch4.html. This resource gives a good overview of the problems of pollution, where the contaminants have come from, and the problems associated with their introduction. For a discussion of how the pollution has affected the ability to eat the fish in the Great Lakes, see the Michigan Department of Community Health's *Eat Safe Fish Guide*, available at http://www.michigan.gov/documents/mdch/MDCH_EAT_SAFE_FISH_GUIDE_-_UPPER_PENINSULA_WEB_455361_7.pdf. This resource details the toxicity of different species of fish in specific lakes and streams and gives guidelines about safe levels of human consumption. While the levels of toxins vary in the fish species from place to place, according to these guidelines no fish should be consumed more than six

times per month. This is a significant loss for people who were accustomed to eating fish almost every day for much of the year. For a discussion of extinct fish species in the Great Lakes, see Extinct Fish in Canada, available at https://www.currentresults.com/Endangered-Animals/North-America/extinct-fish-canada.php. I should also remind the reader that the Great Lakes cover a gigantic watershed that is made up of 21 percent of the world's surface freshwater. This is not a small waterway, but one-fifth of the world's supply of freshwater, which is polluted to the point where the fish, a significant source of lean protein, cannot be safely eaten on a weekly basis. For a breakdown of the lakes, see http://www.epa.gov/greatlakes/basicinfo.html.

CHAPTER 5. A LOGIC OF BALANCE

1. The concept of *mino bimaadiziwin* will be explained in detail later.
2. Treaty of Washington, 1836, online text available at https://www.cmich.edu/library/clarke/ResearchResources/Native_American_Material/Treaty_Rights/Text_of_Michigan_Related_Treaties.
3. Here I am agreeing with Leanne Simpson, who writes that *mino bimaadiziwin* "is becoming almost an overused and oversimplified concept in Nishnaabeg scholarship particularly amongst non-speakers and cultural beginners." Leanne Simpson, *Dancing on Our Turtle's Back: Stories of Nishnaabeg Re-Creation, Resurgence, and a New Emergence* (Winnipeg, MB: Arbeiter Publishing, 2011), 26–27 n. 9. One need only to do a search on *mino bimaadiziwin* to demonstrate the plethora of titles that use the concept in academic and popular writing.
4. John D. Nichols and Earl Nyholm, *A Concise Dictionary of Minnesota Ojibwe* (Minneapolis: University of Minnesota Press, 1995), 32.
5. Nichols and Nyholm, *Concise Dictionary*, 85.
6. It should be noted that even though Basil Johnston has been involved in teaching and writing in Anishinaabemowin for decades, he rarely uses the concept in his work. His 2007 *Anishinaubae Thesaurus* does not include *mino bimaadiziwin*. In the examples he gives for the prefix *mino*, he does not include this concept, even though he certainly is aware of its popularity. Basil Johnston, *Anishinaubae Thesaurus* (East Lansing: Michigan State University Press, 2007), 168. This is curious, but can be explained by the regional diversity inherent in Anishinaabemowin dialects. While he does not use the wording *mino bimaadiziwin*, he does cover similar concepts in some of his later writings. I will discuss his use of those concepts further.
7. Winona LaDuke, *All Our Relations: Native Struggles for Land and Life* (Cambridge, MA:

South End Press, 1999), 132.

8. LaDuke, *All Our Relations*, 133. In 1999, some 50,000 sturgeon hatchlings were returned to White Earth.

9. LaDuke, *All Our Relations*, 133.

10. LaDuke, *All Our Relations*, 133.

11. LaDuke, *All Our Relations*, 134. *Mi'iw* in this sense would translate as "that is all."

12. Dumont quoted in LaDuke, *All Our Relations*, 132.

13. Simpson, *Dancing on Our Turtle's Back*, 27 n. 18.

14. Simpson, *Dancing on Our Turtle's Back*, 27 n. 18.

15. Amy Christine McCoy, "Minobimaadiziwin: Perceiving the Good Life through Anishinaabe Language" (master's thesis, Michigan State University, 2007), 5.

16. McCoy, "Minobimaadiziwin," 5–6.

17. McCoy, "Minobimaadiziwin," 5.

18. That these narratives are in print is a double-edged sword in that while there is a greater access for Anishinaabeg and non-Anishinaabeg alike, they are written in English, which often takes some of their meaning out of context. Other times the narratives that are written down are largely fabricated. For a collection indicative of these fabrications and euroforming, see Henry Rowe Schoolcraft, *Schoolcraft's Indian Legends*, ed. Mentor L. Williams (East Lansing: Michigan State University Press, 1991). For an early written version of narratives by an Anishinaabe person, see William Jones, *Ojibwa Texts Collected by William Jones*, ed. Truman Michelson (New York: E.J. Brill, 1917). Even though Jones was himself Ojibwa, his English translations often fall into the trap of capitulating to a euroformed framework of religion.

19. I use Johnston's narratives here not only for their accessibility for readers to seek out for themselves, but also to follow a consistent trajectory of scholarly work.

20. Basil Johnston, *Walking in Balance: Meeyau-ossaewin* (Wiarton, ON: Kegedonce Press, 2013), 43. In this section I will stick with Johnston's pronunciation and spelling of *Nana'b'oozoo*, to make the text more readable. I still prefer the term *Nanapush*; however, the brevity of this section suggests keeping with his spelling.

21. Johnston, *Walking in Balance*, 44. It may seem out of balance to suggest that *Nana'b'oozoo* should fend for himself, but as a trickster figure he often struggles to follow directions or pay heed to warnings from the rest of life. There is an understanding in the culture that he would be thought of as suspect in this scenario. In this way, it is important that *Nana'b'oozoo* has a family that he is caring for because it invokes a larger Anishinaabeg community.

22. Johnston, *Walking in Balance*, 44.

23. There is a narrative about the deer being taken away by the crows because they were being taken for granted by the Anishinaabeg. The deer only returned when they were promised that they would again be respected by having ceremony and protocols adhered to when they were killed. See Basil Johnston, *Ojibway Heritage* (Lincoln: University of Nebraska Press, 1990), 55–57.

24. Basil Johnston, *Living in Harmony: Mino-nawae-indawaewin* (Wiarton, ON: Kegedonce Press, 2011), 56. The full narrative is on pages 56–60.

25. *Pukawiss* is the second son of *Winona* and *Aepingushmook*, the West Wind. He is known to be the progenitor of dancing and performances in Anishinaabeg culture. For a longer discussion of *Pukawiss*, see Basil Johnston, *The Manitous: The Spiritual World of the Ojibway* (St. Paul: Minnesota Historical Society Press, 2001), 27–35.

26. Johnston, *Living in Harmony*, 58.

27. Johnston, *Living in Harmony*, 59.

28. Johnston, *Living in Harmony*, 60.

29. The closest that we have to these social gatherings today is the powwow. However, it is important to remember that these gatherings are a contemporary take on an older dynamic of social gatherings including society dances, community celebrations, and political gatherings.

30. These brief discussions are only the tip of the iceberg of the full meaning of these narratives. Especially in their longer versions, they are much richer in detail and drenched with multiple layers of meaning. My discussions are strictly focused on the concepts of balance and harmony in Anishinaabeg communities.

31. This is not to suggest that *mino bimaadiziwin* is not an old concept as well; it has just received so much attention in the last couple of decades that it has taken on a life of its own. *Mino bimaadiziwin* is also discussed in A. I. Hallowell's article "Ojibwa Ontology, Behavior, and World View" as "life in the fullest sense, life in the sense of longevity, health and freedom from misfortune." A. I. Hallowell, "Ojibwa Ontology, Behavior, and World View," in *Contributions to Ojibwe Studies: Essays, 1934–1972*, ed. Jennifer S. H. Brown and Susan Elaine Gray (Lincoln: University of Nebraska Press, 2010), 559. Hallowell's research was among the Berens River Anishinaabeg near Lake Winnipeg.

32. Johnston, *Living in Harmony*, 3.

33. *Collins English Dictionary* (New York: HarperCollins Publishers, 2012).

34. "Equilibrium," in American Heritage, *Stedman's Medical Dictionary* (New York: Houghton Mifflin, 2002).

35. Recall the narrative that William Berens tells of the tent shaking ceremony where the moose and wolf *ogimaag* come to tell the man that he needs to stop leaving the

moose carcasses in the woods and use them appropriately. See William Berens and A. I. Hallowell, *Memories, Myths, and Dreams of an Ojibwe Leader*, ed. Jennifer S. H. Brown and Susan Elaine Gray (Montreal: McGill-Queen's University Press, 2009), 87.

36. "Homeostasis," in *The American Heritage Science Dictionary* (New York: Houghton Mifflin Co.); Dictionary.com, http://dictionary.reference.com/browse/homeostasis.

37. For those not familiar with life in the north woods, when deer die in the winter their bodies are quickly frozen by the below-freezing temperatures and often quickly covered by snow. In the spring when the snow melts, these well-preserved bodies are easily uncovered and eaten by bears, foxes, crows, and a lot of other animals in search of an easy source of protein.

38. This is clearly an oversimplification as the factors affecting deer and bear populations are far more complex than there is room to present here. The ability of deer to last through the winter is first affected by the quantity and quality of their food supply in the fall, the depth of the snow, the duration of the cold, and how quickly the snow melts in the spring. However, this example suffices to demonstrate the signs that can be read by the Anishinaabeg and other animals in the forest.

39. For example, recall the efforts of the Michigan Department of Environmental Quality (DEQ) and their denial of the Anishinaabeg challenge to the mine opening at *Migizi Sin*, or Eagle Rock near Keweenaw Bay, Michigan. Their legal brief denied the religious claim because there was no building for human occupancy; they did not have to consider it a place of worship. This example shows the enmeshed nature of the political (Michigan DEQ) and the economic (mining company). See State of Michigan, Department of Environmental Quality, File No. GW1810162, http://turtletalk.files.wordpress.com/2010/01/kennecott-fdo.pdf.

40. It is important here to state again that I am describing Anishinaabeg village life in its early treaty form. This is not to suggest that ethical standards have always been static within our communities. Quite the contrary. As I have noted in this and in previous chapters, our ethical narratives dealing with appropriate relationships to the rest of life are grounded in instances when we failed to follow through with our ethical responsibilities. It would be an interesting study to look at Anishinaabeg responses to the fur trade as it went through its stages of early contact to depletion of indigenous species, as many Anishinaabeg participated in the fur trade and helped to facilitate the destruction of some fur-bearing species. There were multiple responses and it ultimately ended poorly for all of the life involved. Furthermore, in a contemporary setting, there often are competing ethical concerns in the struggle for traditional culture to be incorporated into federally recognized tribal governments in their decision-making

process.

41. Here we can think of such legislative acts as the development of the Environmental Protection Agency (EPA) and the Wilderness Act. While they certainly demonstrated a move in the right direction at the time, when we consider the plethora of environmental problems that have ensued even with these measures in place, their limits in power can be seen.

CONCLUSION

1. Treaty of Washington, 1836, online text available at https://www.cmich.edu/library/clarke/ResearchResources/Native_American_Material/Treaty_Rights/Text_of_Michigan_Related_Treaties.

2. For a useful discussion of a similar treaty time and complex set of circumstances, see Anton Treuer, *The Assassination of Hole in the Day* (St. Paul, MN: Borealis Books, 2011). This book is a deeper elaboration of the complex set of circumstances around the shift from *doodem* leadership of crane and loon clans to the election of other leaders, and the courting of some of these leaders by the U.S. Government for treaty signing.

3. Treaty of Washington, Article 13.

4. John D. Nichols and Earl Nyholm, *A Concise Dictionary of Minnesota Ojibwe* (Minneapolis: University of Minnesota Press, 1995), 15.

5. Article 8 states that "a deputation shall be sent to the southwest of the Missouri River, there to select a suitable place for the final settlement of said Indians, which country, so selected, and of reasonable extent, the United States will forever guaranty and secure to said Indians." Treaty of Washington, 1836.

6. A. I. Hallowell, "Temporal Orientation in Western Civilization and in a Preliterate Society," in *Contributions to Ojibwe Studies: Essays 1934–1972*, ed. Jennifer S. H. Brown and Susan Elaine Gray (Lincoln: University of Nebraska Press, 2010), 126.

7. For a discussion of the boarding school experience in the United States, see Ward Churchill, *Kill the Indian, Save the Man: The Genocidal Impact of American Indian Residential Schools* (San Francisco: City Lights Books, 2004). See especially the preface to this book, written by Tink Tinker. The preface, titled "Tracing the Contours of Colonialism: American Indians and the Trajectory of Educational Imperialism," explains this cycle of violence being perpetrated in our communities very well.

8. For a copy of the official court record, see http://1836cora.org/documents/peoplevsleblanctext.pdf. This is a digital copy on the website of the Chippewa-Ottawa Resource Authority (CORA), an Indigenous-run consortium of the Anishinaabe Nations

that had signed the 1836 Treaty of Washington. This organization helps to oversee Indigenous-run fisheries in the waters of what is now the State of Michigan. For an overview of *State of Michigan v. Leblanc*, and the two subsequent federal cases (*U.S. v. Michigan* 471 and *U.S. v. Michigan* 653), the negotiated settlement, see https://www.cmich.edu/library/clarke/ResearchResources/Native_American_Material/Treaty_Rights/Contemporary_Issues/Fishing_Rights/Pages/default.aspx. This resource describes the lead-up to the court cases and Great Lakes fisheries as a whole.

9. For a discussion of the fishing rights issues, see Larry Nesper, *The Walleye War: The Struggle for Ojibwe Spearfishing and Treaty Rights* (Lincoln: University of Nebraska Press, 2002).

10. For a copy of the Inland Consent Decree, see the Turtle Talk blog at https://turtletalk.wordpress.com/2007/11/07/inland-settlement-consent-decree-materials. This is an Indigenous-run legal website.

11. Treaty of Washington, Article 13.

12. *Lyng v. Northwest Indian Cemetery Protection Association*, 485 U.S. 451.

13. Vine Deloria Jr., *The World We Used to Live In: Remembering the Powers of the Medicine Men* (Golden, CO: Fulcrum Press, 2006), xvii–xviii.

14. Leanne Simpson, *As We Have Always Done: Indigenous Freedom through Radical Resistance* (Minneapolis: University of Minnesota Press, 2017), 6.

REFERENCES

Alfred, Taiaiake. *Peace, Power, Righteousness: An Indigenous Manifesto*. New York: Oxford University Press, 1999.

———. *Wasáse: Indigenous Pathways of Action and Freedom*. Peterborough, ON: Broadview Press, 2005.

Allen, Paula Gunn. *The Sacred Hoop: Recovering the Feminine in American Indian Traditions*. Boston: Beacon Press, 1992.

Angel, Michael. *Preserving the Sacred: Historical Perspectives on the Ojibwa Midewiwin*. Winnipeg: University of Manitoba Press, 2002.

Baierlein, Ralph. *Newton to Einstein: The Trail of Light*. New York: Cambridge University Press, 1992.

Bailey, Garrick. *The Osage and the Invisible World: From the Works of Francis La Flesche*. Norman: University of Oklahoma Press, 1995.

Bakhtin, M. M. *The Dialogic Imagination: Four Essays*. Edited by Michael Holquist. Translated by Caryl Emerson and Michael Holquist. Austin: University of Texas Press, 1981.

Baraga, Frederic. *A Dictionary of the Ojibway Language*. St. Paul: Minnesota Historical Society Press, 1992.

Basso, Keith. *Wisdom Sits in Places: Landscape and Language among the Western Apache*. Albuquerque: University of New Mexico Press, 1996.

Benton-Benai, Edward. *The Mishomis Book: The Voice of the Ojibway.* Hayward, WI: Indian
   Country Communications, Inc., 1988.

Berens, William, and A. I. Hallowell. *Memories, Myths and Dreams of an Ojibwe Leader.* Edited
   by Jennifer S. H. Brown and Susan Elaine Gray. Montreal: McGill-Queen's University Press,
   2009.

Boyer, Pascal. "Cognitive Limits to Conceptual Relativity: The Limiting-Case of Religious
   Ontologies." In *Rethinking Linguistic Relativity,* edited by John J. Gumperz and Stephen C.
   Levinson, 203–21. New York: Cambridge University Press, 1996.

Brooks, Lisa. *The Common Pot: The Recovery of Native Space in the Northeast.* Minneapolis:
   University of Minnesota Press, 2008.

Byrd, Jodi A. *The Transit of Empire: Indigenous Critiques of Colonialism.* Minneapolis: University
   of Minnesota Press, 2011.

Chidister, David. *Savage Systems: Colonialism and Comparative Religion in Southern Africa.*
   Charlottesville: University Press of Virginia, 1996.

Churchill, Ward. *Fantasies of the Master Race: Literature, Cinema, and the Colonization of
   American Indians.* San Francisco: City Lights Books, 1998.

———. *Kill the Indian, Save the Man: The Genocidal Impact of American Indian Residential
   Schools.* San Francisco: City Lights Books, 2004.

———. *A Little Matter of Genocide: Holocaust and Denial in the Americas, 1492 to the Present.*
   San Francisco: City Lights Books, 1997.

———. *Since Predator Came: Notes from the Struggle for American Indian Liberation.* Littleton,
   CO: Aegis Publications, 1995.

———. *Struggle for the Land: Indigenous Resistance to Genocide, Ecocide and Expropriation in
   Contemporary North America.* Monroe, ME: Common Courage Press, 1993.

———, ed. *Marxism and Native Americans.* Boston: South End Press, 1989.

Churchill, Ward, and Glenn Morris. "Key Indian Laws and Cases." In *The State of Native
   America,* edited by M. Annette Jaimes. Boston: South End Press, 1992.

Coleman, Sister Bernard, Ellen Frogner, and Estelle Eich. *Ojibwa Myths and Legends.*
   Minneapolis, MN: Ross and Haines, Inc., 1962.

Cooper, John M. *The Northern Algonquian Supreme Being.* New York: AMS Press, 1978.

Coulthard, Glen Sean. *Red Skin, White Masks: Rejecting the Colonial Politics of Recognition.*
   Minneapolis: University of Minnesota Press, 2014.

Deloria, Vine, Jr. *Behind the Trail of Broken Treaties: An Indian Declaration of Independence.*
   New York: Delacorte Press, 1974.

———. *Custer Died for Your Sins: An Indian Manifesto.* Norman: University of Oklahoma
   Press, 1988.

————. *Evolution, Creationism, and Other Modern Myths: A Critical Inquiry.* Golden, CO: Fulcrum Publishing, 2002.

————. *For This Land: Writings on Religion in America.* New York: Routledge, 1999.

————. *God Is Red: A Native View of Religion.* Golden, CO: Fulcrum Publishing, 1992.

————. *The Metaphysics of Modern Existence.* San Francisco: Harper and Row, 1979.

————. *Red Earth, White Lies: Native Americans and the Myth of Scientific Fact.* Golden, CO: Fulcrum Publishing, 1997.

————. *Spirit and Reason: The Vine Deloria Jr. Reader.* Edited by Barbara Deloria, Kristen Foehner, and Sam Scinta. Golden, CO: Fulcrum Publishing, 1999.

————. *The World We Used to Live In: Remembering the Powers of the Medicine Men.* Golden, CO: Fulcrum Publishing, 2006.

Deloria, Vine, Jr., and Daniel R. Wildcat. *Power and Place: Indian Education in America.* Golden, CO: Fulcrum Publishing, 2001.

Densmore, Frances. *Chippewa Customs.* St. Paul: Minnesota Historical Society Press, 1979.

Doerfler, Jill, Niigaanwewidam James Sinclair, and Heidi Kiiwetinepinesiik Stark, eds. *Centering Anishinaabeg Studies: Understanding the World through Stories.* East Lansing: Michigan State University Press, 2013.

Dobyns, Henry F. *Their Number Become Thinned: Native American Population Dynamics in Eastern North America.* Knoxville: University of Tennessee Press, 1983.

Fanon, Frantz. *Black Skin, White Masks.* New York: Grove Press, 1967.

————. *A Dying Colonialism.* New York: Grove Press, 1965.

————. *The Wretched of the Earth.* New York: Grove Press, 1963.

Foucault, Michel. *The Order of Things: An Archaeology of the Human Sciences.* New York: Vintage Books, 1994.

Gawboy, Carl, and Ron Morton. *Talking Sky: Ojibwe Constellations as a Reflection of Life on the Land.* Duluth, MN: Rockflower Press, 2014.

Geertz, Clifford. *The Interpretation of Cultures.* New York: Basic Books, 1973.

Grounds, Richard A., George E. Tinker, and David E. Wilkins, eds. *Native Voices: American Indian Identity and Resistance.* Lawrence: University Press of Kansas, 2003.

Gumperz, John J., and Stephen C. Levinson, eds. *Rethinking Linguistic Relativity.* New York: Cambridge University Press, 1996.

Gyekye, Kwame. *African Cultural Values: An Introduction.* Philadelphia: Sankofa Publishing Co., 1987.

————. *An Essay on African Philosophical Thought: The Akan Conceptual Scheme.* Philadelphia: Temple University Press, 1995.

————. *Beyond Cultures: Perceiving a Common Humanity.* Accra, Ghana: Ghana Academy of

Arts and Sciences, 2004.

———. *Tradition and Modernity: Philosophical Reflections on the African Experience*. New York: Oxford University Press, 1997.

Hall, Anthony J. *The American Empire and the Fourth World*. Montreal: McGill-Queen's University Press, 2003.

———. *Earth into Property: Colonization, Decolonization, and Capitalism*. Montreal: McGill-Queen's University Press, 2010.

Hallowell, A. Irving. *Contributions to Ojibwe Studies: Essays, 1934–1972*. Edited by Jennifer S. H. Brown and Susan Elaine Gray. Lincoln: University of Nebraska Press, 2010.

———. *The Role of Conjuring in Saulteaux Society*. Philadelphia: University of Pennsylvania Press, 1942.

Hawkins, Mike. *Social Darwinism in European and American Thought, 1860–1945: Nature as Model and Nature as Threat*. New York: Cambridge University Press, 1997.

Hernández, Albert. *Subversive Fire: The Untold Story of Pentecost*. Lexington, KY: Emeth Press, 2010.

Hiebert, Paul G. *Transforming Worldviews: An Anthropological Understanding of How People Change*. Grand Rapids, MI: Baker Academic, 2008.

Holland, Dorothy, and Naomi Quinn. *Cultural Models in Language and Thought*. New York: Cambridge University Press, 1987.

Huhndorf, Shari M. *Going Native: Indians in the American Cultural Imagination*. Ithaca, NY: Cornell University Press, 2001.

Jaimes, Annette M. *The State of Native America*. Boston: South End Press, 1992.

Johansen, Bruce E., ed. *Enduring Legacies: Native American Treaties and Contemporary Controversies*. Westport, CT: Praeger, 2004.

Johnston, Basil H. *Anishinaubae Thesaurus*. East Lansing: Michigan State University Press, 2007.

———. *Honour Earth Mother*. Lincoln: University of Nebraska Press, 2003.

———. *Living in Harmony: Mino-nawae-indawaewin*. Wiarton, ON: Kegedonce Press, 2011.

———. *The Manitous: The Spiritual World of the Ojibway*. St. Paul: Minnesota Historical Society Press, 2001.

———. *Ojibway Ceremonies*. Lincoln: University of Nebraska Press, 1990.

———. *Ojibway Heritage*. Lincoln: University of Nebraska Press, 1990.

———. *Walking in Balance: Meeyau-ossaewin*. Wiarton, ON: Kegedonce Press, 2013.

Jones, William. *Ojibwa Texts Collected by William Jones*. Edited by Truman Michelson. New York: E.J. Brill, 1917.

Kalu, Ogbu. "The Sacred Egg: Worldview, Ecology and Development in West Africa." In

Indigenous Traditions and Ecology, edited by John A. Grim. Cambridge, MA: Harvard University Press, 2001.

Kearney, Michael. *World View*. Novato, CA: Chandler and Sharp Publishers, 1984.

Kelly, Leah Renae. *In My Own Voice: Explorations in the Sociopolitical Context of Art and Cinema*. Edited by Ward Churchill. Winnipeg, MB: Arbeiter Ring Publishing, 2001.

Kidwell, Clara Sue, Homer Noley, and George E. "Tink" Tinker. *A Native American Theology*. Maryknoll, NY: Orbis Books, 2001.

Kohl, Johann Georg. *Kitchi-Gami: Life among the Lake Superior Ojibway*. Translated by Lascelles Wraxall. St. Paul: Minnesota Historical Society Press, 1985.

Kramsch, Claire. *Language and Culture*. New York: Oxford University Press, 1998.

LaDuke, Winona. *All Our Relations: Native Struggles for Land and Life*. Cambridge, MA: South End Press, 1999.

———. *Last Standing Woman*. Stillwater, MN: Voyageur Press, 1997.

———. *Recovering the Sacred: The Power of Naming and Claiming*. Cambridge, MA: South End Press, 2005.

———. *The Winona LaDuke Reader: A Collection of Essential Writings*. Edited by Margret Aldrich. Stillwater, MN: Voyageur Press, 2002.

Lakoff, George. *Moral Politics: What Conservatives Know That Liberals Don't*. Chicago: University of Chicago Press, 1996.

Lakoff, George, and Mark Johnson. *Philosophy in the Flesh: The Embodied Mind and Its Challenge to Western Thought*. New York: Basic Books, 1999.

Landes, Ruth. *Ojibwa Religion*. Madison: University of Wisconsin Press, 1968.

Lee, Annette S., William Wilson, Jeffrey Tibbetts, and Carl Gawboy. *Ojibwe Sky Star Map Constellation Guide: An Introduction to Ojibwe Star Knowledge*. North Rocks, CA: Lightning Source–Ingram Spark, 2014.

Long, Jerome H. "Symbol and Reality among the Trobriand Islanders." In *The History of Religions: Essays in Divinity*, edited by Joseph M. Kitagawa. Chicago: University of Chicago Press, 1967.

Lucy, John A. *Grammatical Categories and Cognition*. New York: Cambridge University Press, 1992.

———. *Language Diversity and Thought: A Reformulation of the Linguistic Relativity Hypothesis*. New York: Cambridge University Press, 1992.

Lyng v. Northwest Indian Cemetery Protection Association, 485 U.S. 439 (1988). United States Supreme Court.

Lyons, Scott Richard. *X-Marks: Native Signatures of Assent*. Minneapolis: University of Minnesota Press, 2010.

Lyotard, Jean-François. *The Postmodern Condition: A Report on Knowledge*. Translated by Geoff Bennington and Brian Massumi. Minneapolis: University of Minnesota Press, 1984.

Mann, Barbara Alice, ed. *Daughters of Mother Earth: The Wisdom of Native American Women*. Westport, CT: Praeger, 2006.

———. "A Failure to Communicate: How Christian Missionary Assumptions Ignore Binary Patterns of Thinking within Native-American Communities." In *Remembering Jamestown: Hard Questions about Christian Mission*, edited by Amos Yong and Barbara Brown Zikmund, 29–41. Eugene, OR: Pickwick Publications, 2010.

———. *George Washington's War on Native America*. Lincoln: University of Nebraska Press, 2008.

———. "The Greenville Treaty of 1795: Pen-and-Ink Witchcraft in the Struggle for the Old Northwest." In *Enduring Legacies: Native American Treaties and Contemporary Controversies*, edited by Bruce E. Johansen, 135–202. Westport, CT: Praeger, 2004.

Masuzawa, Tomoko. *The Invention of World Religions: Or, How European Universalism Was Preserved in the Language of Pluralism*. Chicago: University of Chicago Press, 2005.

Mbembe, Achille. *On the Postcolony*. Berkeley: University of California Press, 2001.

Mbiti, John S. *African Religions and Philosophy*. Portsmouth, NH: Heinemann Educational Publishers, 1999.

McCoy, Amy. "Minobimaadiziwin: Perceiving the Good Life through Anishinaabe Language." Masters' thesis, Michigan State University, 2007.

McKim, Donald K. *Westminster Dictionary of Theological Terms*. Louisville, KY: Westminster John Knox Press, 1996.

McLoughlin, William G. *The Cherokees and Christianity, 1794–1870: Essays on Acculturation and Cultural Persistence*. Athens: University of Georgia Press, 1994.

McNally, Michael D. *Ojibwe Singers: Hymns, Grief, and a Native Culture in Motion*. New York: Oxford University Press, 2000.

Memmi, Albert. *The Colonizer and the Colonized*. Boston: Beacon Press, 1991.

Miller, Cary. *Ogimaag: Anishinaabeg Leadership, 1760–1845*. Lincoln: University of Nebraska Press, 2010.

Moore, Marijo, ed. *Genocide of the Mind: New Native American Writing*. New York: Thunder's Mouth Press/Nation Books, 2003.

Naugle, David. *Worldview: The History of a Concept*. Grand Rapids, MI: Wm. B. Eerdmanns Publishing Co., 2002.

Neihardt, John G. *Black Elk Speaks: Being the Life Story of a Holy Man of the Oglala Sioux*. Lincoln: University of Nebraska Press, 1979.

Nesper, Larry. *The Walleye War: The Struggle for Ojibwe Spearfishing and Treaty Rights*. Lincoln:

University of Nebraska Press, 2002.

Newcomb, Steven T. *Pagans in the Promised Land: Decoding the Doctrine of Christian Discovery.* Golden, CO: Fulcrum Publishing, 2008.

Nichols, John D., and Earl Nyholm. *A Concise Dictionary of Minnesota Ojibwe.* Minneapolis: University of Minnesota Press, 1995.

Noodin [Noori], Margaret. *Bawaajimo: A Dialect of Dreams in Anishinaabe Language and Literature.* East Lansing: Michigan State University Press, 2014.

———."*Beshaabiiag G'gikenmaaigowag*: Comets of Knowledge." In *Centering Anishinaabeg Studies: Understanding the World through Stories*, edited by Jill Doerfler, Niigaanwewidam James Sinclair, and Heidi Kiiwetinepinesiik Stark. East Lansing: Michigan State University Press, 2013.

Ortiz, Alfonso. *The Tewa World*. Chicago: University of Chicago Press, 1969.

Overholt, Thomas W., and J. Baird Callicott. *Clothed-in-Fur and Other Tales: An Introduction to an Ojibwa World View.* New York: University Press of America, 1982.

Peacock, Thomas, and Marlene Wisuri. *Waasa Inaabidaa: We Look in All Directions.* Afton, MN: Afton Historical Society Press, 2002.

Purves, William K., Gordon H. Orians, and H. Craig Heller. *Life: The Science of Biology.* Sunderland, MA: Sinauer Associates, Inc., 1992.

p'Bitek, Okot. *African Religions in European Scholarship*. New York: ECA Associates, 1990.

———. *Religion of the Central Luo*. Nairobi: East African Literature Bureau, 1971.

———. *White Teeth*. Nairobi: Heinemann Kenya, 1989.

Radin, Paul. *Primitive Religion*. New York: Dover Publications, 1957.

———. *The Trickster: A Study in American Indian Mythology*. New York: Schocken Books, 1973.

Redfield, Robert. *The Primitive World and Its Transformations*. Ithaca, NY: Cornell University Press, 1953.

Schach, Paul, ed. *Languages in Conflict: Linguistic Acculturation on the Great Plains.* Lincoln: University of Nebraska Press, 1980.

Schoolcraft, Henry Rowe. *Algic Researches: North American Indian Folktales and Legends.* Mineola, NY: Dover Publications, 1999.

———. *Schoolcraft's Indian Legends*. Edited by Mentor L. Williams. East Lansing: Michigan State University Press, 1991.

———. *Schoolcraft's Ojibwa Lodge Stories: Life on the Lake Superior Frontier.* Edited by Phillip P. Mason. East Lansing: Michigan State University Press, 1997.

Silko, Leslie Marmon. *Ceremony*. New York: Penguin Books, 1977.

Simpson, Leanne. *As We Have Always Done: Indigenous Freedom through Radical Resistance.* Minneapolis: University of Minnesota Press, 2017.

————. *Dancing on Our Turtle's Back: Stories of Nishnaabeg Re-Creation, Resurgence, and a New Emergence.* Winnipeg, MB: Arbeiter Ring Publishing, 2011.

Sire, James. *Naming the Elephant: Worldview as a Concept.* Downers Grove, IL: InterVarsity Press, 2004.

Skinner, Alanson. "Notes on the Eastern Cree and Northern Saulteaux." In *Anthropological Papers of the American Museum of Natural History*, vol. 9, pt. 1. New York: American Museum of Natural History, 1911.

Skutnall-Kangas, Tove. *Linguistic Genocide in Education—or Worldwide Diversity and Human Rights?* Mahway, NJ: Lawrence Erlbaum Associates, Publishers, 2000.

Smart, Ninian. *Worldviews: Crosscultural Explorations of Human Beliefs.* Upper Saddle River, NJ: Prentice Hall, 2000.

Smith, Andrea. *Conquest: Sexual Violence and American Indian Genocide.* Cambridge, MA: South End Press, 2005.

Smith, Linda Tuhiwai. *Decolonizing Methodologies: Research and Indigenous Peoples.* New York: Zed Books, 2006.

Teasdale, G. R., and Z. Ma Rhea, eds. *Local Knowledge and Wisdom in Higher Education.* Oxford: Pergamon, 2000.

Tinker, George E. (Tink). *American Indian Liberation: A Theology of Sovereignty.* Maryknoll, NY: Orbis Books, 2008.

————. *Missionary Conquest: The Gospel and Native American Cultural Genocide.* Minneapolis: Fortress Press, 1993.

————. "The Romance and Tragedy of Christian Mission among American Indians." In *Remembering Jamestown: Hard Questions about Christian Mission*, edited by Amos Yong and Barbara Brown Zikmund, 13–28. Eugene, OR: Pickwick Publications, 2012.

————. *Spirit and Resistance: Political Theology and American Indian Liberation.* Minneapolis, MN: Fortress Press, 2004.

————. "Why I Do Not Believe in a Creator." In *Buffalo Shout, Salmon Cry: Conversations on Creation, Land Justice, and Life Together*, edited by Steve Heinrichs. Waterloo, ON: Herald Press, 2013.

Treuer, Anton, ed. *The Assassination of Hole in the Day.* Saint Paul, MN: Borealis Books, 2011.

————, ed. *Living Our Language: Ojibwe Tales and Oral Histories.* St. Paul: Minnesota Historical Society Press, 2001.

Turner, Dale. "Perceiving the World Differently." In *Intercultural Dispute Resolution in Aboriginal Contexts*, edited by Catherine Bell and David Kahane, 57–69. Toronto, ON: UBC Press, 2004.

————. *This Is Not a Peace Pipe: Towards a Critical Indigenous Philosophy.* Toronto: University of Toronto Press, 2006.

Underhill, James W. *Humboldt, Worldview and Language.* Edinburgh: Edinburgh University Press, 2013.

Underhill, Ruth M. *Red Man's Religion.* Chicago: University of Chicago Press, 1974.

Vecsey, Christopher. *Traditional Ojibwa Religion and Its Historical Changes.* Philadelphia: American Philosophical Society, 1993.

Wa Thiong'o, Ngũgĩ. *Decolonising the Mind: The Politics of Language in African Literature.* Portsmouth, NH: Heinemann Educational Books, 1989.

Weaver, Jace, ed. *Native American Religious Identity: Unforgotten Gods.* Maryknoll, NY: Orbis Books, 1998.

————. *Notes from a Miner's Canary: Essays on the State of Native America.* Albuquerque: University of New Mexico Press, 2010.

————. *Other Words: American Indian Literature, Law, and Culture.* Norman: University of Oklahoma Press, 2001.

————. *That the People Might Live: Native American Literatures and Native American Community.* New York: Oxford University Press, 1997.

Weber, Max. *The Protestant Ethic and the Spirit of Capitalism: The Relationships between Religion and the Economic and Social Life in Modern Culture.* Translated by Talcott Parsons. New York: Charles Scribner's Sons, 1976.

White Hat, Sr., Albert. *Zuya, Life's Journey: Oral Teachings from Rosebud.* Edited and compiled by John Cunningham. Salt Lake City: University of Utah Press, 2012.

Williams, Robert A., Jr. *The American Indian in Western Legal Thought: The Discourses of Conquest.* New York: Oxford University Press, 1990.

————. *Like a Loaded Weapon: The Rehnquist Court, Indian Rights, and the Legal History of Racism in America.* Minneapolis: University of Minnesota, 2005.

————. *Linking Arms Together: American Indian Treaty Visions of Law and Peace, 1600–1800.* New York: Routledge, 1999.

Wilson, Shawn. *Research Is Ceremony: Indigenous Research Methods.* Winnipeg, MB: Fernwood Publishing, 2008.

Wiredu, Kwasi. *The Akan Worldview.* Washington, DC: Smithsonian Libraries, 1985.

————. *Cultural Universals and Particulars: An African Perspective.* Bloomington: Indiana University Press, 1996.

————. *Philosophy and an African Culture.* New York: Cambridge University Press, 1980.

Whorf, Benjamin Lee. *Language, Thought and Reality: The Selected Writings of Benjamin Lee*

Whorf. Edited and with an introduction by John B. Carroll. New York: MIT Press, 1956.

Wub-E-Ke-Niew. *We Have the Right to Exist.* New York: Black Thistle Press, 1995.

Yong, Amos, and Barbara Brown Zikmund, eds. *Remembering Jamestown: Hard Questions about Christian Mission.* Eugene, OR: Pickwick Publications, 2010.

INDEX

A

aadizookaan (single origin story), 64, 177 (n. 19), 178 (n. 20)

aadizookaanag (origin and ideological narratives), 65, 67, 74, 85, 121–22, 150; as both narratives and characters, 78, 79, 177 (n. 19); Hallowell on, 64, 179 (n. 24); in *mewinzha*, 63, 66–68, 79; regeneration theme in, 64, 185 (n. 82); told only in winter, 55, 64, 68, 178 (n. 23). See also *Giizhigokwe* narratives

aadizookewinini (storytellers), 178 (nn. 22–23)

Aazheyaadizi ("living in a way that extends back in time"), xxi

Ackerknecht (Edwin H.), 188 (n. 19)

Aepingushmook (West Wind), 110, 199 (n. 25)

agriculture, 47, 76, 175 (n. 72), 181;

monocropping in, 54, 175 (n. 73)

AIRFA (American Indian Religious Freedom Act), viii, 158 (n. 4)

Akan (culture): dualism in, 19–20; and eurowest, 18, 19, 92; in Ghana, 18; material in, 92; natural as concept in, 18, 92, 163 (n. 65); origin narratives, 18; spatiality in, 18, 19, 44, 45, 49, 93; time in, 77; worldview in, 19, 92–93, 163 (n. 67)

Akan (language): cogito translated into, 44–45; conceptions of, 92; conceptual colonization of, xi, xii; on creation/*oboade*/God, xi, xii, 18–19; "divining" as infinite future in, 185 (n. 81); and logic of intension versus extension, 92; space in, 93; specific location structure in, 45; time in, 49, 67, 77, 179 (n. 32); "to be" not used in, 44; and worldview, 92. *See also*

Washington, vii–viii, xiv–xv, 1, 157 (n. 3), 201–2 (n. 8)

I

idealism, 15

ideologies: competing, 126; changing, 27; compared to worldview, xvi; definitions of, xvi, 7, 24–25; science, 123–25, 126; compared to worldview, xvi

Indian agents, xiv, 187 (n. 4)

Indian Removal Act, 62, 85, 149, 155; and boarding schools, 106, 152, 201 (n. 7)

indigeneity, logics of, viii, xiv

Indigenous peoples: frameworks of thought, 3; and Manifest Destiny, 53, 54, 85, 148; as other, 148; as primitive, 11, 148–49, 188 (n. 19)

Indigenous philosophy, 17–22

Indigenous resistance, 192 (n. 46)

Indigenous resurgence, xiv, 83

Indigenous worldview, x, xiv, 2, 3

Inland Consent Decree (2007), viii, xiv–xv, 153, 202 (n. 10)

ishpeming (heaven), 37

Ishpeming ("place above," Upper Peninsula), 43, 171 (n. 36)

J

Jamestown colony, 54, 175 (n. 73)

Jesuit Relations, 175 (n. 74)

Jesuits, 70

Johnston, Basil H. (Anishinaabeg), 167–68 (n. 14), 169 (n. 21); Anishinaabemowin in texts of, 111–12; on balance, 134–36, 138; Christian framework of, 110, 111, 173 (n. 58); and creation narratives, 33–34, 109, 111; decolonization thought of, 49, 107–8, 109, 112; and double-vowel orthography, 173 (n. 57), 192 (n. 48); on the flooded world, 33, 107; gendering by, 108; Honour Earth Mother, 184 (n. 64); on *Kitche Manitou*, 107, 109, 170 (n. 29); on *kitchi manidoo* as creator, 107–13; on *Kitchi-Manitou*, 108, 113; linguistic conceptual moves of, 110; on manidoo, 49, 109–10, 173 (n. 57), 192 (n. 48); on *manidoog*, 110, 111; on *manitouwun*, 49, 110; and *mino bimaadiziwin*, 197 (n. 6); on *Mishi-Waub-Kaikak*, 111; and *Nanapush* as *Nana'boo'zoo*, 111, 184 (n. 64), 198 (n. 20); narrative style of, 110–12; on reciprocal relationships, 109; on *Shkaakaamikwe* as life giving, 189 (n. 22); on Sky Woman, 33–34, 36, 37; time concepts used by, 110–11. Works: *Anishinaubae Thesaurus*, 113, 168 (n. 17), 169 (n. 22), 172 (n. 51), 197 (n. 6); *Living in Harmony*, 134, 135, 138, 144; *The Manitous*, 107, 108–9, 110; *Ojibway Ceremonies*, 111; *Ojibway Heritage*, 107–9, 170 (n. 29); *Walking in Balance*, 134–35, 141, 198 (nn. 20–21)

Jones, Peter (Anishinaabeg): as missionary, 37, 106–7, 192 (n. 47); Bible translations by, 37–38, 106–7, 192 (n. 44)

Jones, William (Ojibwa), 198 (n. 18)

K

Kadabendjiget (K'tchi-ma'ni-tu, Creator, Supreme Power), 101

Kagame, Alexis, 44–45, 164 (n. 76)

kamig (land), 34, 36–37, 39, 168 (n. 17)

20, 24, 98, 115, 131, 148; methodological lens of, xi, xiv, 34; in natural selection, 8, 161 (n. 25); Naugle on, 3, 4–6, 22, 160 (n. 2); redefining, 149; Redfield on, 12, 14, 15; and relatedness, 23, 87, 91, 99, 117; and relationship with land, xi, xvi, 20, 23; shifts in, 27; and space, xvi, 20, 21, 23, 85; theory of, xv; and time, xi, xvi, 12, 23, 61, 83–85; and Underhill, 9–10, 161 (n. 32), 161–62 (nn. 33–34); and weltanschauung, 2–3, 22, 160 (n. 2), 161 (n. 32), 162 (n. 34); and weltansicht, 8–10, 161 (n. 32), 162 (n. 34); and white supremacy, 3, 11, 148. *See also* Indigenous worldview

World We Used to Live In, The (Deloria), 154

Wounded Knee Occupation, 152

Z

zhitoon (make or create), 37–38, 39, 191 (n. 37)